DISABILITY AS DIVERSITY IN HIGHER EDUCATION

Addressing disability not as a form of student impairment—as it is typically perceived at the postsecondary level—but rather as an important dimension of student diversity and identity, this book explores how disability can be more effectively incorporated into college environments. Chapters propose new perspectives, empirical research, and case studies to provide the necessary foundation for understanding the role of disability within campus climate and integrating students with disabilities into academic and social settings. Contextualizing disability through the lens of intersectionality, *Disability as Diversity in Higher Education* illustrates how higher education institutions can use policies and practices to enhance inclusion and student success.

Eunyoung Kim is Associate Professor in the Department of Education Leadership, Management, and Policy at Seton Hall University, USA.

Katherine C. Aquino is Adjunct Professor and Program Specialist for Accreditation and Assessment at New Jersey City University, USA.

DISABILITY AS DIVERSITY IN HIGHER EDUCATION

Policies and Practices to Enhance Student Success

Edited by
Eunyoung Kim and Katherine C. Aquino

Routledge
Taylor & Francis Group

NEW YORK AND LONDON

First published 2017
by Routledge
711 Third Avenue, New York, NY 10017

and by Routledge
2 Park Square, Milton Park, Abingdon, Oxon, OX14 4RN

Routledge is an imprint of the Taylor & Francis Group, an informa business

Library of Congress Cataloging in Publication Data
A catalog record for this book has been requested

ISBN: 978-1-138-18617-0 (hbk)
ISBN: 978-1-138-18618-7 (pbk)
ISBN: 978-1-315-64400-4 (ebk)

Typeset in Bembo
by diacriTech, Chennai

CONTENTS

Acknowledgments   *ix*
Preface   *xi*

PART I
Theoretical Lenses and Application   **1**

1 Supporting Students with Non-Disclosed Disabilities:
   A Collective and Humanizing Approach   3
   Christina Yuknis and Eric R. Bernstein

2 A Different Diversity? Challenging the Exclusion of Disability
   Studies from Higher Education Research and Practice   19
   Lauren Shallish

3 Queering Disability in Higher Education: Views from the
   Intersections   31
   Ryan A. Miller, Richmond D. Wynn, and Kristine W. Webb

PART II
College Experiences of Students
with Disabilities   **45**

4 "Does Disability Matter?": Students' Satisfaction
   with College Experiences   47
   Katherine C. Aquino, Taghreed A. Alhaddab, and Eunyoung Kim

5 Engaging Disability: Trajectories of Involvement for College
Students with Disabilities 61
Ezekiel Kimball, Rachel E. Friedensen, and Elton Silva

6 College Students with Learning Disabilities: An At-Risk
Population Absent from the Conversation of Diversity 75
Wanda Hadley and D. Eric Archer

7 Using a Spatial Lens to Examine Disability as Diversity
on College Campuses 89
Holly Pearson and Michelle Samura

PART III
**Perspectives of Faculty and
Higher Education Administration** **105**

8 Faculty and Administrator Knowledge and
Attitudes Regarding Disability 107
Allison R. Lombardi and Adam R. Lalor

9 Working It Backward: Student Success through
Faculty Professional Development 122
Cali Anicha, Chris M. Ray, and Canan Bilen-Green

10 "It's a Very Deep, Layered Topic": Student Affairs
Professionals on the Marginality and
Intersectionality of Disability 138
Annemarie Vaccaro and Ezekiel Kimball

11 Tools for Moving the Institutional Iceberg:
Policies and Practices for Students with Disabilities 153
Jacalyn Griffen and Tenisha Tevis

PART IV
Institutional Programs and Initiatives **169**

12 Disability, Diversity, and Higher Education: A Critical Study of
California State University's Websites 171
Susan L. Gabel, Denise P. Reid, and Holly Pearson

13 Encountering Institutional Barriers and Resistance: Disability
    Discomfort on One Campus   185
    Heather Albanesi and Emily A. Nusbaum

14 Access Ryerson: Promoting Disability as Diversity   200
    Denise O'Neil Green, Heather Willis, Matthew D. Green,
    and Sarah Beckman

15 Thinking and Practicing Differently: Changing the
    Narrative around Disability on College Campuses   216
    Sue Kroeger and Amanda Kraus

About the Contributors   *230*
Index   *238*

ACKNOWLEDGMENTS

Editor Eunyoung Kim's Acknowledgments

Any collaborative writing project requires the commitment, energy, and enthusiasm of individual contributors who go above and beyond ordinary limits. That being said, I would like to thank all those who generously gave their time and intellectual rigor to explore the disability-diversity discourse—especially for their commitment and passion for promoting the success of students with disabilities in college and beyond. This volume is a testament to your dedication to the notion of disability as diversity. Thank you for taking the journey with us and seeing it through to the end.

Second, I would like to thank Heather Jarrow, our editor at Routledge, who trusted our vision of the book from the beginning and kept us on track with her patience and support. I would also be remiss if I didn't thank Katherine C. Aquino, my co-editor, for her keen eye and patience, which were instrumental to the completion of this project.

Finally, I would like to thank my parents and Danny for their encouragement, support, and confidence, which have inspired me to overcome any setbacks I encountered during my scholarly journey.

Editor Katherine C. Aquino's Acknowledgments

From a very early age, my mother has played an integral role at teaching me the importance of acceptance and awareness. As an elementary school teacher, she highlighted equity in the classroom, addressing student functioning level or overall ability positively and constructively. My mother, Cathie, continues to inspire my research work through our ongoing conversations that bridge theory to practical application.

To our amazing contributing authors: thank you for sharing your incredible ideas and passion on such a significant, and timely, topic. I am privileged to call you my colleagues and I am so happy to know that, through our work, we can add to this important conversation. Additionally, thank you to the Routledge team, Heather and Rebecca, for being as excited about this project as we are! You provided an incredible amount of positive guidance and we were so fortunate to have had your support throughout the length of the project. Lastly, thank you to my co-editor, Dr. Eunyoung Kim, for providing the confidence to take our conversation on this topic to the actuality of this text.

Lastly, I would like to thank my husband, Salvatore, for his love, kindness, support, and encouragement. I do not know if I will ever truly be able to articulate how grateful I am for you. Having you as my best friend is my life's greatest blessing. Thank you for everything, but, most importantly, thank you for being you.

PREFACE

Within the higher education system, approximately 11 percent of undergraduate students identify as having a disability (National Center for Education Statistics, 2015; Raue & Lewis, 2011). Despite over one in ten college students with a documented disability, disability remains a neglected component of student diversity (Olkin, 2002). Aquino (forthcoming) notes there is significant variation in what is included in the literature as a standard element of student diversity, with race and ethnicity most commonly a focus for student diversity literature (Hurtado, Alvarado, & Guillermo-Wann, 2015). As such, an overarching trend excluding student disability from student diversity research is apparent (Davis, 2011; Darling, 2013; Devlieger, Albrecht, & Hertz, 2007; Linton, 1998). "Diversity" has come to represent race, ethnicity, gender, sexual orientation and, *at times*, disability (Linton, 1998); holistically, there continues to be a lack of cohesion between student disability and diversity, with a frequent misconstruction and misplacement of disability outside of the diversity construct (King, 2009; Linton, 1998; Reid & Knight, 2006). Disability is itself multifaceted, a characteristic that should be understood as more than just a single entity, with variations in type, onset, and overall level of functionality.

The approach to and overall understanding of student disability has centered on disability as a potential limitation for college success and has remained rooted within the medical model of disability. The traditional understanding of disability in academic settings was framed by a model that focuses on "impairments, activity limitations, and participation restrictions" (World Health Organization, 2014, para. 1), greatly influencing legislation applied in the postsecondary setting (e.g., Americans with Disabilities Act) and the mandated disability accommodation process. This model created the assumption that disability is to be fixed, improved, and deviates from the typical human experience (Artiles, 2013; Watermeyer,

2013). Seeing disability as a form of impairment prevents disability from serving as an empowering characteristic of an individual's identity, and therefore further separates disability and other demographic characteristics that are seen as traditional forms of diversity. Moreover, this perpetuates segregation between disability and other social identity memberships (Artiles, 2013).

Critiquing the stigmatizing components brought forth through by the medical model of disability, several approaches address how disability is viewed within social and cultural environments. This has allowed for a shift in understanding student disability through a lens that is significantly different from the medical model. One approach that attempts to disconnect potential stigmatization related to an individual's disability and reframe it as a product of the overall environment is the social model of disability (Barnes, 1991; Barnes, 2004; Martin, 2012; Oliver, 1990; Oliver & Barnes, 1993). This theoretical perspective addresses the notion of disability as an interaction with social environment, mirroring other forms of diversity and how they can be socially constructed. Additionally, the minority group model understands disability as a stigmatizing and oppressed characteristic (Hahn, 1985; 1986; 1996) and addresses the lack of equity for individuals with disabilities. This allows for conversation about individuals with disabilities and of minority group statuses having similar life experiences, and that both are considered characteristics of diversity. Although minority groups may also experience stigmatization, this model bridges student disability with other forms of student diversity.

Focus of the Book

The focus of this volume is on a greater, more in depth conversation about how disability can be better addressed, as a form of student diversity within the postsecondary setting through the lens of intersectionality. The theory of intersectionality establishes the vital junctures that bridge disability and diversity, and promotes the identification of multiple diversity memberships. The intersectionality framework provides the foundation to explore potential connections and divergences occurring with and within a disability, and the complexities of other cultural-social identities in higher education contexts (Mereish, 2012). Although disability has been considered a limiting, "lesser than" membership among other diversity characteristics (Hirschmann, 2013), disability nevertheless intersects with other forms of diversity such as racial or ethnic backgrounds, gender, sexual orientation, and/or religious affiliation. Viewing disability as a characteristic of diversity and examining how it intersects with other diversity memberships may not only share revealing information related to the potential salience of diversity identities, but also elucidate the role of disability in overall identity development, self-perception, and success in college. This volume therefore addresses the current disconnect between perceptions of disability and student diversity in higher education, and (re)establishes the ground for how disability is and should be interpreted within the postsecondary environment.

The text highlights a unique angle of higher education and how it continues to allow student disability to remain stigmatized and marginalized. Several chapters featured in this volume report in-depth qualitative studies that focus on the collegiate experiences of students with disabilities, and the faculty and administrators who serve them. Given the nature of disability studies, these studies are important because they provide a deeper understanding about the complex intersection between disability and other dimensions of diversity, and highlight the structural factors that influence the dynamic of disability-diversity discourse. Other chapters in the volume feature a critical literature review and theoretical lenses related to disabilities within the discourse of diversity in higher education, and offer validation for disability as part of diversity dimensions. Certain chapters in the volume focus on the equally important institutional initiatives that promote disability as a part diversity. These chapters describe how one university's policy and practice with students with disabilities has been developed and implemented, and offer an in-depth look at an institutional way of being "inclusive." Considering the scarcity of adequate information on students with disabilities' college transitions, performance, and completion rate at the national, state, and institutional levels, we include a chapter that focuses on students' satisfaction with collegiate experiences and campus climate, using a nationally representative sample compared with the general student population and students with other diversity categories. Some chapters in this volume feature self-reflective qualitative studies that powerfully demonstrate struggles, challenges, and a deep level of understanding of oneself and one's assumptions while engaging in working with students with disabilities.

Organization of the Book

This volume consists of four parts: (1) theoretical lenses and application, (2) college experiences of students with disabilities, (3) perspectives of faculty and higher education administration and (4) institutional programs and initiatives.

Substantial progress has been made in advocacy for, and support of, students with disabilities in the postsecondary environment. For example, federally mandated policies, such as the reauthorization of the Higher Education Opportunity Act of 2008, promote postsecondary integration and have reduced numerous barriers faced by college students with disabilities (Hendrickson et al., 2013). Legislation such as Section 504 of the Rehabilitation Act of 1973 and the Americans with Disabilities Act established a guided approach to disability services and accommodation support within the college environment. Policies such as these provide opportunities to adequately support student needs within a higher education setting, better allowing students to acclimate to the overall institutional dynamic and diversity milieu. Part I introduces disability-related theoretical frameworks as a form of diversity in higher education and addresses how the higher education community interprets and implements policies and how these theoretical lenses are applied in the empirical research of disability-diversity context.

Many factors combine to make an individual's higher education experience unique, greatly influencing educational outcomes and the overall experience of students with disabilities. Limited social opportunities and lack of service use may contribute to high rates of students with disabilities not completing degree requirements and leaving college early (Quick, Lehmann, & Deniston, 2003). Obstacles and procedures faced by students with disabilities while negotiating academic and social success may make these students feel unwelcomed or unaccepted within the institution's interpretation of student diversity (e.g., Mamiseishvili & Koch, 2012). Part II addresses the unique college experiences of students with disabilities and the various factors impacting these experiences.

Although institutions are required by law to provide accessible options for students with disabilities, colleges and universities may only be providing the bare minimum due to limited staffing and/or the perceived unimportance of accessibility. Additionally, despite faculty members indicating a positive perception of assisting students with disabilities, a disconnect may occur between the desire to help and the actual implementation of accommodation supports (Brockelman, Chadsey, & Loeb, 2006; Murray, Wren, & Keys, 2008). Research notes the importance of higher education administration in how students with disabilities transition into and integrate with the higher education environment (Belch, 2011; Korbel, McGuire, Banerjee, & Saunders, 2011). Institutions must be made aware of the role they play in the successful passage through the educational experience of students with disabilities. Additionally, student affairs administration must take up the task of promoting a sense of community and equity, in order to promote these students' academic retention and success (Bogue, 2002). Chapters in Part III discuss how faculty and administration apply federal policy and institutional protocols related to postsecondary student disability, integrating various initiatives to improve the student disability-diversity connection.

Many colleges and universities have acknowledged the vital role of disability support services in facilitating the transition from secondary school to college life, eliminating the barriers these students encounter, and providing equal opportunities within inclusive and supportive campus environments. Due to the passage of legislation protecting the rights of persons with disabilities, higher education institutions are now responsible for providing accessible education to students with disabilities by making appropriate academic adjustment, such as providing course substitutions, adapting instructional methods, and modifying the length of time allotted for the completion of requirements. Given the growing presence of students with learning disabilities on college campuses (Capps, Henslee, & Gere, 2002), for example, many colleges and universities have created campus-wide centers where faculty and instructional staff work collaboratively to improve instruction (e.g., finding resources, assembling feedback from students) and address the changing diversity and learning needs of students (Ouellett, 2004). Given the often inconsistent and reactive efforts by institutions to assist students with disabilities, chapters in Part IV present a variety of innovative programs and practices to address disability proactively, describing the educational components of institutional disability support programs and services.

Intended Audiences

The primary audience for this edited volume includes but is not limited to: higher education researchers, institutional administrators, student affairs professionals, faculty, academic advisors at the postsecondary level, disability studies educators and researchers, national and institutional policy makers, and general readers who are interested in disability and diversity issues in higher education. Certainly students with disabilities themselves and parents of students with disabilities should be interested in reading this book, as well as graduate and undergraduate students who are pursuing related courses (diversity, multiculturalism, special education, disability studies).

References

Artiles, A. J. (2013). Untangling the racialization of disabilities. *Du Bois Review, 10*, 329–347.

Aquino, K. C. (forthcoming). The disability-diversity disconnect: Redefining the role of student disability within the postsecondary environment (Unpublished doctoral dissertation). Seton Hall University: South Orange, NJ.

Barnes, C. (1991). *Disabled people in Britain and discrimination*. London, United Kingdom: Hurst.

Barnes, C. (2004). Disability, disability studies, and the academy. In J. Swain, S. French, C. Barnes, & C. Thomas (Eds.), *Disabling barriers, enabling environments* (pp. 28–33). London, United Kingdom: Sage.

Belch, H. A. (2011). Understanding the experiences of students with psychiatric disabilities: A foundation for creating conditions of support and success. *New Directions for Student Services, 2011*(134), 73–94.

Bogue, E. G. (2002). An agenda for common caring: The call for community in higher education. In W. M. McDonald & Associates (Eds.), *Creating campus community: In search of Ernest Boyer's legacy*. San Francisco, CA: Jossey-Bass.

Brockelman, K. F., Chadsey, J. G., & Loeb, J. W. (2006). Faculty perceptions of university students with psychiatric disabilities. *Psychiatric Rehabilitation Journal, 30*(1), 23–30.

Capps, S. C., Henslee, A. M., & Gere, D. R. (2002). Learning disabilities within postsecondary education: Suggestions for administrators and faculty members. *Journal of Social Work in Disability & Rehabilitation, 1*(3), 15–24.

Darling, R. B. (2013). *Disability and identity: Negotiating self in a changing society*. Boulder, CO: Lynne Rienner Publishers.

Davis, L. J. (2011, September 25). Why is disability missing from the discourse on diversity? *The Chronicle of Higher Education*. Retrieved from http://chronicle.com/article/Why-Is-Disability-Missing-From/129088/.

Devlieger, P. J., Albrecht, G. L., & Hertz, M. (2007). The production of disability culture among young African–American men. *Social Science & Medicine, 64,* 1948–1959.

Hahn, H. (1985). Changing perceptions of disability and the future of rehabilitation. In L. G. Pearlman & G. F. Austin (Eds.), *Societal influences in rehabilitation planning: A blueprint for the 21st century* (pp. 53–64). Alexandria, VA: National Rehabilitation Association.

Hahn, H. (1986). Disability and the urban environment: A perspective on Los Angeles. *Society and Space, 4,* 273–288.

Hahn, H. (1996). Antidiscrimination laws and social research on disability: The minority group perspective. *Behavioral Sciences and the Law, 14,* 41–59.

Hendrickson, J. M., Carson, R., Woods-Groves, S., Menhenhall, J., & Scheidecker, B. (2013). UI REACH: A postsecondary program serving students with autism and intellectual disabilities. *Education and Treatment of Children, 36*(4), 169–194.

Hirschmann, N. J. (2013). Disability, feminism, and intersectionality: A critical approach. *Radical Philosophy Review, 16,* 649–662.

Hurtado, S., Alvarado, A. R., & Guillermo-Wann, C. (2015). Thinking about race: The salience of racial identity at two- and four-year colleges and the climate for diversity. *Journal of Higher Education, 86*(1), 127–155.

King, K. A. (2009). A review of programs that promote higher education access for under-represented students. *Journal of Diversity in Higher Education, 2*(1), 1–15.

Korbel, D. M., McGuire, J. M., Banerjee, M., & Saunders, S. A. (2011). Transition strategies to ensure active student engagement. *New Directions for Student Services, 2011*(134), 35–46.

Linton, S. (1998). *Claiming disability.* New York, NY: New York University Press.

Martin, N. (2012). Disability identity-disability pride. *Perspectives: Policy and Practice in Higher Education, 16*(1), 14–18.

Mamiseishvili, K., & Koch, L. C. (2012). Students with disabilities at two-year institutions in the United States: Factors related to success. *Community College Review, 40*(4), 1–20.

Mereish, E. H. (2012). The intersectional invisibility of race and disability status: An exploratory study of health and discrimination facing Asian Americans with disabilities. *Ethnicity and Inequalities in Health and Social Care, 5*(2), 52–60.

Murray, C., Wren, C. T., & Keys, C. (2008). University faculty perceptions of students with learning disabilities: Correlates and group differences. *Learning Disability Quarterly, 31*(3), 95–113.

National Center for Education Statistics. (2015). *Digest of Education Statistics, 2013* (NCES 2015-011), Table 311.10.

Oliver, M. (1990). *The politics of disablement.* Basingstoke, United Kingdom: MacMillan.

Oliver, M., & Barnes, C. (1993). Discrimination, disability, and welfare: From needs to right. In D. Swain, V. Finkelstein, S. French, & M. Oliver (Eds.), *Disabling barriers, enabling environments* (pp. 267–277). London, United Kingdom: Sage.

Olkin, R. (2002). Could you hold the door for me? Including disability in diversity. *Cultural Diversity & Ethnic Minority Psychology, 8,* 130–137.

Ouellett, M. L. (2004). Faculty development and universal instructional design. *Equity & Excellence in Education, 37*(2), 135–144.

Quick, D., Lehmann, J., & Deniston, T. (2003). Opening doors for students with disabilities on community college campuses: What have we learned? What do we still need to know? *Community College Journal of Research & Practice, 27,* 815–827.

Raue, K., & Lewis, L. (2011). *Students with disabilities at degree-granting postsecondary institutions* (NCES 011–018). Washington, DC: U.S. Government Printing Office.

Reid, D. K., & Knight, M. G. (2006). Disability justifies exclusion of minority students: A critical history grounded in disability studies. *Educational Research, 35*, 18–23.

Watermeyer, B. (2013). *Towards a contextual psychology of disablism.* New York, NY: Routledge.

World Health Organization. (2014). Health topics: Disabilities. Retrieved from http://www.who.int/topics/disabilities/en/.

PART I
Theoretical Lenses and Application

1

SUPPORTING STUDENTS WITH NON-DISCLOSED DISABILITIES

A Collective and Humanizing Approach

Christina Yuknis and Eric R. Bernstein

Introduction

Along with the increased frequency of disability identification in elementary and secondary schools (Wagner, Newman, Cameto, & Levine, 2005), students receiving special education services are also increasingly enrolling in postsecondary education (Council for Exceptional Children, 2014). Although students with disabilities are attending higher education in larger numbers than before, a disproportionate number do not graduate compared to their nondisabled peers (Barber, 2012; Hudson, 2013).

While attending postsecondary institutions, not all of students disclose their disability to their subsequent institutions of higher education (Richardson, 2009). There are a number of reasons for this including fears of "the social stigma, the loss of esteem by professors, and the fear that future employers will have access to their record" (Lauffer, 2000, p. 42). Those concerns and the widely held perception that postsecondary faculty do not accommodate or understand the needs of students with disabilities (Barnard-Brak, Lechtenberger, & Lan, 2010; Burgstahler, 2006), contribute to postsecondary students with disabilities withholding that information from faculty or administrators. This withholding of information means that students may not be receiving the accommodations or supports that they need to access educational opportunities, and this could be a reason why students with disabilities do not persist to graduation.

The objective of this chapter is to propose a framework that expands the construction of culturally relevant pedagogy to include cultural dimensions of disability and that recognizes the intersectionality of disability with other identities. Postsecondary faculty can then use this framework to evoke instructional practices that are inclusive for all students in their classes in a collective and humanizing way, thus reducing the need to rely on self-disclosure of a disability before accommodating.

We begin by providing background on the intersection of disabilities with other identities and identify some of the issues surrounding disclosure of disability. We then offer one way of understanding culturally relevant pedagogy and propose expanding this understanding of culturally relevant pedagogical framework to include disability. Finally, we discuss practices that may facilitate the implementation of this framework within postsecondary environments.

A New Framework

Ladson-Billings (1995) has described culturally relevant pedagogy, in part, as being "committed to collective, not merely individual, empowerment" (p. 160). She supports Bartolome's (1994) argument for a "humanizing pedagogy that respects and uses the reality, history, and perspectives of students as an integral part of educational practice" (p. 173). We propose extending the assertions of culturally relevant pedagogy around collective empowerment and humanization that respects students as whole people and includes diversity of (dis)ability.

This framework, which we are calling *Culturally Relevant Disability Pedagogy*, makes use of culturally relevant pedagogy principles but applies them to people with disabilities, while simultaneously recognizing the intersectionality of the human experience. Goodley (2013) notes "Intersectionality is not simply about bringing together these markers but to consider how each supports or unsettles the constitution of one another" (p. 636). The markers he is referring to are the markers of a person's identity. Each part of a person's identity—gender, race, ethnicity, background experiences, and so on—works to bolster or disrupt the workings of the other identities. Until recently, disability was not a part of the discourse surrounding diversity, although bodily experiences differ. To illustrate, we offer an example from gender and disability, and the ways they are linked because bodily ways of being are situated within gendered experiences. For example, mental illness in women is typically couched in terms of madness or sanity, but for men, it is typically described in terms of criminality (Goodley).

We are proposing a new framework that we term Culturally Relevant Disability Pedagogy, because the discourse around disability is often framed in a deficit narrative. Culturally Relevant Disability Pedagogy seeks to change that narrative by building on the prior work of other theorists (such as Ladson-Billings) on the overlap between culturally relevant pedagogy and critical disability studies. The central idea is to create positive, affirming environment not just for people from a variety of cultures, but also along dimensions of disability. This requires some recognition of the ways in which bodily ways of being are influenced and interact with culture.

Intersectionality

Banks (2013) notes that intersectionality is an emerging area of study within multicultural education, having grown since the beginning of the 21st century. Gillborn (2015), citing the African American Policy Forum, best articulates the rationale for our reliance on an intersectional approach in considering the development of a new framework to include disability. Our intersectional approach "goes beyond conventional analysis in order to focus our attention on injuries that we otherwise might not recognize . . . to 1) analyze social problems more fully; 2) shape more effective interventions; and 3) promote more inclusive coalitional advocacy" (p. 278). The connection between problem analysis and intervention development is especially central to our proposed framework.

Disability studies, specifically, is an emerging field in critical theory that seeks to define disability outside of the traditional medical view and in terms of the social construction of disability. The main posit is that society is set up in such a way as to be oppressive to people with various physical or cognitive characteristics, and as such *disables* them (Goodley, 2013). Critical disability studies take the field one step further by examining disabling forces through political, theoretical, and practical lenses (Goodley). Hegemonic ideas of disability both within and outside of disability studies are raised for inspection and analysis, because bodies that are disabled challenge ideas of what it means to be nondisabled. The idea of *normal* is questioned, defined, and redefined when varied bodily abilities are introduced for inspection.

Goodley (2011, as cited in Goodley, 2013) notes the emergence of a "carnal sociology," a notion that explores the importance of the body in understanding how one self interacts with society. The body cannot be ignored or disregarded. Critical disability studies acknowledge that people with disabilities are multidimensional beings with many different identities and theorizes about the role of the body in the human experience. Each identity falls along a spectrum of capital and interacts with other identities and the body in complex ways. For example, a person may be White, male, and have a learning disability. While the learning disability gives this individual lower academic capital (and therefore, lower status) than a person who does not have a learning disability, his Whiteness and maleness cannot be disregarded as they provide a certain amount of privilege. These characteristics interact to give the person a certain amount of status, and that status can vary depending on whether the individual is a student in a classroom, an athlete on the field, or a consumer in a shop.

Disability Disclosure

For many people with disabilities, the idea of when and how to disclose their disability to others, whether for school, work, or social purposes, is a difficult one. Research shows that people struggle with choosing the appropriate time to disclose their disability (Jans, Kaye, & Jones, 2012), but nondisclosure comes at a cost for higher education. Students with disabilities who do not disclose to their postsecondary institution are at a higher risk of dropping out (Hudson, 2013).

Several studies have shown that most course instructors do not receive training on how to accommodate students with disabilities (Asuncion et al., 2010; Gladhart, 2010) nor do they understand the needs of students with disabilities (Asuncion et al., 2010; Barnard-Brak et al., 2010, Burgstahler, 2006; Cole & Cawthon, 2015; Rao, 2004). Faculty members often rely on disability support services for information on how to work with students with disabilities, but those offices utilize boilerplate templates to distribute a list of accommodations for a specific student (Orr & Hammig, 2009). Due to their perception that faculty members rarely have a deep understanding of how to support students with disabilities, the participants in Burgstahler's (2006) study did not disclose their disabilities unless they absolutely needed accommodations. In Cole and Cawthon's (2015) study, students with learning disabilities shared that when they approached faculty members about accommodations, many of them did not know what to do. The students then had to assume the responsibility for assisting the faculty members in understanding the disability support process, a responsibility that students felt strained the professor-student power dynamic.

This perception of faculty knowledge surrounding disability is noted in existing research. Some studies have found that a substantial portion of the teaching faculty do not know whether students with disabilities are treated fairly in the classroom (Bruder & Mogro-Wilson, 2010). Others have found that faculty do not know how to interact with people with disabilities (Lombardi, Murray, & Dallas, 2013). Interestingly, Cole and Cawthon (2015) found that students who had professors whose demeanors were more positive toward disability were more willing to disclose the disability and to do so more deeply (via personal conversations in addition to a letter).

Orr and Hammig (2009) also note that the use of boilerplate accommodations for a specific student does little to address the needs of students who have undisclosed disabilities or who may need additional support. Additionally, when faculty choose to not comply with the university accommodations policy (as found in Bruder & Mogro-Wilson, 2010) or to wait for students to approach them regarding needed accommodations, it sets up an environment where students perceive that accommodations are unavailable while also putting the onus on the student for disclosing. This does not encourage students to disclose, and thus students would rather wait until they are on the brink of failing before asking for accommodations (Burgstahler, 2006).

Providing instruction that meets the needs of a broader group of students, instead of accommodations for select individuals would go a long way to supporting those students who do not disclose their disabilities. For example, Gladhart (2010) found that fewer than half of instructors never provided advanced organizers, large print handouts, captioned materials, or captioned or scripted audio for their students. Instructors surveyed by Asuncion et al. (2010) indicated that ensuring accessibility was the role of someone else on campus. As Rao (2004) notes, faculty "need to be better informed about disabilities and students with disabilities" (p. 197).

Stigma and Disability

Individuals with disabilities face a similar potential threat as people from traditionally marginalized racial and ethnic groups—stigma. Several decades ago, Goffman (1963) describes stigma as an attribute that reduces "a whole and usual person to a tainted, discounted one," ultimately discrediting the individual based largely, if not entirely, on perceptions of that attribute alone (p. 3). Later, Steele and Aronson (1995) studied the ways that stigma led to a vulnerability that impacted Black students' academic experiences and performance, or stereotype threat. They explained that stereotype threat was the "risk of confirming, as self-characteristic, a negative stereotype about one's group" (p. 797).

Stereotype threat theory may help inform the basis for non-disclosure of disability and the reasons that disability should be conceptualized as a form of diversity in the higher education classroom. It is essential to note that stereotype threat theory does not consider the "internalization of inferiority images or their consequences" (Steele & Aronson, 1995, p. 798). Rather, it "derives from the broad dissemination of negative stereotypes about one's group—the threat of possibly being judged and treated stereotypically, or of possibly self-fulfilling such a stereotype" (p. 798). Students with disabilities, similar to students from traditionally racially and ethnically marginalized groups, face the vulnerabilities these stereotypes threaten (Greenbaum, Graham, & Scales, 1995).

Particularly salient in the context of higher education, stereotype threat is heightened when the domain is an area of interest. Each subsequent level of higher education involves greater self-selection and less compulsion. The nature of the effects of stereotype threat in compulsory PK-12 education may differ from the impact of those same threats in higher education contexts, specifically because of the students' inherent heightened interest and self-selection in their higher education programs. Students in graduate and professional programs, even further self-selected, may feel increased psychological pressures associated with stereotypes and, thus, may further resist the revelation of their disability status (e.g., Griffin, 2002; Pontius & Harper, 2006).

The words one chooses and how a disability is framed makes a difference. Stigma and discrimination, even decades after the passing of the Americans with Disabilities Act (ADA), are rampant and can influence how people with disabilities experience the world. People with non-apparent disabilities, such as learning disabilities or mental health disorders, are often viewed unfavorably due to negative stereotypes and misunderstandings, which results in an increased reluctance to disclose (e.g., Cole & Cawthon, 2015; Sniatecki, Perry, & Snell, 2015). Whereas people whose disabilities are more apparent are given more empathy and opportunities to choose whether or not to disclose—though still facing threats from the stereotypes associated with their disabilities.

Bruder and Mogro-Wilson (2010) surveyed students and faculty at a university to assess the attitudes, beliefs, and knowledge of people with disabilities.

Of note is that the majority of students (both undergraduate and graduate) and faculty reported that they felt pity, awkwardness, and/or embarrassment often or occasionally when they met a person with a disability. There was a fear of doing or saying the wrong thing, and there were feelings of uncertainty about how to behave around people with disabilities. Additionally, approximately half of undergraduate students reported less than enthusiastic feelings when encountering people with disabilities, an attitude that students with disabilities themselves pick up on (Cole & Cawthon, 2015).

Sniatecki, Perry, and Snell (2015) also examined faculty attitudes and beliefs around disability and reported that faculty generally held positive views about the place for students with disabilities in higher education, but those views were significantly different based on the type of disability. Faculty held students with physical disabilities in higher favor than students who had mental health or learning disabilities. These views play a role in the way that students with disabilities experience postsecondary education.

Culturally Relevant Pedagogy

The search for the "right" teaching strategies that acknowledge and humanize all students and their histories is a challenge for educators. Culturally relevant teaching is recognized as a way of empowering students to bring their realities and perspectives to the classroom and to recognize the perspectives of their peers (Ladson-Billings, 1995; 2014). Ladson-Billings found through her work that teachers are primarily concerned with academic achievement, regardless of a student's culture, so that feel-good types of pedagogy are not central. The challenge then is how culturally relevant teaching can be designed to get students to a place where they want to excel academically.

Culturally relevant pedagogy and culturally responsive classroom are often centered on the creation of a positive and affirming environment. Teacher characteristics associated with culturally relevant pedagogy and the culturally responsive classroom, include "empathy, caring, the ability to create a healthy classroom climate, leadership skills, humor, and involvement with . . . social relations" (Cartledge & Kourea, 2008, p. 353).

Moll, Amanti, Neff, and Gonzalez (1992) used the term "funds of knowledge" when describing "historically accumulated and culturally developed bodies of knowledge and skills essential for household or individual functioning and well-being" (p. 133). Bridging home and school cultures, representing students' funds of knowledge in the curriculum, and incorporating cultural practices are the ways that instructors have used culturally relevant pedagogy with success (Banks, 2013; Moll, 2015). Gay (2013) suggests that culturally relevant pedagogy is about connecting the learning that happens in school with life outside of school, and that it empowers students to exert agency and self-determination. Culturally relevant pedagogy is teaching "diverse students *through* their own cultural filters"

(Gay, p. 49, emphasis original). Cultural differences and cultural knowledge are viewed as assets in a culturally responsive classroom and are used to challenge stereotypes, prejudices, and oppression as well as promoting ideals of social justice.

Where students with disabilities do not necessarily share a culture (the exception being American Deaf Culture), there are ways to include their ways of knowing into the classroom experience. Students with disabilities may not share similar types of struggles, but they do all struggle with academic and social life. The qualities of a culturally responsive classroom identified above are also qualities that best support students with disabilities. This parallel underlines the appropriateness of a (re)construction of culturally relevant pedagogy to explicitly include disability. Where exceptionality has been included in multicultural education and recognized as one part of a person's intersectional identity, ways of incorporating the experiences of people with disabilities into the college classroom, beyond providing post hoc accommodations, have been largely ignored.

Definition of Culturally Relevant Disability Pedagogy

The extension and adaptation of culturally relevant pedagogy to include disability is a natural one. Ladson-Billings (1995) defines three criteria upon which culturally relevant pedagogy rests, "(a) Students must experience academic success; (b) students must develop and/or maintain cultural competence; and (c) students must develop a critical consciousness through which they challenge the status quo of the current social order" (p. 160). These are the bedrocks upon which we will integrate concepts of disability studies. The obvious place to start is to say that all students, including those with disabilities, must experience academic success. However, it is not enough to just include students with disabilities into the classroom and provide them with accommodations. That does not meet their needs of being accepted for who they are or weaving them into the classroom tapestry.

In order to ensure students experience academic success, the environment must be welcoming and supportive. By setting students with disabilities apart, with the mere label of "students with disabilities," there is the established idea that they are different or may not be like the other students in very important ways. Instead, we propose the notion of considering the ways in which the environment disables students. For example, what are sightlines like from each of the desks in the room, what sounds are there that might be distracting or cover up a speaker's voice, how is information presented to students so that all can understand it? These are elements of the classroom which not only alienate students who are labeled with disabilities, but they can alienate other students, too. It is important to identify the barriers to learning that each of our students face and to try to minimize them as much as possible. Once barriers are reduced, then it is possible for students to learn which then is followed with academic success.

It is easy to discuss the reduction of physical barriers to success, but there are also attitudinal and behavioral barriers as well. Once a student receives a label, there is an automatic response by school personnel as to how that a student will behave, and he/she is treated accordingly. Think about this: a student with an IEP arrives in a school, and the student's label is Emotional and Behavior Disorder. The automatic assumption is that the child will be behavior problem, and the teachers assigned to work with the student prepare to fortify their classroom management and mitigate the damage the student will do to the classroom environment. There is usually little consideration given to the idea that perhaps the environment set the student up to fail. There may not have been structures in place for the student to follow, the student may not have understood the rationale for the structures, or the environment was set up in a way that prevented the student from participating fully in the class so the student responded in ways that an IEP team deemed socially unacceptable.

Additionally, the personnel may have negative connotations or feelings about students with that particular label and begin a process of resistance (Gay, 2013). They set themselves up internally for a fight and prepare for the negative behaviors they will encounter. The student enters the school and is automatically confronted with people who are expecting the worst. How they must feel to be greeted by people who may outwardly say warm things, but who are on edge and maybe even a little standoffish. Perhaps the words are not negative, but the tone is a littler sterner or harsher than the tone used for other students. This does not make a recipe for success.

We propose changing the framework from personalizing the disability in an individual, as in something is wrong with the individual that must be remedied or accommodated, to recognizing the disability of the environment, as in identifying the parts of the environment that prevent a person from being able to do what s/he needs to do. This reframing moves the onus from the individual with the disability to a collective responsibility for creating a humanized environment that more effectively meets the needs of all students across the spectrum of learning differences. This major shift in today's education world removes much of the individual adaptations typically associated with teaching and supporting students with disabilities and, instead, focuses the entire community, collectively, on ensuring that there is nothing disabling in the environment for the student with a particular disability to encounter.

The second part of Culturally Relevant Pedagogy as defined by Ladson–Billings (1995) is that students develop and maintain cultural competence. Gay (2013) notes that many teachers shy away from this notion, because they mistakenly equate recognition of differences as discriminatory or they feign ignorance without making an effort to become culturally competent themselves. They may stick to superficial celebrations of culture, customs, and food or discuss only the ways in which people from various cultures get along without recognizing the struggle. When it comes to people with disabilities, they are typically shown inspirational stories of overcoming, what has been termed "inspiration porn" (Young, 2012). The purpose of inspiration porn, according to Young, is so that non-disabled people can put their worries into perspective. So they can go, "Oh well if that kid who doesn't have any legs can smile while he's having an awesome time, I should never, EVER feel bad about my life." It's there so that non-disabled people can look at us and think "well, it could be worse . . . I could be that person."

In this way, these modified images exceptionalize and objectify those of us they claim to represent. It's no coincidence that these genuinely adorable disabled kids in these images are never named: it doesn't matter what their names are, they're just there as objects of inspiration.

But using these images as feel-good tools, as "inspiration," is based on an assumption that the people in them have terrible lives, and that it takes some extra kind of pluck or courage to live them.

In her TED talk, Stella Young (2014) discussed an experience she had while teaching. One of her students raised his hand and asked when she was going to do her speech. After questioning him a bit, she came to the realization that his only experience with people with disabilities was for them to come to the school and give an inspirational speech. He did not have experience with people with disabilities in his daily life, and was confused by anything outside of the inspirational talk. The disconnect between recognizing the difference—Young goes about her day sitting (while many people do so by walking) and objectifying her experience: it must be so difficult to be "confined" to a wheelchair—does not do anything to improve students' cultural competence when it comes to disability.

Gay's (2013) response is that we need to teach students how to grapple with the troubling issues of injustice, oppression, and inequities of life while also recognizing the contributions of people who are different from them. She argues that difference is neither inherently good nor inherently bad; they are present in our everyday experiences and should be recognized for what they are. By bringing difference out into the open and exploring it from all angles, not just the smooth, shiny side, we can become culturally competent and move our students toward becoming culturally competent in a truly humanistic way.

The third criterion for culturally relevant pedagogy identified by Ladson-Billings (1995) is that students become aware of the inequities of society and begin to challenge the status quo. The "students" Ladson-Billings refers to here is inclusive of all students in the community. Here again, culturally relevant pedagogy shifts the paradigm from the "different student" bearing the burden to fight for change to a paradigm where the community, collectively, works to disrupt stereotypes and discrimination and all members of the community become critically conscious of barriers or unearned advantages present in the existing social order. For example, a student who uses a wheelchair is often the one who assumes responsibility for requesting access or advocating for themselves when that access is denied. If all students are taught to understand the barriers—both physical and attitudinal—faced by students in wheelchairs, they are then empowered to disrupt discriminatory practices and challenge discriminatory beliefs. Social justice cannot be achieved without everyone's participation.

Finally, despite the legal definitions of disability as using terms such as "impairment" and viewing through a lens of what people cannot do, we are choosing to adopt Gay's (2013) approach of moving beyond the negative view of deficit. We prefer to look at the potential and promise of what students can do. This is a challenge since the word "disability" calls up negative perspectives for many teachers, but this shift in thinking is required in order to be a culturally relevant instructor for students with unique learning needs.

Culturally Relevant Disability Pedagogy in Practice

As we established, it is important to the success of students with disabilities for faculty to be cognizant of the impact of disability on learning and to design instruction that is inclusive for all students. Lombardi, Murray, and Dallas (2013) conducted a study of faculty attitudes around disability when they have and have not received training. They found that regardless of whether the training was low intensity (e.g., reading an article about disability) or high intensity (e.g., attending a workshop), faculty reported a significantly higher willingness to incorporate inclusive strategies into their instruction. They propose that a starting place to increase the awareness and willingness of faculty to support students with disabilities is just to provide a range of resources. The resources can include articles or books available on a shared faculty site, workshops provided on campus, large multi-day training events, or assigning a contact person to reach out to faculty. It is more important to provide a variety of resources that faculty can access in different ways (Lombardi et al., 2013).

Additionally, in order to encourage the disclosure of disabilities, a reduction in stereotyping is critical. Culturally relevant disability pedagogy can succeed at enhancing outcomes for students with disabilities in the same ways that culturally relevant pedagogy has succeeded at supporting the outcomes of students from traditionally marginalized racial and ethnic groups. In practice, culturally relevant pedagogies have led to "strategies that have reduced negative stereotyping and secured students in an academic domain where they are valued, challenged, and supported" (Taylor & Antony, 2000, p. 195). A good place to start might be with Cole and Cawthon's (2015) recommendations for faculty: (1) increase their knowledge level of disability and accommodations, (2) work with students to develop an accommodation plan to be used consistently throughout the semester, (3) make an effort to appear open and willing to accommodate students with disabilities, and (4) try to teach to different learning styles.

Bartolome (1994) has decried the search for the "right" teaching strategies and argued for an approach that emphasizes the inclusion of diverse perspectives and histories into pedagogical practice. Culturally relevant teaching does not intend to essentialize any single culture. Rather, it is about bringing in the knowledge and experiences of people who belong to a group that is often oppressed and using those ways of being and knowing to connect to the academic content. They experience and know the world in different ways than the White, Euro-centric model expected in most classrooms in the United States. This is also true for people with disabilities. They may not fit precisely into the able-bodied mold that schools were designed for. While they participate in the culture, maybe even the dominant culture, they are often still considered less-than and treated to a whole host of injustices and oppressions.

The threat of negative stereotyping after being labeled with a disability, as discussed earlier, is among the first barriers that students with disabilities must face. Instructors can do much to reduce the stigma of "disability" for their students. Teachers can design instruction that reduces the extent to which the person's disability is on display, as Ladson-Billings (2014) calls it "consistently marginalized students are repositioned into a place of normativity—that is, that they become subjects in the instructional process not mere objects" (p. 76). Much like how Stella Young (2012; 2014) stated that she is not the inspiration for able-bodied people, merely pointing out the ways that students are different or highlighting their differences in class turns people with disabilities into objects to be viewed. However, leveraging the principles of Universal Design for Learning (UDL) can help to move instruction from objectifying to being inclusive.

UDL eschews the idea that students fall into one of two groups: having disabilities or not having disabilities. Instead, UDL starts with the premise that all learners fall on a continuum of learning needs, and that classrooms and instruction need to be reconstructed to support students on the entire continuum (Orr & Hammig, 2009). Environments can be designed in a way that every student is able to demonstrate what they know and can do without privileging one type of ability over another. When students are provided information several different ways and given opportunities to demonstrate what they know in ways that are meaningful to them, then the impact of different ways of learning and knowing is reduced.

Often, higher education classrooms rely on a series of lectures and tests for student learning (Chao, DeRocco, & Flynn, 2007). These approaches are not appropriate for many types of learners to demonstrate what they know. Take, for example, the brother of the lead author. This brother (let's call him D) has been identified with a learning disability from a very young age. D registered for a math course his first semester of college, and failed it despite being able to demonstrate a high level of math competency in the class. The course instructor even commented on D's uncanny ability to think in mathematical terms. However, D has always struggled with tests, the sole way that grades were determined in this particular math course. The use of paper-and-pencil tests may be ubiquitous, but it is not the only way to assess student learning of concepts. In fact, Orr and Hammig (2009) consider paper-and-pencil tests to be outmoded, based on their review of the literature of pedagogy in higher education.

Thomas Scruggs and Margo Mastropieri have researched a series of techniques that support the learning of all students in the classroom without watering down the curriculum. They call these techniques *differentiated curriculum enhancements* (Scruggs & Mastropieri, 2013, p. 70). Through a series of studies (see, for example, Marshak, Mastropieri, & Scruggs, 2011; Mastropieri, Scruggs, Norland, Berkeley, McDuffie, Tornquist, & Connors, 2006; Scruggs, Mastropieri, & Marshak, 2012), they found that all students in the classroom benefit from these techniques, but students with learning disabilities showed a greater relative benefit (Scruggs, 2012). Additionally, these strategies allow for content standards to remain at a high level while also reducing the stigma of being singled out as the student who needs help.

Scruggs (2012) also suggests that instruction that focuses on specific skill or strategy building had strong effect sizes, thus interventions that support students in attending to the content or in thinking more systematically are more appropriate. Additionally, these strategies reduce the cognitive load that students need in order to process content. A number of strategies are identified by Scruggs as fitting into this mold. They include:

- Peer-mediated learning
- Hands-on learning
- Computer-assisted instruction
- Spatial learning strategies, such as using tables and charts
- Study aids, such as highlighting and structured notes
- Learning strategy instruction, such as study skills and note-taking skills
- Mnemonic instruction
- Systematic, explicit instruction in specific contexts

Although these strategies have been tested by Scruggs and Mastropieri in secondary settings, they are still effective strategies for postsecondary students as well. The Scholarship of Teaching and Learning is the framework used by postsecondary institutions for promoting effective instructional strategies for their students. Clickers and other active learning strategies have been shown to improve student attitudes toward content and course performance (Shuster & Preszler, 2014). For example, Shuster and Preszler (2014) found that using peer-mediated instruction, in the form of peer facilitators and peer-facilitated small, resulted in improved student performance, particularly for minority and female students, in one biology class. In another biology class, they found that the peer workshop model was not as successful, so they experimented with supplementing the traditional lecture with case studies that were designed to encourage students to apply processes and explain their answers.

Explicit instruction on specific skills or strategies is also effective for postsecondary students (Thomas & Sondergeld, 2015). For example, Thomas and Sondergeld worked with pre-service teachers on assessing student performance and providing constructive feedback as part of an instructional methods course.

The preservice teachers received explicit instruction on how to give feedback to students and then were given opportunities to apply the skills in a real-world context. They found that the preservice teachers in this course demonstrated higher achievement on the program's primary performance assessment than preservice teachers who did not take the course.

These strategies have not been researched specifically with students who have disabilities in postsecondary classrooms, but they serve to illustrate the ways in which strategies that are effective in secondary classrooms can apply to postsecondary settings. These are teaching techniques that support the learning of all students, including those who have disabilities.

Importance of the Argument for Higher Education

From a social justice perspective, it is critical to higher education for the fact that students with disabilities are attending and will continue to attend postsecondary institutions in growing numbers. In order to achieve the ideal of equal participation in society and bridge the opportunity gaps between people with disabilities and people without disabilities, faculty members must provide an education that is accessible to all of their students. Applying Culturally Relevant Disability Pedagogy as they plan curriculum for a course or program of studies will ensure a more friendly experience for students with disabilities and encourage persistence through graduation.

Perhaps even more urgent in the context of higher education is the increasing pressure for accountability (Hillman, Tandberg, & Fryar, 2015). Expanding supports and structures to enhance student learning outcomes and completion rates will be significant as institutions of higher education are increasingly called to task on those types of measures. The increase in outcome accountability for institutions of higher education coupled with the increasing percentages of people enrolling in undergraduate and post baccalaureate programs makes it critical for those institutions to become more effective at serving students with different learning needs.

Conclusion

Recognizing the barriers to success that students with disabilities often face in higher education classrooms creates a moral imperative for developing new ways of supporting those students. The commonly held assumption that "all of the [student]'s difficulties reside solely within the [student]" (Cartledge & Kourea, 2008, p. 353) is particularly pervasive in higher education. In order to shift that mindset, while maintaining high expectations of all students, faculty must be given the opportunity and encouragement to develop cultural awareness (including awareness of different disabilities), exploring different pedagogical approaches to reach the wider swath of learners, and begin to consider ways of adjusting curriculum content to meet different learners' needs (Banks et al., 2005). In the same ways that culturally relevant pedagogy has become a rallying cry to support the success of students from diverse ethnic and racial backgrounds, this new framework of a culturally relevant disability pedagogy can bring together theory and practice to support the success of students with various disabilities in the higher education classroom.

References

Asuncion, J. V., Fichten, C. S., Ferraro, V., Chwojka, C., Barile, M., Nguyen, M. N., & Wolforth, J. (2010). Multiple perspectives on the accessibility of e-learning in Canadian colleges and universities. *Assistive Technology, 22*, 187–199. doi: 10.1080/10400430903519944.

Banks, J. A. (2013). The construction and historical development of multicultural education, 1962–2012. *Theory into Practice, 52*, 73–82.

Banks, J., Cochran-Smith, M., Moll, L., Richert, A., Zeichner, K., LePage, P., et al. (2005). Teaching diverse learners. In L. Darling-Hammond & J. Bransford (Eds.), *Preparing teachers for a changing world: What teachers should learn and be able to do* (pp. 232–274). San Francisco, CA: Jossey-Bass.

Barber, P. (2012). College students with disabilities: What factors influence successful degree completion? A case study. Retrieved from http://www.heldrich.rutgers.edu/sites/default/files/products/uploads/College_Students_Disabilities_Report.pdf.

Barnard-Brak, L., Lechtenberger, D., & Lan, W. Y. (2010). Accommodation strategies of college students with disabilities. *The Qualitative Report, 15*(2), 411–429.

Bartolome, L. I. (1994). Beyond the methods fetish: Toward a humanizing pedagogy. *Harvard Educational Review, 64*(2), 173–195.

Bruder, M. B., & Mogro-Wilson, C. (2010). Student and faculty awareness and attitudes about students with disabilities. *Review of Disability Studies: An International Journal, 6*(2). Retrieved from http://www.rds.hawaii.edu/ojs/index.php/journal/article/view/169.

Burgstahler, S. (2006). The development of accessibility indicators for distance learning programs. *Research in Learning Technology, 14*, 79–102. doi: 10.1080/09687760500479753.

Cartledge, G., & Kourea, L. (2008). Culturally responsive classrooms for culturally diverse students with and at risk for disabilities. *Exceptional Children, 74*(3), 351–371.

Chao, E. L., DeRocco, E. S., & Flynn, M. K. (2007). *Adult learners in higher education: Barriers to success and strategies to improve results.* A report prepared for the U.S. Department of Labor, Employment and Training Administration. Retrieved from http://files.eric.ed.gov/fulltext/ED497801.pdf.

Cole, E. V., & Cawthon, S. W. (2015). Self-disclosure decisions of university students with learning disabilities. *Journal of Postsecondary Education and Disability, 28*(2), 163–179.

Council for Exceptional Children. (2014). *Advancing higher education & employment opportunities for individuals with disabilities.* Arlington, VA: Council for Exceptional Children.

Gay, G. (2013). Teaching to and through cultural diversity. *Curriculum Inquiry, 43*(1), 48–70. doi: 10.1111/curi.12002.

Gillborn, D. (2015). Intersectionality, critical race theory, and the primacy of racism race, class, gender, and disability in education. *Qualitative Inquiry, 21*(3), 277–287.

Gladhart, M. A. (2010). Determining faculty needs for delivering accessible electronically delivered instruction in higher education. *Journal of Postsecondary Education and Disability, 22*(3), 185–196.

Goffman E. (1963). *Stigma: Notes on the management of spoiled identity*. New York, NY: Prentice Hall.

Goodley, D. (2013). Dis/entangling critical disability studies. *Disability & Society, 28*(5), 631–644. doi: 10.1080/09687599.2012.717884.

Greenbaum, B., Graham, S., & Scales, W. (1995). Adults with learning disabilities: Educational and social experiences during college. *Exceptional Children, 61*(5), 460–471.

Griffin, B. W. (2002). Academic disidentification, race, and high school dropouts. *High School Journal, 85*(4), 71–81.

Hillman, N. W., Tandberg, D. A., & Fryar, A. H. (2015). Evaluating the impacts of "new" performance funding in higher education. *Educational Evaluation and Policy Analysis, 37*(4), 501–519.

Hudson, R. L. (2013). The effect of disability disclosure on the graduation rates of college students with disabilities (Doctoral dissertation). Retrieved from https:// vtechworks.lib.vt.edu/bitstream/handle/10919/24072/Hudson_RL_D_2013. pdf?sequence=1&isAllowed=y.

Jans, L. H., Kaye, H. S., & Jones, E. C. (2012). Getting hired: successfully employed people with disabilities offer advice on disclosure, interviewing, and job search. *Journal of Occupational Rehabilitation, 22*(2), 155–165.

Ladson-Billings, G. (2014). Culturally relevant pedagogy 2.0: Aka the remix. *Harvard Educational Review, 84*(1), 74–84.

Ladson-Billings, G. (1995). Toward a theory of culturally relevant pedagogy. *American Educational Research Journal, 32*(3), 465–491.

Lauffer, K. (2000). Accommodating students with specific writing disabilities. *Journalism & Mass Communication Educator, Winter 2000*, 29–46.

Lombardi, A., Murray, C., & Dallas, B. (2013). University faculty attitudes toward disability and inclusive instruction: Comparing two institutions. *Journal of Postsecondary Education and Disability, 26*(3), 221–232.

Marshak, L., Mastropieri, M. A., & Scruggs, T. E. (2011). Curriculum enhancements in inclusive secondary social studies classrooms. *Exceptionality, 19*(2), 61–74. doi: 10.1080/09362835.2011.562092.

Mastropieri, M. A., Scruggs, T. E., Norland, J. J., Berkeley, S., McDuffie, K., Tornquist, E. H., & Connors, N. (2006). Differentiated curriculum enhancement in inclusive middle school science: Effects on classroom and high-stakes tests. *Journal of Special Education, 40*(3), 130–137.

Moll, L. C. (2015). Tapping into the "hidden" home and community resources of students. *Kappa Delta Pi Record, 51*(3), 114–117.

Moll, L. C., Amanti, C., Neff, D., & Gonzalez, N. (1992). Funds of knowledge for teaching: Using a qualitative approach to connect homes and classrooms. *Theory into Practice, 31*(2), 132–141.

Orr, A. C., & Hammig, S. B. (2009). Inclusive postsecondary strategies for teaching students with learning disabilities: A review of the literature. *Learning Disability Quarterly, 32*(3), 181–196.

Pontius, J. L., & Harper, S. R. (2006). Principles for good practice in graduate and professional student engagement. *New Directions for Student Services, 2006*(115), 47–58.

Rao, S. (2004). Faculty attitudes and students with disabilities in higher education: A literature review. *College Student Journal, 38*(2), 191–198.

Richardson, J. T. E. (2009). The attainment and experiences of disabled students in distance education. *Distance Education, 30*(1), 87–102.

Scruggs, T. E. (2012). Differential facilitation of learning outcomes: What does it tell us about learning disabilities and instructional programming? *International Journal for Research in Learning Disabilities*, *1*(1), 4–20.

Scruggs, T. E., & Mastropieri, M. A. (2013). Individual differences and learning challenges. *Theory into Practice*, *52*, 63–72. doi: 10.1080/00405841.2013.795443.

Scruggs, T. E., Mastropieri, M. A., & Marshak, L. (2012). Peer-mediated instruction in inclusive secondary social studies learning: Direct and indirect learning effects. *Learning Disabilities Research & Practice*, *27*(1), 12–20.

Shuster, M. I., & Preszler, R. (2014). Introductory biology course reform: A tale of two courses. *International Journal for the Scholarship of Teaching and Learning*, *8*(2), Article 5. Retrieved from http://digitalcommons.georgiasouthern.edu/ij-sotl/vol8/iss2/5.

Sniatecki, J. L., Perry, H. B., & Snell, L. H. (2015). Faculty attitudes and knowledge regarding college students with disabilities. *Journal of Postsecondary Education and Disability*, *28*(3), 259–275.

Steele, C. M., & Aronson, J. (1995). Stereotype threat and the intellectual test performance of African Americans. *Journal of Personality and Social Psychology*, *69*(5), 797–811.

Taylor, E., & Antony, J. S. (2000). Stereotype threat reduction and wise schooling: Towards the successful socialization of African American doctoral students in education. *Journal of Negro Education*, *69*(3), 184–198.

Thomas, A. F., & Sondergeld, T. (2015). Investigating the impact of feedback instruction: Partnering preservice teachers with middle school students to provide digital, scaffolded feedback. *Journal of the Scholarship of Teaching and Learning*, *15*(4), 83–109. doi: 10.14434/josotl.v15i4.13752.

Wagner, M., Newman, L., Cameto, R., & Levine, P. (2005). *Changes over time in the early postschool outcomes of youth with disabilities: A report of findings from the National Longitudinal Transition Study (NLTS) and the National Longitudinal Transition Study-2 (NLTS2)*. Retrieved from http://www.nlts2.org/reports/2005_06/nlts2_report_2005_06_complete.pdf.

Young, S. (2012, July 2). *We're not here for your inspiration*. Retrieved from http://www.abc.net.au/rampup/articles/2012/07/02/3537035.htm.

Young, S. (2014). *I'm not your inspiration, thank you very much*. TED Talk. Retrieved from http://www.ted.com/talks/stella_young_i_m_not_your_inspiration_thank_you_very_much.

2

A DIFFERENT DIVERSITY?

Challenging the Exclusion of Disability Studies from Higher Education Research and Practice

Lauren Shallish

Introduction

The 1960s and 1970s civil rights movements required colleges and universities to address social and educational inequality and respond to changing demographics of college-going populations. As such, categories of race, gender, sexual orientation, and ethnicity were used in hiring and recruitment practices, enrollment management policies, and retention initiatives. Disability, however, was largely relegated to the margins. In a *Chronicle of Higher Education* article Lennard Davis (2011) explicitly asked, "Why is disability missing from the discourse of diversity?" Scholars and practitioners argued this is reflective of disability's position as the "Last civil rights movement," citing that better-known groups have had long(er) established legal statutes, fields of study, scholarship, and activism; yet disability studies contends this exclusion is not an issue of timing but structural inequality (Davis, 2015). A contributing factor to the persistent and structural exclusion of disability within postsecondary diversity efforts has been the lack of understanding of persons with disability as having social group status.

In "Five Faces of Oppression" (1990), Iris Marion Young defined a social group as a "special kind of collectivity" whose affinity is shaped by similar experiences. The history of social forces constitutes a group rather than any inherent feature of the individuals who make up the collective. As social groups are defined by their difference from the norm, Guldvik and Lesjo (2014) argued that disability should be considered as one such entity; yet scholars, practitioners, faculty, and administrators largely identify disability as an individualized, biomedical issue. Diversity and disability, therefore, continue to remain separate concerns.

As scholars and practitioners work to increase educational opportunities for historically underserved populations and a growing body of research indicates that being part of a diverse college community can enhance development in leadership skills, critical thinking, and cross-cultural communication (Clark, 2011; Gurin, Dey, Hurtado, & Gurin, 2002; Smith, 2015; Winkle-Wagner & Locks, 2014), there is little inquiry into how disability is situated within post-secondary diversity work. Even as students with disabilities attend college in greater numbers, and the National Center for Education Statistics reported that 11% of undergraduates report having a disability (NCES, 2010), this group often remains segregated in both academic and cocurricular settings (Tregoning, 2009). Data disaggregated by disability category further indicates disparities in representation among various campus sectors including residential life, athletics, and student and alumni affairs (Collins & Mowbray, 2005; Denhart, 2008; Mock & Love, 2012).

Research indicates that barriers for students with disabilities include minimal financial support, difficulty seeking accommodations, subtle obstacles to full participation including lack of peer awareness, and diminished representation in academic fields (Barnar-Brak, Lectenberger, & Lan, 2010; Holloway, 2001). Institutions are required to meet legal requirements for access and as participation outlined in Section 504 of the Rehabilitation Act of 1973 and the Americans with Disabilities Act (1990; 2008), yet research and case law indicate universities are still establishing compliance practices (Harbour, 2013). Even as compliance standards are met, de facto experiences of segregation persist:

> Although similar forms of segregation are no longer tolerated on the basis of race or ethnicity, seating for students using wheel chairs is often limited to the rear of the classroom. Like students who are not native speakers of English, students who communicate via interpreter or speech synthesizer find themselves excluded from class discussion if the faculty member does not control the pace of the conversation so that their voices can be heard… Furthermore, like students for whom English is a "foreign language", students who use American Sign Language (ASL) face additional challenges because ASL is not bound by the same conventions as spoken and written English.
>
> (Higbee, Katz & Shultz, 2010, p. 8)

Inquiry on disability and higher education finds that the most common institutional barriers include a lack of understanding of the disabled experience or the ableist perception that related services provide an unfair advantage (Williams & Ceci, 1999). While legal statutes provide the most basic civil rights, the social and cultural skepticism of individualized accommodations posit differences from normative presentations of ability (Emens, 2013). The perpetuation of disability as an individualized, medical condition maintains its devaluation within diversity efforts and obstructs the understanding of persons who identify as disabled as a valued social group.

Diversity, Legal Discourse, and Research

Diversity in educational settings is generally understood as the "body of services and programs offered to groups of students, faculty and staff that seek to ensure compliance with non-discrimination and related policy and law, and to affirm social membership group differences (broadly considered) in curricular, co-curricular and workplace contexts" (Clark, 2011, p. 57). Diversity work, as it is used in this study, involves the perspectives, cultures, and histories experienced by non-privileged groups and the act(s) of integrating and embedding this work into or disrupting existing institutional structures and practices (Ahmed, 2012). While growing bodies of research examine diversity in higher education and first-person experiences of marginalization in postsecondary settings (Brown, Hinton, & Howard-Hamilton, 2007; Cuyjet, Howard-Hamilton, & Cooper, 2011; Gurin, Dey, Hurtado, & Gurin, 2002; Moses & Chang, 2006; Swartz, 2009), there has been limited inquiry into disability apart from the administration of services and experience of accommodations provided by the offices of disability services (Burgstahler & Cory, 2008). As numbers of students, faculty, and staff with disabilities are growing, and increasingly diverse, there is a demonstrated need for inquiry into experiences of disability beyond legal compliance and service provision (McCune, 2001). Studies on experiences of racial or ethnic marginalization focus on sociological inquiry, academic and social supports, identity centers, scholarships, and alumni events (Lee & LaDousa, 2014; Patton, 2010; Smith, 2015); yet a majority of literature on disability in higher education addresses a singular focus on service delivery in accordance with disability law (Simon, 2011).

For colleges and universities considered "public entities" under the ADA, anti-discrimination is defined as "no qualified individual with a disability shall, by reason of such disability, be excluded from participation in or denied the benefits of any such entity" (ADA, Sec. 12131). While this is consistent with other antidiscrimination statutes, a person must first provide medical documentation of their physical or mental impairment in order to qualify for legal protection. This qualification differs from protections for other classes that, for example, do not have to provide strict medical evidence of their racialized or gendered identity. Additionally, other social groups do not run the risk of not being raced or gendered "enough" as the definition of disability involves time limitations and medical evidence vis-à-vis major life activities (ADA, Sec. 12102).

Disconnects between the spirit of antidiscrimination law and social and cultural acceptance are not unfamiliar to other social groups, yet the interpretation of the ADA by colleges and universities requires a different kind of interaction (Spade, 2011). Argued Emens (2013), the "United States antidiscrimination statutes covering classifications like race and sex—such as Title VII of the Civil Rights Act of 1964—involved costs to the employer and changes to policies and practices that operated *like* an accommodation (e.g., putting women's restrooms in a formerly all-male work place may cost money)" (p. 45). However, "The ADA obliges employers to respond to *individual* requests, supported by medical documentation, initiated by the students and employees themselves, thereby requiring a different kind of interaction" (Emens, 2013, p. 45). Here, the individualized requirement to provide medical documentation to secure accommodation makes the category of disability stand apart from other social group identities. Even as scholars challenge wholesale assumptions about identity and essentialism (May, 2015), disability remains constructed as an individual request with generalized beliefs about capability that are attached to one's label (Oliver, 1990). In every sense, disability meets Young's (1990) criteria for social group status but the largest minority group in the United States is hardly known as such.

Numbers of persons with disabilities attending, teaching, and working in higher education have tripled over the past twenty-five years, but the majority of research on disability and higher education consists of longitudinal surveys, quantitative studies, and case law which maintains a singular focus on compliance with legal regulations (Olney, Kennedy, Brockelman, & Newsom, 2004). In Peña's (2014) review of the four top-tier journals in higher education, scholarship on students with disabilities yielded 25 results out of 2,308 total articles representing 1% of the total work in the last two decades. Almost two-thirds of disability-focused inquiry was quantitative in nature and used surveys to analyze participation, needs, and experiences of students (Peña, 2014). Furthermore, studies on the experience of requesting and administering accommodations highlighted the influence of the medicalized discourse, legally mandated practice of individualized inquiry, and documentation of impairment.

Despite legislative advancements and increased enrollments, faculty, and administrators are not required to address disability or participate in related training (Harbour, 2013). As teachers of K-12 students must participate in disability or diversity training, there is no formal requirement for college or university faculty to understand disability awareness (Lombardi & Murray, 2011). Disparities between IDEA's Part B Child Find mandate and the ADA's individual mandate can also make transition to higher education challenging (Higbee, Katz, & Schultz, 2010). Under the ADA, college students must seek out services and accommodations and in K-12 schools, students meet annually with a multidisciplinary team to review and assess Individualized Education Plans (IEPs). The differences between K-12 and higher education also represent a point of difference that other categories like race and gender do not have to account for in their civil rights statutes. This maintains an individual focus on disability rather than an understanding of how this category functions as a group identity.

Disability Studies Theory

This research is grounded in a disability studies analysis of diversity work so as to challenge the purported neutrality of legal statues and medical classifications of disability and impairment. Disability studies understands the category of disability as a social phenomenon rather than a biomedical deficit that exists solely within the person (Taylor, 2011). This framework contests unquestioned norms about ability, competence, and participation that occur within social, environmental, educational, legal, and attitudinal barriers—part of a larger system of inequality known as ableism (Davis, 2015; Emens, 2013; Linton, 1998). Both scholars and activists in disability studies work to expose the ideologies and institutional systems that marginalize people who have been labeled or become subject to inequality based on being perceived as having a mental or physical impairment.

By employing a disability studies framework, disability is increasingly regarded as a socio-political issue. Growing literature on the complexities of the "disablement process" have emerged from a variety of academic disciplines including geography, philosophy, psychology, and sociology (Barnes, 1999). Disability studies has argued for a social model of disability, one that identifies the category of disability as a construct defined by norms and preferences that do not account for bodily or psycho-social difference. The social model opposes the medical model by arguing impairment is the product of disabling environments and therefore requires interventions at the level of social justice (Siebers, 2008). Disability studies served as the lens by which this study was able to deconstruct the culture of discussion on topics about diversity, education, access, and participation for both persons labeled with a disability and other marginalized groups in higher education.

Methods

Both quantitative and qualitative studies have examined the changing demographics of faculty, students, and staff; however, few projects have investigated the area of disability in postsecondary education beyond the management of offices and services. This is an interview-based qualitative study that sought to understand participants' perceptions of their experiences as diversity workers and how disability was situated within their work. The research design employed a disability studies approach and was based on the assumption that "disability is not a condition characterizing individuals who have limited functioning but is also the product of interaction between individuals and their surroundings" (O'Day & Killeen, 2002, p. 9). Qualitative methods work to expose systems and hierarchies imbued with power and, specific to disability, address how the label of disability has served as a regulatory function of a medical category. This work employed the following research questions:

1. How do diversity workers understand their roles in higher education?
2. What are the ways participants conceptualize disability in relation to other diversity endeavors?
3. In what ways do diversity workers interact with systems of power—including ableism?

4. In what ways have participants' experiences of privilege and inequality informed their work?
5. What efforts do diversity workers utilize to establish a more disability-affirmative agenda?

The study took place with participants from six different college campuses in the northeast United States. The sites were chosen for their representation of differing institutional structures (e.g. women's college, Research One, community college), their commitment to diversity in higher education, and relative geographic proximity. Participants were identified using publically available information on their colleges' websites. Their professional biographies included the following titles: chief diversity officers, chancellor or president, director, dean, senior administrator, compliance officer, faculty, research assistant, and staff. The following descriptors were also identified in the job descriptions of potential participants: diversity, race, gender, sexual orientation, nationality, social inequality, ethnicity, religion, disability, culture, social justice, equity, participation, justice, and inclusion. These key words were adopted from Ahmed's (2012) qualitative research study on diversity workers in higher education. The initial selection criteria included the chancellor or president, the highest-ranking administrator with diversity-related responsibilities, faculty whose scholarship or committee work addressed underrepresented groups in higher education, and staff members who ran identity centers, cocurricular programs, or served as research assistants. These four positions of employment were chosen to gather data from different stratifications within the administrative and leadership structures at each research site. A total of 43 e-mails were sent, 30 replies were received, and 23 interviews were conducted. All names and references to places, events and people have been changed to protect the confidentiality of participants.

Findings: Points of Convergence

The findings in the study address the narrowness of medical interpretations of disability and the ways in which ableism is entrenched with other oppression(s) experienced on college campuses. Participant testimonies demonstrated the social construction of identity categories themselves and the limitations of promoting single-axis thinking. May (2015) described dominant logics about identity as ones that tend to make sense without "Much cognitive effort and that power [itself] operates to continually deny complexity and delay social transformation" (p. 67). In this sense, diversity work and disability were "denied complexity" which, in turn, delayed institutional transformation on the campuses where participants worked.

Robert was a staff member at Eastern State who acknowledged that disability shared similarities with other historically marginalized groups but that this understanding was often thwarted by a focus on medical diagnoses:

I remember early on there was some resistance or just questioning from some other groups on campus, especially the centers that maybe focused on students of color who wondered about that, how disability was a part of diversity. Early on, again, many people we worked with saw disability as a medical issue. A lot of our work was to, hey wait a minute, that may be an aspect of it, but the students themselves represent a particular kind of diversity.

When probed further about how Robert viewed the "medical issue" as an impediment and how he worked to overcome this barrier, he stated:

> Well, our president oversees all diversity efforts so we invited his chairperson for diversity and people on his staff to our staff meetings, trainings, activities. We would invite him to join us and I think pretty early on he saw the connections himself. We would talk about the history of the disability rights movement and how it paralleled and grew from the civil rights movement. Again, both in discussions and in actual formal presentations that we put on, we would make those connections for the diversity chairperson and eventually to faculty and others to make those connections. Then we put everything into columns to see what the common themes were. Again, oppression or disempowerment. That kind of thing.

As Robert's experience suggests, disability and related topics in higher education have been perceived as almost exclusively an individualistic medical problem and have been solely attended to by what was referred to as professionals allied to medicine. The medical model inherent in legal statues like the ADA and Section 504 regulates the administration of services and accommodations in higher education. This positioning also works to construct disability as a "serviceable condition" in higher education, which provides for substantial reason to maintain disablement as a commodity (Baglieri, 2016). Robert and his staff challenged the pervasive medical interpretation. They instead situated disability rights within a civil rights discourse thereby making apparent the histories of social group experience.

Dan was a member of a committee to address admissions recruitment and retention for underrepresented groups at Seneca State. In the committee's work to provide scholarships, cocurricular and academic supports, and financial assistance, Dan acknowledged that "disability fit perfectly into that" even though it was never mentioned as part of the committee's charge. For all the ways disability appeared to fit logically within his colleagues' efforts, both disability and socioeconomic status were still interpreted as negative prospects for the university:

> Economic diversity's a hard sell. There's been a lot of resistance because many people equate poverty or economically poor students with lowering standards. And in the case of disability, the people who make it are more likely from middle or upper class because their parents had the resources

to fight with them and for them, whereas poor people with disabilities it's much harder for them to get access.

Dan saw responses to "poor students" as incorporating deficit beliefs about ability, although ableism was not explicitly named as a marker. Issues of access for persons with disabilities intersected with questions of class and access to resources. In this sense, perceptions about socioeconomic status entwined with ableism. These intersecting oppressions represented structural inequalities that diversity scholars have identified as the false conflict between merit and diversity in higher education. Rather than understanding these intersecting issues as a matter of structural deficits, the blame for academic lack is often placed on students.

Studies on student experiences of disability and accommodations in higher education also focus on the act of having to disclose one's disability status (Higbee, Katz & Schultz, 2010). Findings included student accounts of feeling exposed, having to negotiate complicated decisions about "passing," and sharing potentially private information with a complete stranger (e.g., meeting a faculty member for the first time in the semester). These experiences reflect and connect to many similarities for LGBTQQA students in higher education who feel as though they are in the position of having to "come out" or disclose their sexual orientation (Renn, 2000). As some disability studies scholars contend that accommodations serve to normalize or assimilate students with disabilities into higher education culture, so too have Queer theorists found the act of coming out as one that accommodates normative structures of sexuality. Nelly was a staff and faculty member at Ontario Community College and highlighted the discourse of "curing" or "overcoming" for LGBT groups to be similar to ways in which persons with disability negotiated the influence of the medical model of disability:

> Something else that comes to mind, for disabled individuals, is the whole cure concept. Somebody trying to fix the disabled person to fit into a nondisabled world, which ties in quite a bit with the LGBT community, you know, trying to make gay people straight… Another one—about being out, has been an interesting, mini discussion, we've had with some students who have either ADHD or some non-apparent disability and [their] being afraid to share that with faculty or somebody… and tying that into gay-lesbian people who also have the same process.

The very act of having to disclose or come out signaled an institutional preference for normativity, both about sexual orientation and ability. In this way, diversity work to address LGBTQQA advocacy and disability rights could be shared. By examining this complexity, this expands the existing research on coming out scripts for sexual minorities and for students with disability who feel the must negotiate their disability status both in classroom and nonacademic settings.

The social construction of disability was also influenced by student self-perceptions as described by diversity workers in this study. Particular cultural or religious beliefs were maintained by ableism, though not this was not named explicitly. In the following example, Nelly described how one student's identity was informed by facets of religious and cultural beliefs that denounced disability, specifically psycho-social impairment. Nelly's example of a male student showed the complexity of how ability, race, religion, culture, and gender intersected to inform how the student navigated his identity in higher education:

> We had a very bright man from the inner city. In his teens he started experiencing some unexpected mood swings and this became worse over time to the point where he wouldn't really be able to move off the couch. His family, I don't know if they didn't know they could ask for a medical opinion or were ashamed, it was never real clear on that part but his family told him he should pray. It wasn't until his 30s that he was finally diagnosed with bipolar and then was placed on a medical regimen that worked for him. He was able to enter college, he had a GPA of 3.8 in our mechanical engineering program, which is probably one of our most difficult majors. It took a long time for him to gain any self-confidence. We had many, many conversations because there was still a lot of pain in him. We often had conversations about this and he said for a black man to admit having a mental health diagnosis, he said it just couldn't happen. He would say he would be shunned and he knew that people wouldn't understand. His own family still doesn't understand… he felt, well, he used the terminology for it, I wish I could repeat it, so passing. He said he always felt like he had to try and pass.

The student's experience with a psychosocial disability worked to unsettle his understanding of his gender, culture, and religion and illuminate the ways able-minded norms were embedded within. Ableism featured prominently within his experience of identity. The student felt that disclosing his struggles with psychosocial impairment would compromise his sense of belonging in his other reference groups. The intersection of masculinity and race, as defined by his cultural and religious background, was in conflict with his desire to address his mental health. Importantly, Nelly's example also provided a counter-narrative to the ways in which the medical model of disability has traditionally been constructed as a resoundingly negative lens in disability studies scholarship (Oliver, 1990). The student acknowledged that the "medical regimen worked for him." It is not to say that he disavowed his diagnosis of bipolar but the medications helped him to manage this identity in a different way. Siebers (2008) acknowledges this as part of the value of what disability studies scholarship can bring to understanding notions of identity: "If the field is to advance, disability studies needs to account for both the negative and positive valences of disability, to resist the negative by advocating for the positive and to resist the positive by acknowledging the negative—while never forgetting that it's reason for being is to speak about, for and with disabled people" (p. 5).

Implications and Conclusion

As colleges and universities have acknowledged the category of disability as the result of hard-fought civil rights campaigns and federal legislation, the close proximity to medicalized discourses has kept this category apart from other work that has been designed to address diversity in higher education. There is small but emerging body of qualitative inquiry into experiences that transcend the mandates required by federal law (Holloway, 2001); yet, first-person and autobiographical accounts address the lack of disability awareness on college campuses and the social constructions of disability but do less to interrogate how disability is positioned in relation to and constituted by other social and cultural identities.

This study provided evidence that disability is in fact very much a part of how other underserved groups are constructed in higher education yet is often overlooked as a marker. Participant experiences illuminated the ways ableism functioned and how oppressions experienced by persons labeled as disabled are shared with other in marginalized groups against unquestioned, privileged norms. Specific to disability and disability studies scholarship, this study also illuminated possibilities to reconsider the function of the medical model of impairment (Oliver, 1990).

College presidents, senior administrators, faculty, and staff who are concerned about academic and social success must examine the ways both disability and diversity are constructed. Members of higher education must also interrogate their own biases and the ways that these uphold discriminatory practices at their institutions. These findings demonstrate how disability should be considered within existing practices attentive to diversity so as to better understand the function of ableism within higher education.

As such, it is key that persons with disability be hired not for purposes of tokenism and quotas but to be allies and to center considerations of disability throughout campus sectors. This would potentially reference groups, notions of disability culture and identity and dismantle deficit-based perceptions about what persons with disabilities are qualified to accomplish. Classrooms and curricula must also be representative of marginalized groups and while individual learners may require different supports these do not provide an unfair advantage but are instead a means to access civil rights and participate in campus life alongside one's peers. Specifically for teaching and instruction in postsecondary life, disability addresses questions of access to and learning about course content in a way that benefits all learners. Teaching strategies associated with ability-difference have the potential to focus on the classroom setting. This can minimize the need for individualized accommodations and principles like Universal Design for Learning (Burgstahler & Cory, 2008) can instead embed these supports into the curriculum for all learners. This research illuminates the need for more research, policies, practices, education, and trainings to address ways in which ableism is embedded in our institutional structures and must be dismantled.

References

Ahmed, S. (2012). *On being included: Racism and diversity in institutional life.* Durham, NC: Duke University Press.

Baglieri, S. (2016).Toward unity in school reform:What discrit contributes to multicultural and inclusive education. In D. J. Connor, B. A. Ferri, & S. A. Annamma (Eds.), *DisCrit: Disability studies and critical race theory.* New York:Teachers College Press.

Barnes, C. (1999). *Exploring disability: A sociological introduction.* Malden, MA: Blackwell.

Barnar-Brak, L., Lectenberger, D., & Lan,W.Y. (2010).Accommodation strategies of college students with disabilities. *The Qualitative Report, 1.*

Baynton, D. C. (2013). Disability and the justification of inequality in American history. *The Disability Studies Reader, 17,* 33-57.5(2), 411–429.

Brown, O. G., Hinton, K. G., & Howard-Hamilton, M. F. (2007). *Unleashing suppressed voices on college campuses: Diversity issues in higher education.* New York: Peter Lang.

Burgstahler, S. & Cory, R. (2008). From accommodation to universal design. In S. Gabel & S. Danforth (Eds.), *Disability and the politics of education: An international reader* (pp. 561–577). New York: Peter Lang Publishing.

Clark, C. (2011). Diversity initiatives in higher education: Just how important "Is" diversity in higher education? *Multicultural Education, 19*(3), 57–59.

Collins, M. E., & Mowbray, C. T. (2005). Higher education and psychiatric disabilities: National survey of campus disability services. *American Journal of Orthopsychiatry, 75*(2), 304.

Cuyjet, M. J., Howard-Hamilton, M. F., & Cooper, D. L. (2011). *Multiculturalism on campus: Theory, models, and practices for understanding diversity and creating inclusion.* Sterling, VA: Stylus Pub.

Davis, L. J. (2011). Why is disability missing from the discourse on diversity? *Chronicle of Higher Education.* September 25, 2001.

Davis, L. J. (2015). Diversity. In R.Adams, B. Reiss & D. Serlin (Eds.), *Keywords for disability studies* (pp. 61–74). New York: New York University Press.

Denhart, H. (2008). Deconstructing barriers perceptions of students labeled with learning disabilities in higher education. *Journal of Learning Disabilities, 41*(6), 483–497.

Emens, E. (2013). Disabling attitudes: U.S. Disability Law and the ADA Amendments Act. In L. Davis (Ed.), *The disability studies reader* (pp. 42–60). New York: Routledge.

Guldvik, I., & Lesjo, J. H. (2014). Disability, social groups, and political citizenship. *Disability & Society, 29*(4), 516–529.

Gurin, P., Dey, E., Hurtado, S. & Gurin, G. (2002). Diversity and higher education:Theory and impact on educational outcomes. *Harvard Educational Review, 72*(3), 330–367.

Harbour,W. (2013). Inclusion in K–12 and higher education. In A. Kanter & B. Ferri (Eds.), *Righting educational wrongs: Disability studies in law and education* (pp. 294–306). Syracuse, NY: Syracuse University Press.

Hehir,T. (2002). Eliminating ableism in education. *Harvard Educational Review, 72*(1), 1.

Higbee, J. L., Katz, R. E., & Schultz, J. L. (2010). Disability in higher education: Redefining mainstreaming. *Journal of Diversity Management, 5*(2) 7–16.

Holloway, S. (2001).The experience of higher education from the perspective of disabled students. *Disability & Society, 16*(4), 597–615.

Lee, E. M. & LaDousa, C. (2014). *College students' experiences of power and marginality: Sharing spaces and negotiating differences.* New York: Routledge.

Linton, S. (1998). *Claiming disability.* New York: New York University Press.

Lombardi, A. R. & Murray, C. (2011). Measuring university faculty attitudes toward disability: Willingness to accommodate and adopt universal design principles. *Journal of Vocational Rehabilitation, 34*(1), 43–56.

May, V. M. (2015). *Pursuing intersectionality, unsettling dominant imaginaries.* New York: Routledge.

McCune, P. (2001, May/June). What do disabilities have to do with diversity? *About Campus, 5*(1).

Mock, M., & Love, K. (2012). One state's initiative to increase access to higher education for people with intellectual disabilities. *Journal of Policy and Practice in Intellectual Disabilities, 9*(4), 289–297.

Moses, M. S., & Chang, M. J. (2006). Toward a deeper understanding of the diversity rationale. *Educational Researcher [H. W. Wilson–EDUC], 35*(1), 6.

NCES (National Center for Educational Statistics) (2010). *Enrollment in postsecondary institutions, Fall 2008; graduation rates, 2002 and 2005 cohorts; and financial statistics, fiscal year 2008.* Washington, DC: U.S. Department of Education.

O'Day, B. & Killeen, M. (2002). Research on the lives of persons with disabilities: The emerging importance of qualitative research methodologies. *Journal of Disability Policy Studies, 13*(1), 9–15.

Oliver, M. (1990). *The politics of disablement: A sociological approach.* New York: St. Martin's Press.

Olney, M. F., Newsom, M. A., Kennedy, J., & Brockelman, K. F. (2004). Do you have a disability? A population-based test of acceptance, denial, and adjustment among adults with disabilities in the U.S. *Journal of Rehabilitation, 70*(1), 4.

Patton, L. (Ed.). (2010). *Culture centers in higher education: Perspectives on identity, theory and practice.* Sterling, VA: Stylus Publishing LLC.

Peña, E. V. (2014). Marginalization of published scholarship on students with disabilities in higher education journals. *Journal of College Student Development, 55*(1), 30–40.

Renn, K. (2000). Patterns of situational identity among biracial and multiracial college students. *Review of Higher Education, 23*(4), 399–420.

Siebers, T. (2008). *Disability theory.* Ann Arbor: University of Michigan Press.

Simon, J. (2011). Legal issues in serving students with disabilities in postsecondary education. *New Directions for Student Services, 134*, 95–107.

Smith, D. (2009; 2015). *Diversity's promise for higher education: Making it work.* Baltimore: Johns Hopkins University Press.

Spade, D. (2011). *Normal life: Administrative violence, critical trans politics, and the limits of law.* Cambridge: South End Press.

Swartz, E. (2009). Diversity: Gatekeeping knowledge and maintaining inequalities. *Review of Educational Research, 79*(2), 1044–1083.

Taylor, S. (2011). Disability studies in higher education. *New Directions for Higher Education, 154*, 93–98.

Tregoning, M. E. (2009). *"Getting it" as an ally: Interpersonal relationships between colleagues with and without disabilities. Making good on the promise: Student affairs professionals with disabilities.* Washington, DC: ACPA–College Student Educators International and University Press of America.

Williams, W. M., & Ceci, S. J. (1999, August 6). Accommodating learning disabilities can bestow unfair advantages. *Chronicle of Higher Education,* B4–B5.

Winkle-Wagner, R. & Locks, A. (2014). *Diversity and inclusion on campus: Supporting racially and ethnically underrepresented students.* New York: Routledge.

Young, I. M. (1990). Five faces of oppression. In *Justice and the politics of difference* (pp. 39–65). Princeton, NJ: Princeton University Press.

3

QUEERING DISABILITY IN HIGHER EDUCATION

Views from the Intersections

Ryan A. Miller, Richmond D. Wynn, and Kristine W. Webb

Citations? Done! . . . Formatting? Complete! . . . Revisions to editor? Done! We heave a heavy sigh as we hit the Submit button on another scholarly piece of work. A mere moment later, we are plotting time in our calendars to work on our next submission, because we are on the publish-or-perish treadmill embedded in academia. Other than formulating a scholarly discussion or crafting a closing that deliberates future implications, we seldom steal time in our scholastic lives to ponder the impact our efforts will produce, either on our study participants, our professional practice, or our field. We may use our study data to enhance our teaching or share information with professionals, but have we used the study "as a pretext for exploring bigger educational, social, cultural, and political issues," a guideline used by Nash (2004, p. 60)?

This chapter provided us the opportunity to tell the story of our experiences interviewing college students with (dis)abilities who identified as lesbian, gay, bisexual, transgender, or queer. Nash (2004) urges us to incorporate narratives that facilitate knowing about ourselves and others, and to unravel difficulties and hindrances. We believe the story of our study may deliver some truth that we are compelled to share with others. The development of this chapter caused us to genuinely reflect in an authentic, honest, and passionate voice about what we absorbed. Our hope is that we will capture our readers and cause them to think— not necessarily in the same vein as we presented, but at least contemplate about what we learned.

Despite the increasing prevalence of intersectional research in higher educa-tion, disability too often remains disconnected from nonnormative gender and sexual identities. Though the convergence of disability and queer identifications may be a site rich with conceptual possibility (Kafer, 2013; McRuer, 2006), too often, practitioners and scholars have ignored this intersection or treated the two dimensions of diversity as additive or evenly mutually exclusive on campus and in the lives of students, faculty, and staff. This chapter employs scholarly personal narratives (Nash, 2004) from three researchers who took up the question of how college students experienced the intersections and disconnects of disability, gender, and sexuality. We critically consider our varied disciplinary, personal, and professional backgrounds, as well as our positionalities along dimensions of race, gender, disability, and sexual orientation—and how these dimensions shaped the study we conducted (Miller, 2015; Miller, Wynn, & Webb, in press) and potentially uncovered and addressed (dis)connections between disability and diversity in higher education.

Disability, Gender, and Sexuality in Context

We approached our study with an understanding of the bioecological variables that influence human development (Bronfenbrenner & Morris, 2007). In addition to our awareness of the individual characteristics and environments that contextualize students' lives, we were cognizant of the social, cultural, and political momentum toward justice and equality in our society and how it shaped students' stories, our interactions with them, and our analysis of the data.

This study takes place against a backdrop of the 25th anniversary of the American with Disabilities Act and an increase in affirming visibility in media and other public spaces of persons with disabilities and of those who identify as LGBTQ. Social activism centered on ability, gender identity, gender expression, and sexual orientation, has kept us engaged on many fronts—individual, social, institutional—in critical analysis of identity. The social movement exposing contemporary manifestations of systemic and structural racism (e.g., Black Lives Matter, 2013) has also furthered the dialogue on intersectionality of race and other aspects of identity. Intersections of identities have also gained traction in discussions of policy, as a recent White House forum addressed LGBT and disability issues and emphasized educational access (Rosenberg, 2014). In 2015, there were unprecedented legal and policy decisions that helped to create a more inclusive society. For example, the Supreme Court ruled in favor of marriage equality for same sex couples (*Obergefell v. Hodges*, 2015); the federal government added protections for LGBT people in civilian employment (U.S. Equal Employment Opportunity Commission, 2015) and is taking action to expand educational and employment opportunities for Americans with disabilities (White House, 2015); a new rule was proposed on the implementation of the Affordable Care Act to include nondiscrimination protections in healthcare on the basis of sex to include gender identity (Federal Register, 2015); and the Secretary of Defense recently announced his directives to revise "outdated" policies regarding transgender service members (U.S. Department of Defense, 2015). The increased attention to mental health in several aspects of our culture also contributes to the shifting social, political, and policy priorities (U.S. Department of Health and Human Services, 2015).

Existing literature on LGBTQ youth with disabilities also helped to frame this line of research. Duke (2011) synthesized 24 journal articles and book chapters on LGBTQ youth with disabilities, though only two specific to higher education were found (Harley, Nowak, Gassaway, & Savage, 2002; Underhile & Cowles, 1998); neither of which were based on original research studies. Additional research has since focused on LGBTQ students with disabilities in primary and secondary schooling (Kahn & Lindstrom, 2015) and in higher education (Henry, Fuerth, & Figliozzi, 2010), including the two studies conducted by the authors of this chapter (Miller, 2015; Miller, Wynn, & Webb, in press).

Methods

The study we reflect upon utilized in-depth interviews with 31 students at two universities in the Southern United States: a mid-size state university ($n = 6$) and a large, research-intensive university ($n = 25$). Students interviewed identified with a wide range of disabilities, most commonly psychological and mental health-related ($n = 21$), and gender and sexual identities. We approached both studies employing critical and postmodern epistemologies, which informed our qualitative approach of conducting semi-structured, one-on-one interviews (Charmaz, 2006; Clarke, 2005; Lather, 1991). We consulted with each other online and via phone calls throughout the process of developing and conducting both studies. Given the centrality of our personal experiences in our narratives and the research process more broadly, it is important to share facets of our personal and professional identities. Kris is a Caucasian woman who identifies as female and heterosexual, has two diagnosed disabilities, and is married, middle-aged, and middle class. She is a professor in special education and has years of experience interacting with individuals who have disabilities. Richmond is African American, gay, cisgender, male, and does not have a disability. He is a married, middle-class, assistant professor and director of an academic program in clinical mental health counseling with several years of experience as a practitioner in the field. Ryan is an assistant professor of higher education with a background in student development and diversity affairs at several institutions. He is a white, middle-class, cisgender, queer person without a diagnosed disability and is a first-generation college graduate.

For the purposes of this chapter, we wrote and analyzed scholarly personal narratives (SPN) on the process of researching intersections of disability, gender, and sexuality in higher education (Nash, 2004). Education researchers have increasingly used SPN to reflect on their positionalities and subjectivities (Reddick & Sáenz, 2012). Operating from a postmodern perspective, Nash (2004) rejects the notion of SPNs providing "bottom lines or final answers" (p. 41). Instead, such narratives highlight the personal and contextual nature of authors' journeys, "not omnisciently removed from what [they] write, but caught up personally in every word, sentence, and paragraph" (Nash, 2004, p. 24). Nash developed several tentative guidelines for writing SPNs that informed our work, including drawing from background knowledge; moving from the particular to the general and back again; telling stories in open-ended ways; attempting to find larger implications from narratives; and showing passion. Possible SPN "truth criteria" include open-endedness, plausibility, vulnerability, narrative creativity, and personal honesty (Nash, 2004). Following Nash's (2004) recommendation to establish clear constructs and questions for our narratives, the guiding questions that we used included:

1.   How do our disciplinary, personal, and professional backgrounds and positionalities/identities shape our approaches to this study?
2.   How do the current cultures around disability and LGBTQ identities affect our engagement in this work?
3.   How did we personally react to the process of interviewing students?

Emergent Themes from Scholarly Personal Narratives

Guided by the questions above, each of the three authors independently wrote her/his scholarly personal narrative. We then initially read each other's narratives before meeting and developing tentative themes based on the collective content emerging from the narratives. Then, each author revised her/his narrative before selecting excerpts that aligned with each theme. Below, we detail several of the themes we found across our stories and present corresponding excerpts from each of our narratives.

Complex Positionalities: "Acknowledging and Embracing My Own Biases"

> *Kris:* I wondered about my own biases as I conducted the interviews. Many students on campus readily connect me with the Disability Resource Center, the campus office that provides support and accommodations for students with (dis)abilities. I was quite comfortable with listening to (dis)ability conversations. I worried that my rapport with participants would not extend far enough when we discussed LGBTQ topics. Knowing that bias is really not dichotomous (Pannucci & Wilkins, 2011), I allowed myself to acknowledge and embrace my known biases; however, I still worried about how I would represent myself to the students. What would our partic-ipants want to say to a middle-aged straight white woman? Would students who experienced the intersection of their LGBTQ and (dis)ability iden-tities have a command of information that I could only hope to compre-hend? I thought about just what our purpose was when we began to design the study, and the description Kvale and Brinkmann (2009) used to define this type of research. They instructed that interviews were research pieces whose purpose is to amass descriptions of the lifeworld of the individuals who were interviewed in order to respectfully and authentically interpret

the significance of what we asked and how the participants responded. I wanted to listen in order to capture this very *lifeworld* of our students.

Richmond: I was trepidatious about not presently having a disability and being cisgender while my interviewees identified as transgender and having disabilities. I was conscious of creating safe space for people I would meet whose salient identities differ from my own. I believed there would be points of connection, particularly in the experience of oppression as identifying as transgender and having a disability positions many on the margins of our society in ways that resemble my experience of identifying as African American and gay. I also thought I would witness the resilience that I see in myself. As I would later discover, the students that I interviewed had faced remarkable challenges and had somehow used these experiences as motivation to live more authentic lives. These parallels notwithstanding, I was keenly aware of not knowing the experience of having a disability or being transgender and wanted to honor the students' lived experience.

Ryan: I sat across the table from some students with very different experiences from my own along dimensions of disability, sexuality, race, gender, socioeconomic status; how could I possibly understand what they were telling me? Conversely, if I did not do this study, did I believe research about disability should always fall only to people with disabilities, to be the ones to take risks, ask questions, force the issue? While I expected that difference from my participants on the axis of disability would cause distance between us (and surely it did, in at least some instances), I was surprised to find that disability and mental health actually became the topics that many participants described in the most depth. By saying at the start of the process that I did not (yet) have a disability, perhaps I swept away the possibility that students could say, "Well, you know what I mean" (Kanuha, 2000, p. 442), around disability, and invited vivid stories that helped to convey to me what disability might mean. Given my disclosure at the start of interview that I did not presently have a disability, no one said, "Well, you know what I mean," when it came to anxiety, depression, OCD, Asperger's, Tourette's, or any other disability being discussed.

We highlighted the ongoing importance of naming, acknowledging, and reflecting upon our multiple biases throughout the research process and in our individual narratives. We considered not only our own social identities, with which some participants might identify, but also our professional and scholarly backgrounds that could help develop rapport with participants or contribute to a sense of distance in an interview. We were heartened by remembering Kanuha's (2000) call for deconstructing the insider/outsider binary so often present in research, a dichotomy by which an "insider" is presumed to possess particular information and understanding than "outsider" does not. We perhaps shifted back and forth as insiders/outsiders from moment to moment while planning our studies, conducting interviews, analyzing data, and eventually writing scholarly personal narratives. As we attempted to understand and honor the lived experiences of LGBTQ students with disabilities, we found it crucial to ask students to share their experiences in depth and not to gloss over experiences relating to disability, gender identity, or sexual orientation, regardless of whether the researcher conducting the interview shared the same identity or affiliation. Too little research in higher education considers the identity development implications of disability, particularly as disabilities intersect with other social identities. Given this, the standpoints and positions each researcher carries undoubtedly contribute to the process and finished products emerging from research that allow practitioners in higher education to understand the experiences of diverse students with disabilities.

Goals for Conducting Research: "Students' Whole Stories"

Ryan: The twists and turns this study took often surprised and delighted me. The study sometimes kept me up at night, frustrated or wondering how I might, in some small way, do justice to participants' words. How would I represent students not as heroes or villains, not as problems or solutions, not merely as risk and resiliency, but as human? What if I messed up or really got it wrong? What gave me the right to *represent* anyone in the first place? Each participant interview added to the complexity of the study's topics and pushed my thinking beyond previous boundaries.

Kris: Was I taking an active role in advancing the reproduction of students' oppression by focusing on only their disabilities? McRuer (2006) argues the flexible body is a concept in which bodies and thoughts about bodies are no longer marked by deviance or deficiencies, but rather are fluid, normal, and accepted. Stated in other words, full participation in their sexual development should not be dependent on ability or a societal chronology of development. I was trained to change behaviors, strategize, record, establish order, and teach students how to reach goals earned by their peers. Crip theory misaligns with all of these ideas; imperfection is accepted, valued, and embraced. Oppression of people who identify as LGBTQ and those with disabilities must be changed to reinforcement, and even desirability (McRuer, 2006). Rather than coming from the "disembodying ivory tower" suggested by Pothier and Devlin (2006), the study propelled me beyond my previous assumptions that included my position of power over individuals who seemingly needed my assistance. In spite of years of training and experiences with viewing people only by their deficits, I wanted to observe people in their entirety.

Richmond: While my intention has always been to understand people who identify in these ways as fully human, there are times when the marginalized identity group membership frame seems to reinforce a deficit perspective that could also be objectifying. While it is important to consider the impact that structural and institutional power dynamics have on identity development, I wanted to be open to hearing students' whole stories and not filter them to fit a deficit framework.

One must ponder if negative commentary about deficits did not occur, members of society would have no need for diversity awareness, affirmative action, or equal rights statements; however, we live in a world that regards differences as deficiencies. Welch (2011) posited that differences are not deficit, and diversity can be found in the mind of the determiner while identity resides in the mind of the beholder. The very foundation of our educational processes is built on a deficit model (Rogers-Sirin & Sirin, 2009), and for students with disabilities, their deficits are identified and addressed through special education services (Smith & Tyler, 2014). Buxton (2000) urged educational systems to emphasize deficits less and hire supportive faculty and staff members who share the same identities as students from oppressed groups. By recognizing and implementing strengths-based academic and support services while deemphasizing deficit, we are confident students would modulate a view of supposed deficits to different but accepted variances. To move beyond deficits, those considering the experiences of students with disabilities must critically reflect on their goals for their own practice, interventions, teaching, and research. Indeed, such reflection must be continuous, as scholars and practitioners may unconsciously adopt harmful discourses into their work over time without acknowledgment.

Professional Philosophies: "Right of Inclusion"

Kris: I softly closed my office door, sat in my office chair, and wept. I had just completed an interview with a student who talked of his anger, relentless oppression, and feelings of hopelessness he felt every day. I wept because of my failure to him and others. Instead of working to weaken the norms, I had spent a lifetime of fixing, teaching strategies, and upholding normalcy. I wept because I heard an original and genuine voice so deserving of progress and change: "So it's isolating. It put me into sort of a permanent isolation, where I don't feel like I'll ever be part of a permanent community. And I'm not certain that that's a bad thing. I think isolation, to this extreme, is a very American condition. And it's not a happy thing, but I think there's some insight and some good that I can take away from this." I thought about his agony and isolation long after the interview.

Richmond: Another consideration I had about my role in the study was about my training and experience as a mental health counselor. I have conducted many structured, semi-structured, and unstructured interviews and have facilitated countless interventions in individual and group settings over the past 25 years. While I believed this experience would be an asset, I also wanted to be mindful of the purpose of these interviews; to understand how college students experience the intersections and disconnects of disability, gender, and sexuality and not to conduct counseling sessions. This had been addressed in our informed consent and supported by providing a resource list to study participants that included information on counseling services on campus. I was committed to respecting the boundary between research and counseling and, at the same time, it was important for me to be authentic and respectfully curious, which could be therapeutic for the participants. The transformative value of storytelling is well documented, nevertheless, I wanted to be clear about the focus of these interactions and maintain the integrity of the research.

Ryan: Several times, we talked about the LGBTQ center on campus, the disability services office on campus, and the difference in the two. While students, almost uniformly, thought it was important to have a disability services office and benefited from the resources it provides, several lamented what they viewed as a transactional, service-oriented model of the office. They were realistic enough to admit the office was probably overworked and understaffed, but some students spoke affectionately and repeatedly about the LGBTQ center as a site for meeting new friends, becoming activists, and building community. Affection for the LGBTQ center was not universal; some students saw it as a divisive place, a site for political conflict and "activist types," a place that induced anxiety and nervousness—thus creating a conflict between sexuality/gender identity and disability. These insights caused me to think more deeply about overlaps and differences in how universities, administrators, and student affairs practitioners have framed disability and LGBTQ identities in response to differing legal mandates, cultural norms, developments, and traditions in academe.

McLeskey, Rosenberg, and Westling (2013) defined inclusion as a philosophy of education where students with disabilities are valued members of the community. As we considered what inclusion might look like on campuses, not only for students with disabilities, but for students from one or more oppressed groups, we asked these questions: What could we do as a body to ensure students with diverse identities were genuinely included? How can we ensure these students belong in communities, that they are actively included in academic and social activities, and establish support that guarantees their inclusion? Could we actually structure our campus to ensure students would authentically belong? By addressing these questions, campuses might venture beyond access, tolerance, civility, and acceptance to unquestioned inclusion. Authentic inclusion happens not by giving supports in isolation or lowering expectations but by maintaining expectations while giving appropriate support (Valls & Kyriakides, 2013). Further, for inclusion to occur, we must be willing to create venues for students to identify their obstacles and strengths so we can comprehend how they interpret their identities (Schroeter, 2013). We believe that with supports, attitudes, and perception changes, we will approach closer to full inclusion. An examination of our professional orientations toward working with students with disabilities (and all students) necessitates consideration of both the positive and negative ways we have been socialized into our professions, campuses, and academia broadly.

Students' Identity Development Journeys: "Commitment to Authenticity"

Ryan: With each interview, I silently critiqued the protocol, and became more aware of the questions I did not ask: questions about diagnosis, medication, accommodations, living situations, partners and significant others, families of origin and of choice, activism, and leadership. Despite the absence of structured protocol questions about these topics, some combination of these topics emerged in nearly every interview. These topics perhaps illustrate the ubiquity and hegemony with which some cultural narratives predominate—such as the coming out story (of which nearly every participant shared some version—whether disclosing to family, friends, or even professors and colleagues—and often coming out multiple times about multiple queer identities and about disabilities) or the medical model of disability (by which most students shared their journey of seeking healthcare, receiving a diagnosis, and determining which medications to take—often intertwined with a difficult process of self-discovery and a changing self-image).

Richmond: I admired the participants' resilience. I respected the confidence in their self-knowledge and the commitment to authenticity. One student discussed how his friend, who was aware of his disabilities questioned his ability to know himself when he disclosed his transgender identity: "They think like well, you know, you do have a lot of things going on in your head and ya know you don't know if you're quite understanding what this is and when in actuality I do—and I am just as capable of learning about who I am inside as everybody else is."

Kris: As I conducted interviews, I was dismayed and heartbroken when students described what many call the taboo mentality they experienced on campus, among family members, and in their communities: "If you had a disability then you were not equal to someone who did not have a disability. On the other side, if you were in the LGBT community there was definitely something wrong with you. So, for me to belong to both it has been challenging and there has to be a level of self-awareness, where at some point, I have to be okay with who I am because otherwise I am going to be miserable trying to be something I am not: trying to pretend I don't have a disability or trying to pretend I'm not LGBT." I wondered if this student's message was similar to the concept of involuntary alienation with a consciousness of being excluded, as Löfgren-Mårtenson (2013) discussed in her article, "'Hip to be crip?' About crip theory, sexuality and people with intellectual disabilities."

Self-determination emerged as a theme related to empowerment, decision-making, and disclosure in students' identity development journeys. Self-determination refers to one's ability to act as the primary causal agent in their own lives and to maintain and improve their quality of life (Wehmeyer, 2005). Abery & Stancliffe (2003) conceptualized a tripartite, ecological model of self-determination that goes beyond personal control taking of all aspects of one's life and involves a shared control with trusted others and takes cultural variables into consideration. Wehmeyer and Abery (2013) summarized research on self-determination in people with intellectual and developmental disabilities (IDD), which shows that people with IDD are less self-determined than their nondisabled peers, that they can become more self-determined if given adequate supports, that environmental and intra-individual factors contribute to or predict the self-determination of people with IDD, and that enhanced self-determination results in more positive school, community, and quality of life outcomes.

In reflecting specifically on students with disabilities in higher education, Getzel (2014) suggests ways to foster self-determination that include use of faculty and peer mentoring programs and education coaches, receiving accommodations, and collaboration across campus. Getzel also recommends continued research to identify evidence-based practices that can serve as predictors of improved outcomes for students with disabilities specifically in their transition to college, retention, and degree completion.

We believe that by conducting the interviews for this study in an intentionally open and thoughtful manner, we fostered students' self-determination by genuinely listening to them and providing space and time for them to develop and express their own authenticity. We implore higher education practitioners in non-research settings to embrace opportunities to foster self-determination in students with disabilities by creating classrooms that give voice to individuals' lived experience, by incorporating empowerment approaches in student support services, and by implementing institutional policies that reflect an unambiguous commitment to diversity and inclusion.

Implications and Conclusion

We use a common language to describe identity. We speak about social group membership, intersectionality, marginalization, power, and privilege. We use descriptors such as persons with disabilities or non-disabled, LGBT, queer, or heterosexual, and we talk about coming out; yet, no two stories of identity are the same. We aimed to hold this observation at the forefront of our minds in research and in working with students, despite the construction of identity development models and typologies, even those which focus on identities and experiences long perceived as non-normative, excluded, or even deficient. The similarities in language and experience provide points of connection whereby we can develop greater empathy and support for others and ourselves. The uniqueness of experience reminds us of the richness of humanity and our connectedness to and not separation from the other. In fact, in honoring authenticity in identity, we realize that there is no "other."

In this chapter, we attempt to provide a multifaceted framework for diversity in higher education that actively centers disability and its convergence with additional dimensions of identity, framing these intersections as sites of productive possibility for re-imagining diversity beyond deficits in working with students with disabilities. To provide one example, institutions often segment services, programming, and resources such as disability and LGBTQ resource centers. Administrators might consider the subtext that such segmenting sends to students who identify within both areas. This challenge might present an opportunity for practitioners to intentionally collaborate across boundaries and how the work of individual units and offices can be made more inclusive. For instance, LGBTQ resource centers (and, indeed, all campus spaces) should be designed with disability in mind—both programmatically and in promoting physically accessible spaces. Likewise, disability services offices might evaluate inclusion of gender and sexual diversity and accessibility present in publications, staff training, and programs. One point of convergence for such collaboration is the provision of gender-inclusive, physically accessible facilities such as restrooms and locker rooms. These spaces would serve the entire campus community as well as help to address specific needs of people with disabilities and transgender and gender non-conforming individuals (groups which, after all, are not mutually exclusive). Initial collaborations on projects such as gender-inclusive facilities might lead to additional projects for improving the campus climate.

This re-imagining of diversity beyond deficits also presents possibilities for future research. Scholars seeking to understand the lived experiences of students with disabilities and their developmental trajectories would be well served by taking a team approach to research, with team members drawing from diverse sources of personal, professional, and background knowledge and experience. Initial hunches and insights from one researcher can be confirmed, contradicted, or expanded by another team member positioned differently according to (dis)ability, social identities, and disciplinary or field-specific background. Indeed, this approach to collaborative, interdisciplinary research would also enhance projects aimed at understanding students' intersectional experiences with multiple social identities. Lastly, the narratives and themes presented in this chapter offer one avenue for scholars seeking to reflect on their roles within research, and a method for intentionally foregrounding discussion of bias, positionality, and reflexivity within research about disability in higher education. We hope this approach of scholarly personal narrative writing coupled with individual and group reflection will benefit practitioners, administrators, policymakers, and students in higher education.

With our diverse skillsets, professional preparation, and identities, we formed a partnership to pursue information from our participants. We realized each of our personal and professional characteristics would embed themselves in our study. What we didn't realize was how professionally nourishing our post-study reflection would be. Nash (2004) counsels us to "be willing to surrender your truth to a better truth, if only for the moment, or maybe even for a longer while" (p. 64). Cognizant that we are novices in our steps to becoming moral activists, we humbly offer our multi-faceted story to you with the hope that we have added our truths to readers who are passionate about the stories, potential, and success of individuals who are marginalized on our college campuses.

References

Abery, B. H., & Stancliffe, R. J. (2003). A tripartite theory of self-determination. In M. L. Wehmeyer, B. H. Abery, D. E. Mithaug, &. R. J. Stancliffe (Eds.), *Theory in self-determination: Foundations for educational practice* (pp. 43–78). Springfield, IL: Charles C Thomas.

Black Lives Matter (2013). Retrieved from http://blacklivesmatter.com/

Bronfenbrenner, U., & Morris, P. A. (2007). The bioecological model of human development. In W. Damon, & R. M. Lerner (Eds.), *Handbook of child psychology* (6th ed.) (pp. 795–825). New York, NY: Wiley.

Buxton, M. (2000). The African-American teacher: The missing link. *The Black Collegian Online*. Retrieved from http://www.black-collegian.com/career/career-reports/misslink2000-2nd.shtml.

Charmaz, K. (2006). *Constructing grounded theory: A practical guide through qualitative analysis.* Thousand Oaks, CA: Sage.

Clarke, A. (2005). *Situational analysis: Grounded theory after the postmodern turn.* Thousand Oaks, CA: Sage.

Duke, T. S. (2011). Lesbian, gay, bisexual, and transgender youth with disabilities: A meta-synthesis. *Journal of LGBT Youth, 8*(1), 1–52. doi: 10.1080/19361653.2011.519181

Federal Register (2015). *Nondiscrimination in health programs and activities.* Retrieved from https://www.federalregister.gov/articles/2015/09/08/2015-22043/nondiscrimination-in-health-programs-and-activities.

Getzel, E. E. (2014). Fostering self-determination in higher education: Identifying evidence-based practices. *Journal of Postsecondary Education & Disability, 27*(4), 381–386.

Harley, D., Nowak, T., Gassaway, L., & Savage, T. (2002). Lesbian, gay, bisexual and transgender college students with disabilities: A look at multiple cultural minorities. *Psychology in the Schools, 39*(5), 525–538.

Henry, W. J., Fuerth, K., & Figliozzi, J. (2010). Gay with a disability: A college student's multiple cultural journey. *College Student Journal, 44*(2), 377–388.

Kafer, A. (2013). *Feminist, queer, crip.* Bloomington, IN: Indiana University Press.

Kahn, L. G., & Lindstrom, L. (2015). "I just want to be myself": Adolescents with disabilities who identify as a sexual or gender minority. *The Educational Forum, 79*(4), 362–376. doi: 10.1080/00131725.2015.1068416

Kanuha, V. K. (2000). "Being" native versus "going native": Conducting social work research as an insider. *Social Work, 45*(5), 439–447.

Kvale, S., & Brinkmann, S. (2009) *InterViews: Learning the craft of qualitative research interviewing* (2nd ed.). Los Angeles, CA: Sage.

Lather, P. A. (1991). *Getting smart: Feminist research and pedagogy with/in the postmodern.* New York, NY: Routledge.

Löfgren-Mårtenson, L. (2013). "Hip to be crip?" About crip theory, sexuality and people with intellectual disabilities. *Sexuality & Disability, 31*(4), 413–424.

McLeskey, J. M., Rosenberg, M. S., & Westling, D. L. (2013). *Inclusion: Effective practices for all students* (2nd ed.). Boston, MA: Pearson.

McRuer, R. (2006). *Crip theory: Cultural signs of queerness and disability.* New York, NY: New York University Press.

Miller, R. A. (2015). "Sometimes you feel invisible": Performing queer/disabled in the university classroom. *The Educational Forum, 79*(4). 377–393. doi: 10.1080/00131725 .2015.1068417

Miller, R. A., Wynn, R. D., & Webb, K. W. (in press). Complicating "coming out": Disclosing disability, gender, and sexuality in higher education. In S. L. Kerschbaum, J. M. Jones, & L. T. Eisenman (Eds.), *Negotiating disability awareness: Disclosure and higher education.* Ann Arbor, MI: University of Michigan Press, forthcoming.

Nash, R. J. (2004). *Liberating scholarly writing: The power of personal narrative.* New York, NY: Teachers College Press.

Obergerfell v. Hodges, 576 U.S. (2015). Retrieved from http://www.supremecourt.gov/.

Pannucci C., & Wilkins, E. (2011). Identifying and avoiding bias in research. *Plastic Reconstructive Surgery, 126*(2), 619–625.

Pothier, D., & Devlin, R. F. (Eds.) (2006). *Critical disability theory: Essays in philosophy, politics, policy, and law.* Vancouver, Canada: UBC Press.

Reddick, R., & Sáenz, V. (2012). Coming home: Hermanos académicos reflect on past and present realities as professors at their alma mater. *Harvard Educational Review, 82*(3), 353–380.

Rogers-Sirin, L., & Sirin, S. R. (2009). Cultural competence as an ethical requirement: Introducing a new educational model. *Journal of Diversity in Higher Education, 2*(1), 19–29.

Rosenberg, A. (2014, June 20). White House forum takes on LGBT and disability issues, with a dose of pop culture. *Washington Post.* Retrieved from http://www .washingtonpost.com/news/act-four/wp/2014/06/20/white-house-forum-takes-on-lgbt-and-disability-issues-with-a-dose-of-pop-culture/.

Schroeter, S. (2013). "The way it works" doesn't: Theatre of the oppressed as critical pedagogy and counternarrative. *Canadian Journal of Education, 36*(4), 394–415.

Smith, D. D., & Tyler, N. C. (2014). *Introduction to contemporary special education: New horizons.* Boston, MA: Pearson.

Underhile, R., & Cowles, J. R. (1998). Gay, lesbian, bisexual, and transgender students with disabilities: Implications for faculty and staff. In R. L. Sanlo (Ed.), *Working with lesbian, gay, bisexual, and transgender college students: A handbook for faculty and administrators* (pp. 267–276). Westport, CT: Greenwood Press.

U.S. Department of Defense (2015). *Statement by Secretary of Defense Ash Carter on DOD transgender policy.* Retrieved from http://www.defense.gov/News/News-Releases/News-Release-View/Article/612778.

U.S. Department of Health and Human Services (2015). *Let's talk about it.* Retrieved from http://www.mentalhealth.gov/.

U.S. Equal Employment Opportunity Commission (2015). *What you should know about EEOC and the enforcement protections for LGBT workers.* Retrieved from http://www .eeoc.gov/eeoc/newsroom/wysk/enforcement_protections_lgbt_workers.cfm.

Valls, R., & Kyriakides, L. (2013). The power of interactive groups: How diversity of adults volunteering in classroom groups can promote inclusion and success for children of vulnerable minority ethnic populations. *Cambridge Journal of Education, 43*(1), 17–33.

Wehmeyer, M. L. (2005). Self-determination and individuals with severe disabilities: Reexamining meanings and misinterpretations. *Research and Practice for Persons with Severe Disabilities, 30*, 113–120.

Wehmeyer, M. L., & Abery, B. H. (2013). Self-determination and choice. *Intellectual and Developmental Disabilities, 51*(5), 399–411. doi: 10.1352/1934-9556-51.5.399

Welch, M. (2011). Different is not deficit: A philosophical view of diversity and identity. *International Journal of Diversity in Organisations, Communities & Nations, 11*(1), 33–45.

White House, The (2015). *Disabilities*. Retrieved from https://www.whitehouse.gov/issues/disabilities.

PART II

College Experiences of Students with Disabilities

4

"DOES DISABILITY MATTER?"

Students' Satisfaction with College Experiences

Katherine C. Aquino, Taghreed A. Alhaddab, and Eunyoung Kim

Having a disability does not indicate that all students will share the same postsecondary experience. Whether it is the student's sense of belonging to their postsecondary environment, commitment to diversity acceptance, or perceived stigmatization, students with disabilities undergo various experiences during their college years that ultimately influence their overall satisfaction with higher education. Students with disabilities may not feel accepted in the college setting, ultimately deterring their perceived inclusion and reinforcing "stereotypical beliefs and discriminatory practices on the part of both professors and fellow students" (Lechtenberger et al., 2012, p. 857). Frustration with lack of support from institutional staff and faculty members may create a negative impression of one's disability and cause students to self-segregate. This "adversarial position" (Devlin & Pothier, 2006, p. 197) institutions create for students may establish that disability should not be a function of diversity as a holistic view of accepting individual differences and positively recognizing individuals' unique characteristics, since students of other diverse backgrounds do not have to endure additional administrative burdens in order to successfully navigate the higher education system.

As cited in Clark, Middleton, Nguyen, and Zwick (2014), institutional integration refers to "a student's ability to adapt to and assimilate into educational environments" (p. 31) and is organized into two specific types—academic integration and social integration (Tinto, 1975; Pascarella & Terenzini, 1980; Astin, 1975). Although academic and social integration both occur within the same postsecondary environment, academic integration focuses on students' academic performance, ability to endure educational demands, and achieve academic goals, while social integration refers to students' involvement with activities and developing social interactions and networks (Pascarella & Terenzini, 1980; Astin, 1975; 1993). Research indicates a potential positive relationship between the two forms of integration that may impact the successful completion of college (Pan et al., 2008; Tinto, 1975; Ullah & Wilson, 2007). However, limited research has investigated the similarities and differences between academic and social experiences of students with and without self-identified disabilities. Utilizing data from the Diverse Learning Environment (DLE) survey, data gathered from the Higher Education Research Institute (HERI), a research institute based within the University of California Los Angeles (UCLA) and home of the Cooperative Institutional Research Program (CIRP), this chapter explores the sense of inclusion, perceptions, and level of satisfaction of the postsecondary experience among different diverse groups, including students with self-identified disabilities.

Abbreviated Review of the Literature

Research has shown that students' ability to integrate both academically and socially within the higher education environment may be dependent on demographic characteristics including gender, socioeconomic status, race, and ethnicity (Jones, 2010; Rubin, 2011; Strage, 1999; Severiens & Wolff, 2008; Morley, 2003). Jones (2010) found that, when surveying 408 first-time, full-time students from eight private, religiously affiliated institutions, that gender impacts students' levels of social integration and subsequent commitment to their institution and postsecondary experience. Jones (2010) noted that differences lie in the level of social integration: "when both male and female students have low levels of social integration, the subsequent institutional commitment of female students appears to be attenuated in comparison to male students" (p. 697). If the level of social integration increases, this attenuation disappears. Similarly, when preforming a meta-analysis of studies that investigate student social integration patterns by different social socioeconomic statuses, Rubin (2011) found a statistically significant positive relationship between college students' social class and social integration tendencies, although statistical testing notes that the effect size of this relationship was small (p. 28). Lastly, research notes variation in higher education integration by students' race and ethnicity, often highlighting negative integration by race and ethnic minority students (Strage, 1999; Severiens & Wolff, 2008; Morley, 2003). After interviewing 23 full-time, first-time, first-year students from racially/ethnically diverse and/or culturally mixed backgrounds throughout their freshmen and early sophomore years, Morley (2003) found that the institutional environment and peer culture strongly affected students' integration within social activities and campus life events, and was often regulated by the race/ethnic hierarchy felt within the students' social environment.

Due to the many additional obstacles and procedures needed to assist in the success of college students with disabilities, this student population may feel not only unwelcomed as a part of student diversity, but also excluded from the overall institutional environment. Using the Beginning Postsecondary Students Longitudinal Study, Mamiseishvili and Koch (2012) identified 90 students self-identifying with a disability who had enrolled in a two-year postsecondary institution in Fall 2003. Of the 90 individuals with self-identified disabilities,

25% did not continue their postsecondary education following the completion of their first year. Additionally, by the end of their third year, 51% of the sample left college indefinitely. The authors noted factors contributing to the students' postsecondary departure, included physical functionality of the disabilities and depression (Mamiseishvili & Koch, 2012). Moreover, multiple 'minority identities' can create a combined foundation for oppression within the higher education environment. In a case study chronicling a gay, male student with a disability, Henry, Fuerth, and Figliozzi (2010) noted that the college student was often unable to obtain the needed (and institutionally created) support services for postsecondary success—specifically, counseling services—to discuss the obstacles he faced due to his disability and sexual orientation. Although the student participant noted that his specific institution's disability support office adequately addressed his disability, he believed the staff was unable to understand him holistically, with disability as a component of his overall identity (Henry, Fuerth, & Figliozzi, 2010). Henry et al.'s study highlights the dichotomy in the theory and function of institutional disability services. If institutions' disability support offices cannot adequately approach students with disabilities as unique and individual cases, students may have additional challenges constructing their disability as a part of their overall diversity identity and perceive this disability as a negative. In order to develop a positive, cohesive disability identity, Weeber (2004) found that the individual must integrate the concept of disability into one's overall identity and his/her surrounding community. However, students may continue to see their disability as a subservient and undesirable factor in how they perceive themselves and how they are perceived by others if the campus environment is not supportive (Weeber, 2004).

Although individuals have the opportunity to integrate either positively or negatively within their surroundings, students' disabilities may create additional components affecting their ability to integrate. Shepler and Woosley (2012) explored whether or not academic and social integration tendencies differed between college students with and without disabilities, as per Tinto's model of student attrition. The researchers surveyed first-time freshmen students via a first-year institution-wide student survey. Of all the respondent ($N = 5,135$), 120 students were identified by the university disability student support office as having a self-identified disability. Utilizing ANOVA testing, the researchers found that there was no significant difference in Tinto's model variables (e.g., variables related to student characteristics, commitment, and involvement) between students with and without disabilities. As noted by the researchers, "earliest college transition issues for students with disabilities are similar to the issues for other students" (p. 37); however, unlike "issues" for students without disabilities, students with disabilities may have ongoing challenges with needed accommodations and support (e.g., advocacy of disability-related support services by family members).

Based on Tinto's (1975) model, Pascarella and Terezini (1980) established scales to measure institutional components related to student integration, including student perceptions of peer group interactions, interactions with faculty,

faculty concern for student development and teaching, academic and intellectual development, and institutional and goal commitments (Fox, 1984, p. 1052). Although federally mandated policies provide an obligatory foundation for higher education institutions in the United States, research has shown varying support by postsecondary institutions for individuals with disabilities. Claireborne (2011) found that students with disabilities' concerns were not always addressed during the accommodation process and that both students and postsecondary staff noted the current disorganization in "when, how, and whether to disclose disability" (p. 524). Surveying 420 faculty members on their knowledge of, attitude toward, and experience with students with disabilities, Leyser, Vogel, Wyland, and Brulle (1998) found that a large portion of the faculty sample had limited training opportunities related to disability policy and postsecondary accommodation services. Due to wavering accommodation service use and/or institutional community members' limited experience with disability, students with disabilities may experience a different, more negative, postsecondary academic journey. In a study exploring whether or not University policies in a large research institution support the needs of individuals with self-identified physical disabilities, Walker (2008) found, through conducting qualitative interviews with 12 students with self-identified physical disabilities, that students with physical disabilities postsecondary experience differs vastly from that of students without disabilities.

Federal policies restrict the discrimination of individuals with disabilities; however, stigmatization of disability continues and may intensify depending on specific disability types. Fearing possible stigmatization by their peers and institutional staff, students with psychiatric disabilities may be less inclined to disclose their diagnoses and not self-advocate for postsecondary disability accommodation services (Knis-Matthew, Bokara, DeMeo, Lepore, & Mavus, 2007). Working with students with episodic mental health conditions (e.g., bipolar disorder, schizophrenia, major depression), Lin (2013) found that individuals with psychiatric conditions attending a large mid-Atlantic state university indicated lower college adaptation ability, such as social and academic adjustment. Fifty-two percent did not believe they had a disability, and 37% thought they were not eligible for accommodation services. This highlighted the need for additional institution-wide information regarding guidelines for accommodation support and what is truly considered a disability in the postsecondary environment. While interviewing state agency officials about initiatives and policies encouraging individuals with psychiatric disabilities to attend higher education institutions, Collins and Mowbray (2005) found that several states provided decreased support for students with psychiatric disabilities at the postsecondary level. Empirical interest on mental health and psychiatric disabilities related to the higher education setting continues to serve as a burgeoning topic and additional research and attention remains necessary for individuals with psychiatric disabilities within postsecondary institutions.

Methodology and Findings

The DLE survey was administrated in Spring 2011 to undergraduates to capture their perceptions about campus climate, institutional practice, and experiences with faculty, staff, and peers. The survey gives special attention to traditionally underrepresented students as its instrument was based on studies of campus diversity (HERI, 2016). This chapter uses the DLE survey to understand the overall experiences of a traditionally underrepresented group (students with disabilities), by examining their perceptions and experiences of campus diversity climate. Results from the survey are used to assess whether or not the presence of a self-identified disability influences students' satisfaction with academic and social experiences more than other diversity categories, such as race/ethnicity and sexual orientation. The following presents selected outcomes that show differences in campus perceptions and experiences among different diverse groups.

The sample in this study (N = 13,844) has more than 16% of its participants self-identify with a disability. The type of a disability differs among participants; 2% identify with attention-deficit/hyperactivity disorder (ADHD), 3% identify with a physical disability such as speech, sight, hearing, etc.; 1% state that they have a learning disability like dyslexia; nearly 8% identify with a psychological disorder such as depression, and 2% state "other disability." Further, 90% of the sample participants chose "heterosexual" as their sexual orientation where 3% stated that they are homosexual, 4% indicated that they are bisexual, and 3% stated "other" as their sexual orientation. About 22% of the sample members identify themselves with a multiracial ethnicity. The racial breakdown of minorities in the sample is as follows: 37% Asians, 18% Latinos, and 3% African Americans.

Viewing disability as a form of diversity, this chapter aims to investigate whether or not students' satisfaction with academic and social experiences on campus is influenced by the presence of a disability, compared to the experiences of other diversity groups. To fulfill this purpose, Factor Scores are used to assess experiences, behaviors, and satisfactions of participants. Factor Scores use a number of items that measure the same construct, followed by Confirmatory Factor Analysis (CFA), which is then used to combine these items into broad tools that capture campus experiences (HERI, 2016). Factor Scores are particularly helpful to assess or benchmark the different experiences of different groups (HERI, 2016). In the current survey, Factor Scores range from 1 to 100 and have a mean value of 50. The DLE survey provides different Factor Scores measurements that capture different experiences, behaviors, and attitudes. The following section presents selected Factor Scores along with their corresponding results.

Sense of Belonging Factor Score

Sense of belonging is used as a psychological measure of integration, which is an important factor in retention (Hurtado & Carter, 1997). When students feel welcomed by their institution, their sense of integration and cohesion increases, which illustrates a higher sense of belonging, and shows that the institution is successful in influencing students' success (Hurtado & Carter, 1997). In the current sample, the Sense of Belonging Factor Score includes the following items: "I feel a sense of belonging to my campus"; "I feel that I am a member of this college"; "I see myself as a part of the campus community"; "I would recommend this college to others." The Sense of Belonging Factor Score for all participants in the sample ranges from 15 to 66, with a mean score of 50.

As shown in Figure 4.1, sense of belonging seems similar across different minority groups, with a mean value of 50 for all participants. Although the scores are generally similar, African American students and students with disabilities have a lower sense of belonging compared to other underrepresented groups; their mean scores are 48.12 and 48.64, respectively. Furthermore, the Sense of Belonging Factor Score varies by disability type. Participants who self-identify with a psychological disability, such as depression, seem to have a lower mean score (47.44) compared to other disability categories. On the other hand, participants identifying with a learning disability, such as dyslexia, show the highest mean score (50.32). Figure 4.2 further shows the differences in Sense of Belonging among participants who self-identify with a disability.

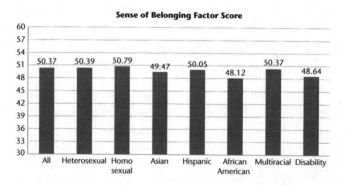

FIGURE 4.1 Sense of Belonging Factor Score (mean) among different underrepresented groups. (*Source*: 2010–2011 Diverse Learning Environments Survey.)

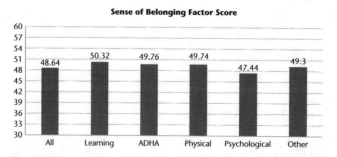

FIGURE 4.2 Sense of Belonging Factor Score (mean) by disability type. (*Source*: 2010-2011 Diverse Learning Environments Survey.)

Furthermore, Figure 4.3 shows whether or not the Sense of Belonging would differ if a student identifies with both a disability and an additional diversity category. As shown in Figure 4.3, the mean score of Sense of Belonging is compared between minority groups: those who identify with a disability and those who did not.

It is clearly shown from Figure 4.3 that once a disability is accompanied with a minority category the Sense of Belonging Factor Score falls lower. For instance, Figure 4.3 indicates a noticeable mean score difference (2.65) for Sense of Belonging between students identifying as Asians and students identifying as Asians with disabilities: 49.47 and 46.82 respectively. The same applies to African-American participants who identify with a disability, compared to African Americans who did not report a disability. In general, African-American students score lower in the Sense of Belonging construct (48.12) compared to other minority groups. Once a disability is associated with African-American students, the mean score of Sense of Belonging falls even lower by more than two scores (mean = 46) (see Figure 4.3).

Institutional Commitment to Diversity Factor Score

The Institutional Commitment to Diversity construct has items that reflect students' views about the diversity of their campus. Such views include the institution's promotion and appreciation of cultural differences, and its commitment to accurately reflect the diversity of the student body (HERI, 2016). The Institutional Commitment to Diversity Factor Score ranges from 13 to 66 with a mean score of 50. As shown in Figure 4.4, the mean score across different minority groups is nearly the same, excluding African-American participants. Similar to the previous construct, African-American students score lower (45.76) in their sense of institutional commitment and promotion of diversity. Participants with a self-identified disability have the next lowest mean score (49.13). However, their mean score is within the average mean of all participants (50.25).

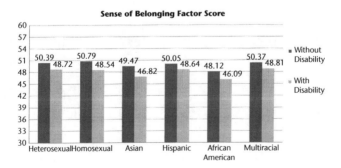

FIGURE 4.3 Sense of Belonging Factor Score (mean) among minorities with/ without a disability. (*Source*: 2010–2011 Diverse Learning Environments Survey.)

Institutional Commitment to Diversity

50.25	50.38	49.81	49.83	49.97	45.76	50.4	49.13
All	Hetero sexual	Homo sexual	Asian	Hispanic	African American	Multiracial	Disability

FIGURE 4.4 Institutional Commitment to Diversity Factor Score (mean) among different underrepresented groups. (*Source*: 2010–2011 Diverse Learning Environments Survey.)

Furthermore, Figure 4.5 presents the Institutional Commitment to Diversity construct divided by disability types. The mean score of the construct is nearly the same across each disability type. Participants self-identifying with a psychological disability, such as depression, show the lowest mean score (48.49) compared to participants with other disabilities. This is similar to the previous construct (Sense of Belonging Factor Score), where participants with psychological disabilities reported the lower mean score compared to other disabilities.

Figure 4.6 shows whether or not the perception of underrepresented minority groups' institutional commitment to promote campus diversity would differ if the student is both a minority and has a self-identified disability. As shown in Figure 4.6, minorities with self-identified disabilities score lower than minorities without self-identified disabilities. The difference in the mean score between the two groups is clearly shown among Asian students, followed by African-American students. Also, Hispanic students identifying with a disability scored lower in the

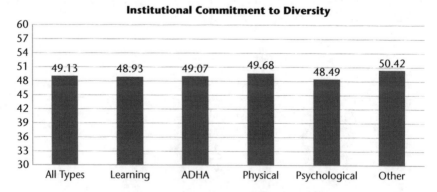

Institutional Commitment to Diversity

49.13	48.93	49.07	49.68	48.49	50.42
All Types	Learning	ADHA	Physical	Psychological	Other

FIGURE 4.5 Institutional Commitment to Diversity Factor Score (mean) by disability type. (*Source*: 2010–2011 Diverse Learning Environments Survey.)

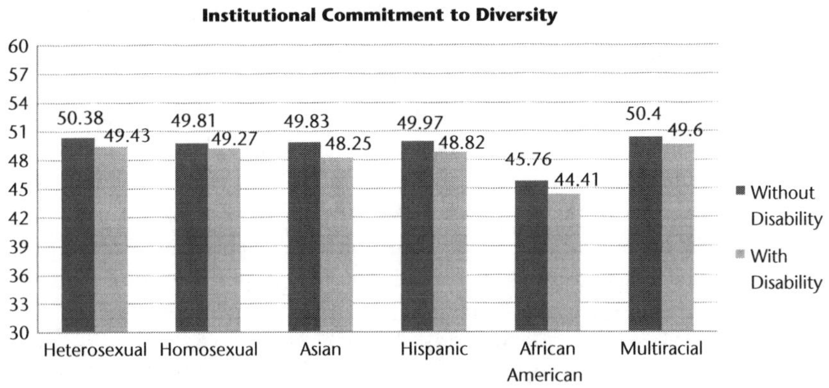

Institutional Commitment to Diversity

FIGURE 4.6 Institutional Commitment to Diversity Factor Score (mean) among minorities with/without a disability. (*Source*: 2010–2011 Diverse Learning Environments Survey.)

Institutional Commitment to Diversity Factor Score than did Hispanic students who did not identify with any type of disability (see Figure 4.6 for more differences). In short, the sense of belonging to the institution and the perception of the institution's commitment to promote diversity decrease once a disability is found in a minority group.

Discrimination and Bias Measurements

The discrimination and bias measurements include items reflecting experiences with offensive verbal and written comments, perceived exclusion from social gatherings and events, witnessing discrimination, and threats of physical violence. Each of the five items asked participants (on a 5-point Likert scale) how often they experience such discriminatory actions on campus. Answers range from "never" to "very often," where "sometimes" is used to measure minorities' perceived campus discrimination and bias. As shown in Figure 4.7, African-American students reported a higher percentage (26%) of witnessing discrimination and of experiencing offensive verbal comments (24%), followed by students with self-identified disabilities: 23% and 22% respectively. Further, students who identified as homosexuals seemed to experience offensive written comments (e.g., e-mails, texts, writing on walls) more than any other minority group; 14% reported that sometimes they receive offensive comments. As for perceived exclusion from social gatherings, both students with self-identified disabilities and homosexual students reported the highest percentage in that category; nearly 16% report that sometimes they have been excluded from social events and gatherings. Furthermore, both Asian participants and homosexual participants reported a higher percentage of "threats of physical violence" compared to other groups. Figure 4.7 illustrates differences in perceived campus discrimination and bias among different underrepresented groups.

Figure 4.8 presents the perceived experiences of campus discrimination and bias among participants with self-identified disabilities to see if such experiences would differ once a disability is introduced. In general, as shown in Figure 4.8, once a disability is combined with a minority status, the perceived sense of discrimination and bias increases. For example, African Americans reported a higher percentage (26%) of witnessing discrimination on campus compared to other minority student groups; African Americans with a disability reported an even higher sense of discrimination (29%).

Moreover, in experiencing offensive verbal comments, it is African-American students who reported the highest percentage (24%); interestingly, once a disability is introduced, it is Hispanic students who reported the highest percentage (27%). Similarly, 14% of homosexual participants reported that they have been excluded from social gatherings—the highest percentage compared to other

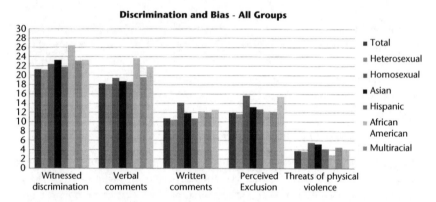

FIGURE 4.7   Perceived Discrimination and Bias among different underrepresented groups (%). (*Source*: 2010–2011 Diverse Learning Environments Survey.)

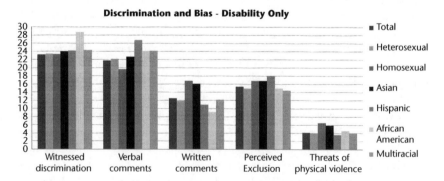

FIGURE 4.8   Perceived Discrimination and Bias among participants with a self-identified disability (%). (*Source*: 2010–2011 Diverse Learning Environments Survey.)

minority groups. However, once a disability is introduced, it is Hispanic students with self-identified disabilities who reported the highest percentage (18%) of being sometimes excluded from social gatherings.

In general, it is clear that once a disability is found in a minority group, the perceived sense of discrimination and bias increases. Table 4.1 demonstrates the differences in perceived campus discrimination and biases between minorities with and without disabilities. As shown in Table 4.1, offensive verbal comments and perceived exclusion from social gatherings are the two categories with stark differences found among minorities with/without disabilities. The highest difference is clear among African Americans with/without disabilities, with more than an 8% difference in their experiences with offensive verbal comments. The same category also shows more than a 4% difference between multiracial participants without/with disabilities. The perceived sense of social exclusion increases as well (by more than 5%) once a disability is found among Hispanic students.

In a few cases, once a disability is found in a minority group, the perceived sense of campus discrimination and bias decreases. For instance, African Americans with disabilities experience less offensive written comments than African Americans without disabilities (3% less). Also, there is a slight decrease in threats of physical violence once a disability is found among Hispanic and multiracial participants.

Conclusion and Implications

In this chapter, we used the Diversity Learning Environment Survey, which was administered in 2011 by the HERI to provide a general overview of students with disabilities perceptions of campus climate, as well as their satisfaction with college experiences compared to the general student population and

TABLE 4.1 Difference in Percentage between Minorities Without/With Self-Identified Disability

	Witnessed discrimination	Verbal comments	Written comments	Perceived Exclusion	Threats of physical violence
Heterosexual	2.26	4.05	1.48	3.29	0.4
Homosexual	0.93	0.18	2.72	1.16	0.99
Asian	0.78	3.98	4.25	3.57	0.68
Hispanic	2.45	8.21	0.25	5.36	−0.54
African American	2.31	0.44	−3.01	2.74	1.63
Multiracial	1.19	4.57	0.07	2.27	−0.48

Source: 2010–2011 Diverse Learning Environments Survey.

other underrepresented student groups (e.g., race/ethnicity, sexual orientation). Given that perceived campus environment, attitude toward campus diversity, interactions with faculty administrators and peers, and behaviors of students are integral to the multifaceted concept of campus climate (HERI, 2016), we used the Factor Scores developed by the HERI to investigate similarities and differences regarding the attitudes and experiences of students with disabilities compared to other minority groups, as well as to students without self-identified disabilities. We looked at how students with disabilities, perceptions of campus diversity vary when combined with other diversity categories, relative to students without disabilities. In addition, we looked at whether or not students' sense of belonging, perceptions of institutional commitment to diversity, and perceptions of discrimination vary within the group of students with disabilities according to different types of disability (psychological, physical, etc.).

Overall sense of belonging, perceived institutional commitment to diversity, and perceived discrimination and bias are lower among students with self-identified disabilities than non-disabled students. Of those minority student groups (race/ethnicity, sexual orientation, disability), African-American students and students with disabilities tend to have lower perceptions of their campus diversity that other minority student groups. Moreover, traditionally underrepresented minority students (e.g., racial/ethnic minorities) with disabilities perceptions of campus diversity are relatively lower than those minority students without disabilities, pointing to the significant role disability plays in influencing student attitudes toward and views of diversity on campus. Students with more than one minority category are more susceptible to having negative college experiences, such as perceived discrimination and bias, particularly African-American students with disabilities. This chapter evidentially highlights that when disability is factored into the diversity dimension, there are varied levels of satisfaction with and perceptions of college campus diversity among minority student groups. These findings call for additional research to investigate why particular minority groups are less likely to perceive campus climate positively—and how their perceived campus environment affects student educational outcomes.

References

Astin, A. W. (1975). *Preventing students from dropping out*. San Francisco, CA: Jossey-Bass.
Astin, A. W. (1993). *What matters in college? Four critical years revisited* (Vol. 1). San Francisco, CA: Jossey-Bass.
Claiborne, L. B., Cornforth, S., Gibson, A., & Smith, A. (2011). Supporting students with impairments in higher education: Social inclusion or cold comfort? *International Journal of Inclusive Education*, 15(5), 513–527.
Clark, M. H., Middleton, S. C., Nguyen, D., & Zwick, L. K. (2014). Mediating relations between academic motivation, academic integration, and academic performance. *Learning and Individual Differences*, 33(2014), 30–38.

Collins, M., & Mowbray, C. T. (2005). Higher education and psychiatric disabilities: National survey of campus disability services. *American Journal of Orthopsychiatry, 75*(2), 304–315. doi:10.1037/0002-9432.75.2.304

Devlin, R. F., & Pothier, D. (2006). *Critical disability theory: Essays in philosophy, politics, policy, and law.* Vancouver, BC, Canada: University of British Columbia Press.

Fox, R.N. (1984). Reliability and discriminant validity of institutional integration scales for disadvantaged college students. *Educational and Psychological Measurement, 44,* 1051–1057.

Henry, W. J., Fuerth, K., & Figliozzi, J. (2010). Gay with a disability: A college student's multiple cultural journey. *College Student Journal, 44*(2), 377.

Higher Education Research Institute (HERI). (2016). *Diverse Learning Environment (DLE) Survey.* Retrieved from http://www.heri.ucla.edu/dleoverview.php

Hurtado, S., & Carter, D. (1997). Effects of college transition and perceptions of the campus racial climate on Latino college students' sense of belonging. *Sociology of Education, 70*(4), 324–345.

Jones, W. A. (2010). The impact of social integration on subsequence institutional commitment conditional on gender. *Research in Higher Education, 51*(7), 687–700.

Knis-Matthews, L., Bokara, J., DeMeo, L., Lepore, N., & Mavus, L. (2007). The meaning of higher education for people diagnosed with a mental illness: Four students share their experiences. *Psychiatric Rehabilitation Journal, 31*(2), 107–114.

Lechtenberger, D., Barnard-Brak, L., Sokolosky, S., & McCrary, D. (2012). Using wraparound to support students with developmental disabilities in higher education. *College Student Journal, 46*(4), 856–866.

Leyser, Y., Vogel, S., Wyland, S., & Brulle, A. (1998). Faculty attitudes and practices regarding students with disabilities: Two decades after implementation of Section 504. *Journal of Postsecondary Education and Disability, 13*(3), 5–19.

Lin, C. (2013). *Predicting college adaptation among students with psychiatric disabilities.* (Order No. 3590768, University of Maryland, College Park). *ProQuest Dissertations and Theses,* 112. Retrieved from http://search.proquest.com/docview/1432192575?accountid= 13793. (1432192575).

Mamiseishvili, K., & Koch, L.C. (2012). Students with disabilities at two-year institutions in the United States: Factors related to success. *Community College Review, 40*(4).

Morley, K. M. (2003). Fitting in by race/ethnicity: The social and academic integration of diverse students at a large predominantly White university. *Journal of College Student Retention: Research, Theory & Practice, 5*(2), 147–174.

Pan, W., Guo, S., Alikonis, C., & Bai, H. (2008). Do intervention programs assist students to success in college? A multilevel longitudinal study. *College Student Journal, 42,* 90–98.

Pascarella, E. T., & Terenzini, P. T. (1980). Predicting freshman persistence and voluntary dropout decisions from a theoretical model. *Journal of Higher Education, 51,* 60–75.

Rubin, M. (2011). Social class differences in social integration among students in higher education: A meta-analysis and recommendations for future research. *Journal of Diversity in Higher Education, 5*(1), 22–38.

Severiens, S., & Wolff, R. (2008). A comparison of ethnic minority and majority students: Social and academic integration, and quality of learning. *Studies in Higher Education, 33*(3), 253–266.

Shepler, D. K., & Woosley, S. A. (2012). Understanding the early integration experiences of college students with disabilities. *Journal of Postsecondary Education and Disability, 25*(1), 37–50.

Strage, A. A. (1999). Social and academic integration and college success: Similarities and differences as a function of ethnicity and family educational background. *College Student Journal, 33*(2).

Tinto, V. (1975). Dropouts from higher education: A theoretical synthesis of recent literature. *A Review of Educational Research, 45*, 89–125.

Ullah, H., & Wilson, M. A. (2007). Students' academic success and its association to student involvement with learning and relationships with faculty and peers. *College Student Journal, 41*, 1192–1202.

Walker, D. K. (2008). *Minority and non-minority students with disabilities in higher education: Are current university policies meeting their needs?* (Doctoral dissertation). Retrieved from ProQuest. (3337955).

Weeber, J. E. (2004). Disability community leaders' disability identity development: A journey of integration and expansion. *Dissertation Abstracts International, 65*, 6074.

5

ENGAGING DISABILITY

Trajectories of Involvement for College Students with Disabilities

Ezekiel Kimball, Rachel E. Friedensen, and Elton Silva

Though often lumped together for convenience or added statistical power (Kimball, Wells, Ostiguy, Manly, & Lauterbach, 2016; Vaccaro, Kimball, Wells, & Ostiguy, 2015), college students with disabilities are a remarkably diverse population (Eagan et al., 2014; NCES, 2014). Disability encompasses a tremendous range of variation in the ways that people might interact with the world, including visual and hearing impairments, cognitive processing issues, mobility restrictions, and psychological conditions. Additionally, individuals assigned the same diagnosis by medical professionals vary in the extent to which they consider their disability a salient part of their sense of self and in the way their disability presents itself in a given context (Dunn & Burcaw, 2013; Riddell & Weedon, 2014). The diversity of disability becomes even more apparent when one begins to consider disability to be just one of many social identities that a person might hold (Jones & Abes, 2013).

When viewed from that perspective, it becomes clear that the lives of students with disabilities warrant an intracategorical approach to intersectional research (McCall, 2005), wherein careful consideration of the impact of disability and other social identities might yield more information about both shared and divergent experiences among people with disabilities. An intracategorical approach to the study of disability will provide new information about the actual experiences of students with disabilities. This information is critical in addressing an ongoing and significant gap in the equity of higher education outcomes for persons with disabilities. While the rate of college participation among students with disabilities is increasing (NCES, 2014), students with disabilities still do not graduate from college at the same rate as their peers (DaDeppo, 2009). A better understanding of who students with disabilities are and what sort of experiences they have will provide those working on college campuses with necessary information to construct evidence-based practices.

In this chapter, we undertake an intracategorical analysis through the lens of student engagement theory (Kuh, 2007; McCormick, Kinzie, & Gonyea, 2013). Drawing on the narrative accounts of eight college students with learning disabilities drawn from one small liberal arts college in the northeast (pseudonym: Meadow College), our analysis helps to explicate connections between disability, other social identities, and engagement. This analysis provides information about an understudied population (Peña, 2014) by focusing on engagement experiences, which have been shown elsewhere to be strongly associated with retention (e.g., Kuh et al., 2005; McCormick et al., 2013; National Survey of Student Engagement, 2013).

Why Does Engagement Matter for Students with Disabilities?

Engagement is a conceptual construct that ties together several theories and empirical findings about student success in higher education. Briefly, it holds that students who engage in a wide range of demonstrably beneficial academic and nonacademic behaviors will experience success at higher rates than they might otherwise (Kuh et al., 2005; Kuh, 2007). For example, researchers have consistently found positive effects, such as increased learning and persistence, among students who join learning communities, regularly receive and respond to instructor feedback, interact with a diverse peer group outside of the classroom, and participate in experiential learning opportunities (Kuh, 2007; McCormick et al., 2013). However, engagement goes beyond mere involvement (Astin, 1993) and also examines the way that students think, feel, and process these beneficial experiences (McCormick et al., 2013), which may explain why not all students having the same experiences see the same results (NSSE, 2013). For example, considerable variation in effect has been documented based on a student's discipline, social identity (e.g., first generation status, race/ethnicity), and institutional type attended.

These variations are particularly important to those doing person-centered research on students with disabilities (Malcolm-Piqueux, 2015). As noted above, while we know that students with disabilities struggle to persist at the same rates as peers without disabilities (DaDeppo, 2009), we actually know little about what happens to them in college (Kimball et al., 2016). Much of the literature that we do have focuses on access to and the efficacy of accommodations (e.g., Cawthon & Leppo, 2013; Grigal, Hart, & Weir, 2012; Hewitt, 2011; Stodden, Roberts, Picklesimer, Jackson, & Chang, 2006). A more limited literature base examines their academic success (e.g., DaDeppo, 2009; Megivern, Pellerito, & Mowbray, 2003; Wessel, Jones, Markle, & Westfall, 2009). Overall, however, there is very little literature that actually looks at what it feels like to be a college student with a disability and how that impacts retention (Kimball et al., 2016).

Thus far, only a handful of pieces have explicitly utilized engagement to frame research on students with disabilities. Nichols and Quaye (2009) and

Brown and Broido (2015) used student engagement as an anchor point to guide the construction of synthetic literature reviews. They demonstrated the extent to which literature on other topics (e.g., study skills, mentoring, climate) related to disability might also be seen as related to engagement. They also provided a series of in-depth recommendations for supporting the engagement of students with disabilities: notably, most of these recommendations are consistent with good practices for student engagement generally—that is, they need not be seen solely as a reflection of the disability of the students in question. That conclusion echoes the empirical findings of Hendrickson and associates (2015), which showed that students with disabilities who participated in an inclusive, holistic postsecondary education program experienced college life in similar ways as students without disabilities, as measured by NSSE. Taken together, these three pieces show not only that engagement is a viable framework with which to study the experiences of students with disabilities, but also that by using engagement as a framework, with appropriate support in place, it is possible for students with disabilities to fully participate in today's higher education environments.

What Do Students with Disabilities Say about Engagement?

To begin exploring disability's connection to engagement, we conducted an exploratory qualitative study involving eight students with learning disabilities enrolled at Meadow College. Participants were recruited using snowball sampling beginning with students known to one or more of the researchers. Each participant was also asked to refer potential participants. At the time we conducted the study, the approximate undergraduate enrollment at Meadow College was 2,500. Roughly 70% of the student body identified as White, while the remaining students self-identified (in order of frequency) as Asian/Asian American, Black/African American, international students, and Latina/o. Nearly 60% of enrolled undergraduate student were female. Thirty percent of all undergraduate students received were Pell eligible and roughly equal numbers were first-generation college students. By limiting the context to a single institution and the range of diagnoses to cognitive disabilities we were better able to identify the differential impact of disability on engagement. All the names contained in Table 5.1 and the discussion of these findings below are pseudonyms.

Each coauthor brought unique perspectives to this study. Ezekiel identifies as a person with a disability, having been diagnosed with obsessive-compulsive disorder at an early age. He also served as the coordinator of disability services for a small college. Elton was an undergraduate student at the time of data collection and therefore was able to connect with participants based on their shared undergraduate experiences. Rachel, a graduate student, is interested in the leaky academic pipeline for people with disabilities. Ezekiel designed the study. Elton was primarily responsible for collecting data and he also assisted Ezekiel with data analysis. Rachel confirmed their findings and interpretations and assisted with the writing process for this chapter.

TABLE 5.1 Participant Demographics

Pseudonym	Age	Gender	Race	Diagnosis	Major
Deion	21	Male	White	Dyslexia	Business
Erin	18	Female	White	Reading Comprehension	Education
Jack	20	Male	White	Dyslexia	Education
Joe	20	Male	White	ADD/Asperger's	Communication
Ralph	20	Male	White	ADD	Communication
Samantha	20	Female	White	Processing Disability	Psychology
Xavier	21	Male	White	Auditory	Business
Zoey	19	Female	White	ADD/ADHD	Sociology

Our study employed narrative research techniques (Gubrium & Holstein, 2009) to explore the way in which our participants told stories about their college engagement. Utilizing semi-structured protocols, we relied on interviews averaging sixty minutes each to seek information from participants about the following topics: the participant's sense of self, the extent to which disability factored into that sense of self, and their academic and nonacademic experiences at Meadow College. We also provided all participants with an opportunity to offer any information that they felt was important for us to understand their experiences. We recorded and transcribed all interviews. Once done, we utilized narrative analysis techniques (Coulter & Smith, 2009; Holley, & Colyar, 2009) to examine both what participants said and how they said it. The findings include (1) the role of disability in mediating classroom engagement, (2) variations in access to institutional support, (3) the importance of supportive peer networks, and (4) the variable salience of disability identity.

The Role of Disability in Mediating Classroom Engagement

For all of the participants in our study, disability shaped their classroom experiences in profound positive and negative ways. The most basic of these impacts is that disability has a real cost in terms of time and money that can make it more complicated to participate fully in curricular and cocurricular engagement opportunities. One participant, Erin, noted that her disability required her to attend off-campus physical therapy appointments twice each week. In addition to a full schedule of classes, schoolwork, club meetings, and other activities, Erin sometimes found herself making difficult decisions about what task to do at any given moment. Indeed, time management was a recurrent theme for participants in our study.

Others noted that their disability impacted their ability to engage in the classroom in less tangible ways. For example, Samantha revealed: "When I'm in the classroom, I just get anxious, I have test anxiety anyway. When everyone starts finishing I get really anxious and I take longer. I do better when I'm by myself at my own table." While that may seem like a small imposition—or for those who have been forced to take a test in a loud classroom, even a benefit—it also means that Samantha is not experiencing the classroom in the same ways as her peers and might be unable to participate as fully in group work. Likewise, Xavier described his struggle to engage with material when presented in certain formats:

> I mean I do have some difficulties because my intro to politics teacher was: you read the material and you sit and listen to him lecture and then you take a test. The same thing the whole semester. It was annoying because I'm not very good with listening. It's part of my disability.

Xavier, though he wished to be successful in the class, could not participate fully in the class due to the fact that he was constantly trying to replay the instructor's words from a moment before. Such a disconnect makes real engagement difficult—if not impossible. Another participant, Ralph, elaborated that he found remaining engaged more difficult when he was not really invested in the class:

> Classes that are required you kind of just get through them rather than enjoy them. [. . .] I'd say a class like sociology, a class that I'm not actively engaged or interested it's a lot harder to focus than it is a class like [cultural studies] where I'm so interested in the actual content of the class is. Classes like science, those are a little bit harder to pay attention. I'm not really interested in them.

While issues like uninspiring classes doubtless plague all college students, they posed a special challenge to the students in our study: since they all had learning disabilities, they required additional time to process some forms of information. When compounded with wandering attention, engagement was particularly unlikely to occur.

Importantly, however, our study also revealed one possible engagement strategy for students with disabilities: providing course content reflective of their experiences. Jack told us that he was taking a course on disability in society and that he found "that class is fun because I've grown up with a disability, so I can actually contribute a lot to the class and give a point of view that most of the kids don't know because they don't have a learning disability." That sentiment echoes literature on campus climate that suggests that students who are able to see themselves reflected in the courses they take and in the instructors that teach them are more successful (Hurtado et al., 2012).

Variations in Access to Institutional Support

Moving beyond the classroom to curricular support, participant responses highlighted the extent to which access to institutional support varied. Meadow College offered two levels of support for students with disabilities. One level of support was designed to meet the institution's legal obligation and, as required, was available to eligible students free of charge. This level included classroom accommodations and access to the institution's tutoring center. The second level of support included fee-based access to a structured disability support program (SDSP) that included formal instruction on academic skills, easier access to academic support professionals, and a variety of technological aids. Generally, students who participated in the SDSP found it beneficial. However, it was quite expensive (costing each student roughly $10,000 per year to participate beyond routine tuition and fees).

There was also considerable diversity within the way that students utilized services within a given level of support. For example, students described a wide range of service utilization patterns in the SDSP. One student, Jack, noted that he required "all the support that I can get." For him, that involved a one-on-one meeting with an academic support professional who provided assistance with academic work. Xavier stated that he met weekly with an academic support professional but found he needed the most support on time management issues. Among our participants, Deion reported the most frequent use of the SDSP but also noted that he had reduced his use of the program over time:

> I'm no longer in [SDSP] now, graduated in a way from [SDSP]. When I was there, I would, for my freshmen year I would meet three times a week. Later on, it got less and less. Back in freshmen year we would go over everything in the week. I was in a management group and we would go over everything. I would usually fly through the stuff because I already knew what we needed to do. I know that time management is the key to college, that was pretty simple. Later on it became: "Can you just read over this paper?" "Can we go over these terms because I have a quiz the next day?" It was little things. It wasn't like I needed her holding my hand and helping me in every way.

Deion's narrative reveals that disability support services represented a catalyst for learning and development that needed to be moderated based on a student's growth trajectory. That finding was echoed by the experience of other students who had been enrolled in the SDSP but found that they did not utilize all of the services at their disposal. For example, Samantha noted that she had left the program because, over time, she realized that she required only extended time on tests.

In short, students with disabilities utilized a wide array of tools and services offered by the institution as they engaged with their college experience. While some students just needed the classroom accommodations provided by the law, others needed more structured and involved assistance. Often, students who utilized more structured services found that they relied less and less on those services and were able to excel on their own.

The Importance of Supportive Peer Networks

A supportive peer environment can facilitate the normalization of disability for students. The development of such an environment necessitates a supportive campus climate with special attention paid to student identities and their interplay with curricular and cocurricular processes (Hurtado et al., 2012; Kimball et al., 2015). Consistent with this literature, students in the SDSP often reported strong connections with the faculty members who met with them one-on-one or taught their smaller classes. However, many participants revealed that they had chosen to attend that institution due to the supportive social network that they perceived to exist at the institution. Joe's admissions experience is quite typical in this regard:

> I like [Meadow College]. I was looking for a college that has a nice community feel where people kind of get to know each other, really support one another and . . . for me, going into it was definitely the community. I really wanted that community feel and a place where I didn't feel lost and over-stimulated.

For Joe, and others, peers were the most tangible part of the social network that supported his success at Meadow College.

Others expanded on this idea by noting that institutional practices—like housing all first-year students together—had contributed to the rapid development of friendships on campus. Importantly, these friendships included connections to people from a wide variety of academic and social backgrounds. Xavier noted:

> I've met some of them through my management courses freshmen year. I've met them through intramurals. I've met my closest friends freshmen year in my dorm . . . We've been close ever since then. I've met people throughout the school just by doing different things or being in different classes.

While Xavier described the importance of his participation in intramurals, others sought different cocurricular engagement opportunities. Erin and Samantha both described involvement in student organizations as critical to their experience on campus and social lives. For example, Erin stated: "I'm involved in clubs. I hang out with people in my clubs. I don't know, I talk to people in classes, other than that, I guess I just have a normal social life."

Importantly, peer networks were connected to the way that our participants described their disability. One of the clubs with which Joe and several other participants volunteered fostered mentoring relationships between college students and school-aged children with learning disabilities. Joe described the experience:

> Every semester we get a new group of 8–9 students with various learning challenges. We go and we have an art project. We don't necessarily care what it looks like in the end. We want them to try and be creative and innovative. It is a mix of anywhere between 6th to 8th grade. As a mentor I am trying to get that student to see a quality they have that they never realized through this project we're doing.

This experience was meaningful on several levels. For some students, it connected with future professional goals—such as Erin's goal of becoming a teacher. For the middle school children involved, it helped them to confront and address the underlying societal stigma toward disability. That effect also carried over to the participants from Meadow College. As Erin noted, her time at Meadow College helped her to address her fears of being thought of as a person with disability: "Because not everyone had a learning disability, I didn't want to be pointed out as someone who did. Now I know that I am not the only one with a learning disability and it's ok to have one." The combined experience of working with younger students with disabilities and interacting with peers with disabilities at Meadow College helped Erin to incorporate her disability into her broader understanding of self.

The Variable Salience of Disability Identity

Even though the participants in our study all had similar diagnoses and Meadow College strove to be inclusive of disabilities, we found that participants reported a diverse range of opinions regarding the salience of that identity. One of the first things that we asked all students in each interview was for them to introduce themselves to the interviewer. In advance of the interviews, all the participants knew the purpose of the study and the general sort of information we would be seeking. Most participants focused on their academic major and hometown. For example, Zoey stated: "I'm a sociology major, I'm a sophomore. I'm Co-President of [Students Against Drunk Driving], I'm involved with [peer tutoring], Alternative Spring Break and a couple of other committees, but I won't name them. I'm from [Virginia]." Similarly, Deion described himself as "a management major" and "big intramural guy."

Most of these introductions were very brief and provided a bulleted list of key facts. We interpreted these lists as the information that the students perceived as the most salient given the context of the interaction. Therefore, these students judged that this information was the most significant to share at the beginning of the interviews. Despite their knowledge that we were interested in better understanding their experiences as students with disabilities, the nature of their disability was not often one of those pieces of information. In fact, only two participants included their disability as part of this introduction. Jack revealed: "Well, I'm 20 years old. I'm from [Delaware] and my learning disability is I am a severe dyslexic. I've been—I was diagnosed with my dyslexia at the age of 5." Likewise, Ralph described himself as "a 20-year-old college student" and "junior" majoring in the social sciences. He only became loquacious when speaking about his disability: "I guess you could say when I was maybe 10 years old I was labeled as ADD and it kind of followed me all the way through high school. It was kind of an obstacle for me, but I seemed to manage to get this far I guess." While most introductions were fairly insubstantial, disability was one of the few times that participants actually added dimensionality—that is, time of diagnosis and impact—to their accounts.

Students varied in the salience that they assigned disability in their lives. For Ralph, it had a very real impact, and it was something that happened to him (i.e., "it kind of followed me"). Other participants were more dismissive of the impact or confident in their ability to determine the course of their own lives. Samantha, for example, stated that she did not really think of herself as a person with a disability: "I don't really like the phrase learning disability; I like learning difference because it's not really a disability. Our brains are just different." Meanwhile, others saw learning disabilities as an obstacle but not determinative part of their experience. When asked whether he sometimes thought of his learning disability as a positive thing, Xavier stated: "I wouldn't say it's an advantage, but it's just another attribute to who I am. Because, for me, I don't really see it as an advantage or a disadvantage or something that slows me down. I just cope with it." Both Zoey and Joe did see positive outcomes from their experiences as people with disabilities. Zoey noted: "Having a disability isn't necessarily bad, it can actually fuel people." Meanwhile, Joe saw his worldview shaped by his disability in important ways. He stated: "I believe that everybody has something good about them, everybody can contribute something no matter what flaws they may appear to have or what challenge they have."

The particular focus on learning disability in our study also revealed an interesting potential insight into how experiences differ based on diagnosis. For example, Xavier stated: "I feel like a learning disability is much harder to overcome than a disability itself because as of now, we have so much technology and medicine that will definitely help you, but from a learning disability standpoint, it's very difficult to overcome it. It depends how you manage it as well." In his narrative, Xavier highlights a theme raised by several participants: a learning disability cannot be easily treated so that a person will be able to meet a normative standard because it fundamentally alters the way that people process letters, numbers, words, equations, sentences, and ideas. While the impossibility of amelioration may also be true of other types of disability as well, the point that

Xavier raises is an important one: it is somewhat difficult to speak of disability as a discrete facet of self when it is integral to the very way that people experience the world. Notably, however, people with learning disabilities do typically have the ability to "hide" that part of themselves from the world. As Ralph stated: "A lot of times I feel like it's easier to hide a learning disability. Someone can hide ADD or ADHD and just by looking at them you wouldn't really know." The ability to "pass" as a person without a disability makes it hard both for those with and those without a disability to identify its impact on the way that people experience the world.

Recommendations to Support Engagement Among Students with Disabilities

The empirical findings offered above show that students with disabilities engage with the college experience in a variety of ways and are influenced by factors inside and out of the classroom. Furthermore, engagement and its mediating factors interact with these students' intersectional identities, of which disability is only one facet. The many ways that students with disabilities engage with college means that there is a great need for intentional and proactive design. There are many vectors for engagement, including academic programs, intramural athletics, and social entities like clubs and student organizations. Fostering inclusive practice and support for students with disabilities means that inclusivity needs to be reflected in every possible engagement vector for all students. We focused on students with language-based learning disabilities; however, academic courses, programs, events, and physical space on a campus need to be accessible to people regardless of disability status or type.

We also suggest that disability awareness and training be incorporated into student affairs professional development. The field currently prepares student affairs professionals to become skilled at navigating conversations about sensitive issues such as gender identity, sexuality, and mental health. In the same way, student affairs professionals need to practice those same principles of destigmatization, honest communication, and support for students with disabilities. Students with disabilities should be able to disclose their disabilities in safe spaces and receive support from student affairs professionals, faculty, and other staff members.

Finally, institutions as a whole need to consider disability access as a part of institutional engagement and include it in their diversity planning attempts. While disability access is often discussed as an important part of institutional diversity and inclusivity, it is rarely systematically addressed in institutional planning. Disability access needs to be incorporated into the fabric of an institution. In other words, institutions need to move beyond the letter of the law and fully engage students with disabilities at every level of institutional planning, engagement, and inclusion.

Conclusion

In many ways, the four themes we identified in our analysis—the role of disability in mediating classroom engagement, variations in access to institutional support, the importance of supportive peer networks, and the variable salience of disability identity—resemble the characteristics of college engagement identified by other scholars. Engagement as a conceptual construct contends that students may take part in a variety of beneficial academic and nonacademic behaviors and the degree, type, and affective experience of those behaviors has a variable impact on academic success (Kuh, 2007; McCormick et al., 2013). Similarly, the students with disabilities in this study found that their engagement with the college experience was mediated by a variety of factors and in a variety of ways. For these students, engagement could take the form of classroom interactions; accommodations for disability; structured peer support groups; clubs and organizations; and interaction with peers, tutors, and faculty members. The way they experienced their disabilities inside and outside the classroom as well as the types of institutional and peer support they were able to access mediated these students' engagement with the college environment. However, because disability identity is not monolithic and each student interfaced with the college environment differently, each student's engagement had unique dimensions. This finding mirrors NSSE's (2013) treatment of engagement as a multidimensional, thematic construct consisting of academic challenge, learning with peers, experiences with faculty, and interactions with campus environment.

We argue that disability is a multi-faceted phenomenon that interfaces with engagement in diverse ways. Participants vary in the way that they describe their disabilities and the relationship those disabilities have to their sense of self. They utilize networks of supportive peers, but those networks do not always look the same—and might not exist in the same way at a different institution. Our participants also encountered a diverse array of support services and sought to make use of them in a manner that made sense to them. All of these elements contribute to the varied capacity of students with disabilities to engage in the classroom. In short, the engagement of students with disabilities is akin to a complex, perhaps unsolvable problem, but that does not mean that we are not obligated to try.

A key first step would be the construction of a relevant theoretical and empirical literature base. Students with disabilities are not presently included in much of the writing on engagement nor are there many empirical pieces on their within-college experiences. Since good practice originates from good research (Kuh et al., 2005), a scholarly literature base that synthesizes disability and engagement is critical for moving forward. As this work is undertaken, care should be taken to distinguish between environments in which and populations for which particular strategies are effective.

Scholars and practitioners alike would do well to be mindful of the fact that "disability" can simultaneously refer to a medical diagnosis, protected legal category, and social identity. Disability is an intersectional identity. Consequently, it is unlikely that there will ever be a unitary best practice for students with disabilities but rather practices that would work well contextually. This conclusion becomes even more apparent when disability is considered in tandem with other social identities. Based on literature that explores disability along with identities related to social class, race/ethnicity, and sexuality (e.g., Haeger, 2011; Kafer, 2013; Stapleton, 2015), we can reasonably conclude that a nuanced understanding of the relationship between disability and engagement must include other elements of a student's background as well. That is, when thinking about the engagement of students with disabilities, we cannot look for a simple pattern shared by all students with disabilities. That conclusion echoes work done elsewhere that demonstrates that adding disability into the mix of theories of student development requires that these theories become more complex to account for both behaviors originated primarily from and those not originating primarily from a student's disability identity.

In the end, however, the main lesson offered by this chapter—and one that subsumes all the implications offered previously—is clear: we think about students with disabilities far too infrequently when thinking about engagement, and as a result, we do not fully appreciate the differing patterns of engagement that might exist on a given college campus. That needs to change, and it can change through an ongoing commitment from scholars and practitioners to hear the voices of students with disabilities.

References

Astin, A. W. (1993). *What matters in college? Four critical years revisited*. San Francisco, CA: Jossey-Bass.

Brown, K., & Broido, E. M. (2015). Engagement of students with disabilities. In S. Quaye & S. Harper (Eds.), *Student engagement in higher education: Theoretical perspectives and practical approaches for diverse populations* (2nd ed., pp. 187–207). New York, NY: Routledge.

Cawthon, S. W., & Leppo, R. (2013). Accommodations quality for students who are d/Deaf or hard of hearing. *American Annals of the Deaf, 158*(4), 438–452.

Coulter, C. A., & Smith, M. L. (2009). The construction zone: Literary elements in narrative research. *Educational Researcher, 38*(8), 577–590.

DaDeppo, L. (2009). Integration factors related to the academic success and intent to persist of college students with learning disabilities. *Learning Disabilities Research & Practice, 24*(3), 122–131.

Dunn, D. S., & Burcaw, S. (2013). Disability identity: Exploring narrative accounts of disability. *Rehabilitation Psychology, 58*(2), 148–157.

Eagan, K., Stolzenberg, E. B., Ramirez, J. J., Aragon, M. C., Ramirez Suchard, M., & Hurtado, S. (2014). *The American freshman: National norms Fall 2014*. Los Angeles, CA: Higher Education Research Institute.

Grigal, M., Hart, D., & Weir, C. (2012). A survey of postsecondary education programs for students with intellectual disabilities in the United States: Survey of postsecondary education programs. *Journal of Policy and Practice in Intellectual Disabilities, 9*(4), 223–233.

Gubrium, J. F., & Holstein, J. A. (2009). *Analyzing narrative reality*. Thousand Oaks, CA: Sage.

Haeger, H. A. (2011). At the intersection of class and disability: The impact of forms of capital on college access and success for students with learning disabilities. Retrieved from http://arizona.openrepository.com/arizona/handle/10150/145292

Hendrickson, J. M., Therrien, W. J., Weeden, D., Pascarella, E. T., & Hosp, J. (2015). Engagement among students with intellectual disabilities and first year students: A comparison. *Journal of Student Affairs Research and Practice, 52*(2), 204–219.

Hewitt, L. (2011). Perspectives on support needs of individuals with autism spectrum disorders: Transition to college. *Topics in Language Disorders, 31*(3), 273–285.

Holley, K. A., & Colyar, J. (2009). Rethinking texts: Narrative and the construction of qualitative research. *Educational Researcher, 38*(9), 680–686.

Hurtado, S., Alvarez, C. L., Guillermo-Wann, C., Cuellar, M., & Arellano, L. (2012). A model for diverse learning environments. In J. C. Smart & M. B. Paulsen (Eds.), *Higher education: Handbook of theory and research* (pp. 41–122). New York, NY: Springer.

Jones, S. R., & Abes, E. S. (2013). *Identity development of college students: Advancing frameworks for multiple dimensions of identity*. San Francisco, CA: Jossey-Bass.

Kafer, A. (2013). *Feminist, queer, crip*. Bloomington, IN: Indiana University Press.

Kimball, E., George-Mwangi, C., Friedensen, R. E., Lauterbach, A., Ostiguy, B., Manly, C., & Wells, R. S. (2015). "I don't see myself as a person with a disability, but technically I am": Extending the Diverse Learning Environments model to students with disabilities in STEM fields. Presented at the Annual Conference of the Association for the Study of Higher Education in Denver, CO, November 8, 2015.

Kimball, E., Wells, R. S., Lauterbach, A., Manly, C., & Ostiguy, B. (2016). Students with disabilities in higher education: A review of the literature and an agenda for future research. In *Higher education: Handbook of theory and research* (Vol. 31) (pp. 91–156). New York, NY: Springer.

Kuh, G. D. (2007). What student engagement data tell us about college readiness. *Peer Review, 9*(1), 4–8.

Kuh, G. D., Kinzie, J., Schuh, J. H., Whitt, E. J., & Associates. (2005). *Student success in college: Creating conditions that matter*. San Francisco, CA: Jossey-Bass.

Malcolm-Piqueux, L. (2015). Application of person-centered approaches to critical quantitative research: Exploring inequities in college financing strategies. In R. S. Wells & F. K. Stage (Eds.), *New scholarship in critical quantitative research—Part 2: New directions for institutional research* (pp. 59–73). San Francisco, CA: Jossey-Bass.

McCall, L. (2005). The complexity of intersectionality. *Signs: Journal of Women in Culture and Society, 30*(3), 1771–1800.

McCormick, A. C., Kinzie, J., & Gonyea, R. M. (2013). Student engagement: Bridging research and practice to improve the quality of undergraduate education. In M. B. Paulsen (Ed.), *Higher education: Handbook of theory and research* (pp. 47–92). New York, NY: Springer.

Megivern, D., Pellerito, S., & Mowbray, C. (2003). Barriers to higher education for individuals with psychiatric disabilities. *Psychiatric Rehabilitation Journal, 26*(3), 217–231.

National Center for Education Statistics. (2014). *Profile of undergraduate students: 2011–2012* (No. NCES 2015-167). Washington, DC: U.S. Department of Education.

National Survey of Student Engagement. (2013). *A fresh look at student engagement: Annual results 2013*. Bloomington, IN: Indiana University Center for Postsecondary Research.

Nichols, A. H., & Quaye, S. J. (2009). Beyond accommodation: Removing barriers to academic and social engagement for students with disabilities. In S. R. Harper & S. J. Quaye (Eds.), *Student engagement in higher education: Theoretical perspectives and practical approaches for diverse populations* (pp. 39–60). New York, NY: Routledge.

Peña, E.V. (2014). Marginalization of published scholarship on students with disabilities in higher education journals. *Journal of College Student Development, 55*(1), 30–40.

Riddell, S., & Weedon, E. (2014). Disabled students in higher education: Discourses of disability and the negotiation of identity. *International Journal of Educational Research, 63*, 38–46.

Stapleton, L. (2015). When being deaf is centered: d/Deaf women of color's experiences with racial/ethnic and d/Deaf identities in college. *Journal of College Student Development, 56*(6), 570–586.

Stodden, R. A., Roberts, K. D., Picklesimer, T., Jackson, D., & Chang, C. (2006). An analysis of assistive technology supports and services offered in postsecondary educational institutions. *Journal of Vocational Rehabilitation, 24*(2), 111–120.

Vaccaro, A., Kimball, E., Ostiguy, B., & Wells, R. S. (2015). Researching students with disabilities: The importance of critical perspectives. In *New scholarship in critical quantitative research—Part 2: New Directions for Institutional Research* (Vol. 163) (pp. 25–41). San Francisco, CA: Jossey-Bass.

Wessel, R. D., Jones, J. A., Markle, L., & Westfall, C. (2009). Retention and graduation of students with disabilities: Facilitating student success. *Journal of Postsecondary Education and Disability, 21*(3), 116–125.

6

COLLEGE STUDENTS WITH LEARNING DISABILITIES

An At-Risk Population Absent from the Conversation of Diversity

Wanda Hadley and D. Eric Archer

The National Center for Education Statistics (NCES, 2012), reports that students with disabilities, specifically learning disabilities, are increasingly enrolling at institutions of higher education. Sparks and Lovett (2009) noted that the enrollment has been excessive even compared to other disability groups. Greenfield, Mackey and Nelson (2016) described students with learning disabilities as the largest federal disability category population. Although there is growing enrollment regarding this student population, typically they have trouble adjusting to and persisting in the college environment (Hamblet, 2014; Balcazar et al., 2012; Hadley, 2009). Students with learning disabilities' first-year retention, four-year progression, and graduation rates are lower than their peers without disabilities (Reiff, 2007). Morris (2014) submitted that fewer students with learning disabilities complete postsecondary education compared to their peers without disabilities. But on average, students with learning disabilities who complete a college program experience significantly better employment and after-graduation living than peers who do not (Leake, Burgstahler, & Izzo, 2011). Additionally, Balcazar et al. (2012) stressed that pursuing a college education increases the possibility that students with learning disabilities will seek out and obtain employment of long-lasting careers, rather than low-skilled entry-level positions. Sparks and Lovett (2009) attribute more students with learning disabilities attending postsecondary education because of more available services. Many college and universities, however, are still unprepared to support students beyond the accommodations required by federal laws (Hong, 2015). While in secondary school systems, students with learning disabilities are provided services according to the mandates of the Individuals with Disabilities Education Act (IDEA) of 1990/Individuals with Disabilities Education Improvement Act (IDEIA) of 2004. Conversely, when students with learning disabilities transition to college, they are assured services according to the expectations of Section 504 of the Rehabilitation Act of 1973 and the Americans with Disabilities Act (ADA) of 1990. Higher education institutions are required by law to offer accommodations and services such as peer tutors, notetakers, and additional time for students to complete exams (Hamblet, 2014; Hadley, Twale, & Evans, 2003). Students with learning disabilities transitioning to higher education could be required to take college preparatory courses, provided peer mentors through the Office for Students with Disabilities (OSD), and/or enrolled in academic support workshops to enhance their study skills. They could also be encouraged to seek counseling from the university counseling center to support emotional and personal needs. Such structured campus supports offered during students' transition to college, could support successful persistence (Wernersbach et al., 2014). Kraus (2010) summarizes the responsibility higher education has in reframing disability as another aspect of diversity:

> Perhaps the role of service provider should not be limited to determining individual accommodations and facilitating campus access, but expanded to that of an ambassador of disability culture. We have the unique opportunity to reframe disability, push forward progressive ways of thinking, and challenge antiquated ideas. In our roles, we represent disability to our campuses and community.
>
> *(p. 28)*

For students with learning disabilities who might be less prepared for college work than students without learning disabilities such academic supports might be helpful. Wernersbach et al. (2014) further found that academic self-efficacy is an essential factor to consider in helping students be successful and persistent in the academic environment. Accommodations such as study skills or developmental courses have shown effectiveness in providing underprepared students with support. Guy, Cornick, Holt, and Russell (2015) established that students with noted learning deficiencies, such as students with learning disabilities, require specific remediation and/or academic support. Guy et al. (2015) further submitted that students who successfully complete, for example, a developmental mathematics course in their fall semester of course work are more likely to register for spring semester courses than those students who do not successfully complete. The requirements at most colleges are that students must complete the developmental course requirements before enrolling in credit-bearing general courses. Developmental course work helps to build a host of skills and increase the student's self-determination. Having self-determination skills helps the student direct their progress and have a vision for their future. Students with learning disabilities transitioning to college have had very little experience directing their future. Self-determination as a construct is multidimensional and representative of psychological and behavioral traits (Cobb et al., 2009). Cobb et al. (2009) further noted that positive self-determination skills are a predictor of successful transition to life after college. Hughes et al. (2013) highlighted growing evidence that suggested the role of self-determination in promoting positive academic, social and post-school outcomes for students with intellectual and developmental disabilities. Hughes et al. (2013) defined self-determination skills as decision making, self-advocating, and the student's active involvement in their educational future. The findings of Hughes et al. were inclusive of ethnically and racially diverse students with severe intellectual disabilities. They further found that students with learning disabilities self-determination skills from high poverty high schools seeking to transition to college may lag behind their peers from more affluent schools with. Schools with inadequate resources may limit opportunities for the necessary experiential pieces for developing self-determination skills. Balcazar (2012) noted the need to develop better support systems to encourage the possibility of ethnic minority students with learning disabilities to enroll and graduate from college. Self-determination outcomes can be taught to students presenting a host of disabilities and learning concerns. Although self-determination is a lifelong process that can be learned through problem solving and varied experiences, for various reasons, it is not always taught (Hughes et al., 2013). The context and structure of developmental courses might influence students' academic self-efficacy as well as self-determination abilities. The acquisition of needed skills and greater self-confidence may move students with learning disabilities toward a more successful college experience. In this chapter, we discuss issues faced by students with learning disabilities in higher education, how social constructions of disability influence the lived experience of these students, and the implications of various perspectives on disability for the postsecondary education professionals who work to support this diverse student population.

The Higher Education Experiences of Students with Learning Disabilities

A learning disability is a diagnosed condition that could limit student participation and learning in the college environment (Remy & Seaman, 2014). Colleges and universities have developed supports to accommodate and include students with "visible" disabilities such as visual impairments and physical disabilities (Crudden, 2012). Learning disabilities, however, are often times referred to as "hidden" or "invisible" disabilities because they may not appear in clear and concrete ways (Reiff, 2007). Learning disabilities may influence the student's aptitude in basic skills such as reading and mathematics, but also skills such as auditory, visual, and/or spatial perception. Additionally, the student's executive functioning skills including problem solving, task organizing and assignment completion might be challenged because of the learning disability. Students with dyslexia, autism spectrum disorder (ASD), and intellectual disabilities (ID) are the increasing categories of learning disabilities anticipating the transition to college (Plotner & Marshall, 2015; Mitchell & Beresford, 2014; and VanBergeijk, Klin, & Volkmar, 2008). Mitchell and

Beresford (2014) informed that students with high-functioning ASD can find the transition to and demands of college expectations very challenging. They further found that the arduous educational curriculum and lack of social skills undermine the confidence students need in their new environment. In their transition to college, students who have these specific cognitive disabilities generally struggle with communication skills, academic tasks, disability disclosure and self-advocacy (Glennon & Marks, 2010). Dyslexia, ASD and ID are disabilities that accompany other concerns such as emotional problems and/or as attention deficit hyperactivity disorder (ADHD). Vickers (2010) submitted that learning disabilities and attention-focus concerns are important issues on college campuses because of the number of students diagnosed with these disabilities. Students with ADHD have trouble focusing and maintaining attention and are frequently impulsive and disorganized. Vickers (2010) further observed that accommodations such as extra time to take exams, alternative exam formats, and notetakers help students a great deal. A misconception about students with learning disabilities is their capacity for learning, but it is their process for learning, that is different. Students' perception and integration skills influence the way they process information. A student with a learning disability who processes information differently must retrieve, assemble, and express information in adaptive methods. Since there may be discrepancies in basic skills and the student's ability to synthesize what they have learned, accommodations/special services might be necessary for the student to express what he or she has learned. Even though students with learning disabilities in the college environment are entitled to reasonable accommodations according to federal laws, they must compete with peers without learning disabilities in inclusive classroom settings.

In transitioning to higher education, students might find college life as unstructured compared to the schedules of the secondary school settings. Higher education administrators and faculty generally view students as adults who are responsible for their own education. Services for students with learning disabilities at the college level differ considerably from services at the high school level. The difference is due to the laws protecting students in the two educational settings. While in secondary schools, students with disabilities, however, receive special education services authorized by IDEA/IDEIA and overseen by a team referred to as the Individual Education Planning (IEP) team. This group of school personnel, parents, and students convene to insure appropriate services provided to the student (Hadley, Twale, & Evans, 2003). The team also assists students in deciding what type of postsecondary possibility makes the most sense for them. At this time, high school counselors may want to have students look at career and interest inventories. Of equal importance, according to Reiff (2007), the student's knowledge, aptitude, and educational preparation are evaluated. The IEP team can be instrumental in assisting the student in their transition to college. When students with disabilities transition to college they are no longer covered by IDEA/IDEIA and IEPS are not applicable (Vickers, 2010). In a college environment, students with learning disabilities are protected by Section 504 of the

Rehabilitation Act of 1973 and the Americans with Disabilities Act (ADA) of 1990. Both 504 and the ADA are civil rights statutes as opposed to educational statutes. Section 504 and the ADA require colleges and universities to make reasonable and necessary modifications to policies and practices to avoid discrimination and ensure access and opportunity for students with learning disabilities. Vickers (2010) defined "equal access and opportunity" as the same access and opportunity available to the general population of students. Since Section 504 and the ADA do not require college and universities to provide a model of special education services like those offered in high school, students with disabilities will most likely need support in their transition and adjustment to college expectations (Madaus, 2011). For students with learning disabilities to receive accommodations and support services in college, they must first provide documentation of their learning disability. Reiff (2007) wrote that an evaluation of learning disabilities typically include results from both an aptitude/intelligence and achievement tests. Additionally, most colleges and universities require documentation that is within three years of the date of the college application. Psychoeducational assessments such as the Wechsler Adult Intelligence Scale (WAIS-IV) and/or the Woodcock-Johnson Cognitive Battery can provide a comprehensive understanding of a student's overall learning style. Reiff (2007) added that although colleges and universities do not use one standard set of credentials, the majority of schools follow guidelines developed by the Association for Higher Education and Disability (AHEAD). The diagnosis of a learning disability is the discrepancy between aptitude and achievement. Further, most colleges and universities request evaluations that use both aptitude and achievement tests. The testing should simply explain any strategies and accommodations necessary for the student. Moving to and thriving in postsecondary education requires students with learning disabilities to practice self-determination behaviors. Self-determined students are able to identify their strengths and weaknesses, manage their lives, and pursue future goals (Ankeny & Lehmann; 2011). Unlike high school in college students with learning disabilities are expected to provide documentation of their learning disability and request services. Developing the self-regulated skills needed for college can be overwhelming for many students with learning disabilities. High school administrators, such as counselors and transition coordinators are essential in helping students acquire information and understand the differences in services and expectations for student advocacy in the college setting. In their move to college, students need to meet university entrance requirements, self-identify as a student with a learning disability, and self-advocate to the campus Office for Students with Disabilities (OSD). The OSD is responsible for maintaining and employing current knowledge and policies about disability issues to the campus community. The staff is responsible for providing advising to students with learning disabilities, programmatic support, and direct services. Without proper documentation of their disability, the student is not legally eligible for accommodations and services from OSD. Vickers (2010) found that accommodations first-year students with learning disabilities requested included notetakers, textbooks on tape, extended time for examinations, and quiet areas for testing. Her findings were that students with learning disabilities and attention deficit disorder (ADD) were most likely than students with physical disabilities to receive services from the disability services office. Her observation was that the learning disabilities and ADD population were more willing to request and receive services. She pronounced that structural adjustments that students with physical disabilities request such as Braille signs and ramps are a part of the universal design, not a student-by-student requested accommodation. Although, according to Reiff (2007), Office of Disability Services (ODS) or Disability Support Services (DSS) is generally the office name and Hadley et al. (2003) noted that at most institutions the office is housed under the umbrella of Student Affairs. Many students transitioning to college can benefit from the services of OSD and the support of their personnel. In their meeting with OSD staff, students can discuss adjustment to college issues, class schedules, specific courses, their syllabi and textbook issues. Students should be encouraged to meet with instructors early in the semester to ensure that they understand course requirements and expectations. This behavior of self-advocacy is required at the postsecondary level for students with learning disabilities. According to Reiff (2007), students with learning disabilities transitioning to college must be self-determined and self-reliant. He added that students needed to learn self-advocacy skills in high school to be successful in college. Additionally, self-advocacy skills assist students in becoming more self-aware and willing to address their learning issues. Practicing and discussing their needs with OSD staff helps students with learning disabilities decide what to say and stress to their professors. Reiff (2007) further noted that this means that in moving to postsecondary education, the student must understand what will assist in their progress and what will not. In addition to supporting students, the OSD staff generally offers outreach, consultation, and presentations to university faculty and staff to facilitate an environment of accessibility and opportunity for students with learning disabilities. In her exploration of faculty's opinions of accommodations for students, Vickers (2010) found them to be largely accepting and cooperative. It was not clear if their cooperation came about because they agreed with the university's request or chose not to oppose it. Granting accommodations that were considered excessive and clearly evaluating "accommodated" student performance were two areas of concern for university faculty.

Developmental Theory and Students with Learning Disabilities

Understanding how students with learning disabilities develop during their college years is important in encouraging and guiding their progress. Transitioning the students into the collegiate culture and supporting their matriculation through student development theory provides a model to monitor and focus programming efforts for them. Student development theory offers a framework for assisting the students and for assessing how they are adjusting to college life (Evans et al., 2010). In addition to evaluating the work with students, theory oftentimes is used to predict student outcomes and explain behaviors. Most developmental theories propose that for growth or development to happen, the student must experience some type of "event" or "crisis." Theory allows for student affairs practitioners to combine ideas and information into a set of constructs that provides for deeper understanding, broader meaning, and more relevance to the student's transition. Developmental theory is based on the premise that as a consequence of the college environment and experiences, students are presented a series of "developmental challenges" to their current identity or being that requires a response. These challenges and responses to the challenges generally happen across a continuum of time and/or stages of development. It is not to suggest, however, that the sum of a student's experiences and development could be understood through one theory or one stage of a specific theory. Each theory and/or stage of development is proposed to capture some defining piece or pieces of the student. As the nature of students with learning disabilities evolve, so too must the theories identified and presented. According to Baxter Magolda (2011), using multiple theories might offer a more holistic perspective in engaging with at-risk populations such as students with learning disabilities. Baxter Magolda wrote that self-authoring ways of knowing emerges from students' willingness to explore new interpersonal experiences as they progress in college. Students with learning disabilities are transitioning to college from a background where there is generally little opportunity for constructing and contextualizing their experiences. Baxter Magolda's definition of self-authorship connects strongly to the skill of self-determination because of the importance of developing decision-making skills for students with learning disabilities. The content of development and the course of development might look differently depending on the actual theory. The common characteristic, however, of developmental movement or growth is along a path or continuum.

Viewing the work with students with learning disabilities through the paradigms of student development theory can also help establish campus policies and procedures for serving students. The transition to college might be a major event for most students. Due to their earlier educational experience of extensive and intensive support mandated by the Individuals with Disabilities Education Act (IDEA) of 1990/Individuals with Disabilities Education Improvement Act (IDEIA) of 2004, transitioning to college may be particularly challenging for students with learning disabilities (Madaus, 2011). Goodman et al. (2006) described transitioning as a change in relationships, routines, and assumptions about the student's life. According to his theory, student maturation is based on the student's management and resolution of crucial issues. Hadley (2009) and Hadley, Twale, and Evans (2003) updated version of Chickering and Reisser's (1993) developmental theories provided the theoretical lens for students with learning disabilities' transition (Evans et al., 2010). Hadley et al. (2003) and Hadley (2009) studied how students with learning disabilities persisted, changed and grew over their four-year college experience and what experiences most influenced that growth. According to Evans et al. (2010), Hadley's (2009) assessment of students with learning disabilities academic adjustment assisted in the evaluation of the transition to college of students with learning disabilities. Hadley's (2009) research found that as students with learning disabilities successfully persisted in the college environment, they needed to develop specific competences, practice emotional maturity, and move away from previous accommodations and services.

Learning Disabilities as a Construct of Diversity

In addition to understanding the individual academic experiences of students with learning disabilities in higher education, it is also critical to understand how societal views on disability serve to influence the academic experiences of these students at a structural level. Johnson (2006) highlights the socially constructed nature of various identity statuses, such as race, ethnicity, and sexual identity, and the privileges and power conferred to individuals who hold identities congruent with majority groups. These privileged identity statuses are linked to and perpetuated by larger systems in our society. As such, the power that comes from privileged identities (e.g., being male, Caucasian, heterosexual) is not nested in the individual but, instead, is conferred to an individual through the larger system when others assume the individual to be part of the dominant group. Although disability, including learning disabilities as a subset of disability, was originally missing from initial conversations on social constructions of identity, the last several decades have seen the category of disability recognized as another source of socially constructed privilege or oppression, depending on the perceived ability status of an individual (Linton, 1998). Ashmore and Kasnitz (2014) outline the development of disability models in higher education and how these models have changed the way faculty and administrators perceive disability. Over time, such perceptions have ranged from a medical model perspective, where ability is solely within the individual domain, to a cultural model of disability, where the nature of ability is a socially constructed phenomenon based upon how individuals are perceived within larger social structures. This shift from a medical model of disability to a cultural model has occurred gradually over the last several decades and have included several iterations of disability models in higher education.

Initially, disability in the United States was understood though a medical model perspective, where characteristics ascribed to ability were a function of "the legal and ideological delineation of those who embodied ableness and thus full citizenship, as apart from those whose bodies and minds were considered deficient and defective" (Nielsen, 2012, p. 50). This perspective was especially problematic for those individuals deemed as "disabled" as they were often denied access to benefits readily available to "able-bodied" individuals including employment, education, and the ability to marry and have a family (Nielsen, 2012). Charlton (1998) discusses how this medical model perspective of disability began to shift as the disability advocacy movement gained momentum in the 1970s, leading to greater rights being afforded to those who had been deemed "deficient" by larger society. This shift toward alternatives to a medical model of disability was further spurred by the passage of the legislation, which afforded rights to the disabled. Such legislation included the Individuals with Disabilities Education Act and Section 504 of the Rehabilitation Act of 1973 (Ashmore & Kasnitz, 2014). Linton (1998) highlights the lasting impact of the medical model perspective on disability studies in the United States as conferring legitimacy to the practice of assigning meaning to disability where none had previously existed in a formal sense.

Ashmore and Kasnitz (2014) discuss two additional perspectives on disability, which serve as alternatives to the medical model of disability in higher education. The first of these two models includes disability as a contextual variable. This model of disability still retains some aspects of the medical model while recognizing the dynamic nature of disability as a socially constructed phenomenon. For example, the World Health Organization (WHO, 2011) defines disability as being linked to a medical condition; however, there is also the recognition that definitions of disabled change over time and are linked to context in which an individual and others he or she may interact with experience a particular disability. In essence, the contextual model of disability views ability as a function of an individual health condition (e.g., being diagnosed with a learning disability) and personal and environmental factors experienced by the disabled individual (e.g., societal attitudes toward disability, challenges faced in accessing services as a result of one's disability). Ashmore and Kasnitz suggest this contextual model has the potential to make positive impacts on our perceptions of disability by allowing for a greater understanding concerning how notions of disability may vary across a variety of contexts, such as in the higher education environment, instead of simply being a static medical condition embedded with universal meaning across all contexts.

The third model of disability discussed by Ashmore and Kasnitz (2014) includes a social and cultural conception of disability. Longmore (2003) links the development of this perspective on disability with the emergence of disability studies in the 1980s. Furthermore, Thomas (2004) describes the contribution this perspective on disability beyond previous models: "In this social relational definition, disability only comes into play when the restrictions of the activities experienced by people with impairment are socially imposed, this is, when they are wholly social in origin" (p. 581). Therefore, instead of focusing on disability as residing in the individual, the social and cultural conception model of [dis]ability views the consequences of differences in ability status (e.g., marginalization, lack of access to resources) as a result of the larger social structures discussed by Johnson (2006). "[D]isability studies [have] demonstrated how the status and assigned roles of disabled people are not inevitable outcomes of impairments but the products of social and political processes" (Linton, 1998, p. 72). By shifting perspectives on disability from a medical model where disability is inherent in the individual to a social and cultural conception of disability, where ability is a socially constructed phenomenon imposed upon individuals who are perceived as "different," disability studies has moved toward the study of disability as a minority model much like other areas of study, which examine the lived experiences of minority groups (Olkin, 1999). Ashmore and Kasnitz view the social and cultural conception of disability as particularly salient to the work of disability services professionals, faculty and staff in higher education as many of the social and cultural conceptions which influence our views of disability are often deeply ingrained in postsecondary institutions. As a result, the way we consider our work with students with disabilities, including those with learning disabilities, may be heavily influenced by social and cultural assumptions often taken for granted.

Implications of Learning Disabilities as a Social Construct for Disability Services

Discussion of the historical development of disability models in higher education has important implications beyond simply engaging in an academic overview of the state of disability studies. The evolution of disability models in higher education have resulted in the development of various strategies used by professionals on college and university campuses to support the needs of students with disabilities (Guzman & Balcazar, 2010). Additionally, in her study of how Chief Student Affairs Officers (CSAOs) make meaning of "students of concern," Tucker (2015) found that policies and campus resources provided to support students of concern (including at-risk students, students with disabilities, et al.) were highly influenced by the way in which CSAO's perspectives on what it meant to be a "concerning" student based on prior experiences, educational background, and their philosophy on student affairs practice. As such, these authors highlight the wide variety of perceptions on disability in higher education and how these perceptions are often shaped by individual and larger society influences.

Guzman and Balcazar (2010) highlight three broad approaches to the provision of disability services, which they see as directly linked to the larger disability models discussed previously. These approaches include an individual approach (medical model), a social approach (disability as a contextual variable, and a university approach) (social and cultural conception of disability) (Guzman & Balcazar, 2010). As such, the way one views disability, ranging from an inherent medical condition to a socially constructed phenomenon mainly existing outside the individual, can have a strong influence on the way postsecondary institutions choose to support students with disabilities on their campuses. Institutions that choose to view disability from a medical model perspective may focus their efforts solely on compliance and provide reactionary services on a case-by-case basis when students with disabilities approach the office for assistance. Alternatively, those institutions that choose a universal approach to the provision of disability services are more likely to go beyond compliance and to view disability as another aspect of diversity and to work to proactively integrate students with disabilities into the larger campus community and to view these students as having important contributions to make to the overall culture of the institution. Cory, White and Stuckey (2010) advocate for the latter approach and encourage institutions to view disability as another aspect of difference; an identity status that some students may hold that can serve to further increase diversity within the campus community and can add to the experiences of all students within the academy. In addition, these authors advocate highlighting disability within campus programs and curricular instead of simply viewing disability as a problem to be managed through individual services and compliance with federal mandates.

Challenges of Serving Students with Learning Disabilities

There is complexity in serving students with learning disabilities on the college campus because of academic, ethical, cultural, and financial issues accompanying this student population. The Americans with Disabilities Act (ADA) of 1990 articulates that students with disabilities are to have equal opportunity to participate fully in campus educational and social programming. Novak (2015) points out that the ADA is more than an anti-discrimination statute. It is recognized as a federal policy commitment to the inclusion of students with disabilities on college campuses. This legislature described discrimination against individuals as a serious and prevalent problem in our country, including our educational system. The ADA requires that public services, including education, be provided in the most integrated setting appropriate to each individual's needs is known as the law's integration mandate (Novak, 2015). This integration mandate recognizes students with learning disabilities as a diverse population on the campus and their rights to pursue a meaningful educational and cocurricular experience. The number of students with learning disabilities has significantly grown over the past 25 years and institutions have often struggled with how to best incorporate this diverse group of students into the academic environment. In addition, the number of students with other learning disabilities classifications such as ADHD, autism spectrum disorders, and intellectual disabilities have increased (Madaus, 2011), leading to greater diversity of students with learning disabilities as a student population and further increasing the challenge for institutions to successfully support and integrate these students into the university community. Because of this growth, institutions of higher education will have more accommodation and service demands to meet for a host of students. However, this potential challenge also provides an opportunity for higher education professionals. As discussed previously, there are a number of approaches institutions of higher education can use when addressing issues concerning students with disabilities, including those with learning disabilities. Authors such as Cory, White, and Stuckey (2010); Guzman and Balcazar (2010); and Kraus (2010) encourage higher education professionals to seize the opportunity to move beyond individual models of disability, which simply focus on compliance, to truly incorporating all students, including those with learning disabilities, as active participators in the campus community who can further enrich our understanding of diversity within postsecondary education.

References

Ankeny, E. M. & Lehmann, J. P. (2011). Journey toward self-determination: Voices of students with disabilities who participated in a secondary transition program on a community college campus. *Remedial and Special Education, 32*(4), 279–289.

Ashmore, J., and Kasnitz, D. (2014). Models of disability in higher education. In M. L. Vance, N. E. Lipsitz, and K. Parks (Eds.), *Beyond the American with Disabilities Act: Inclusive policy and practice in higher education* (pp. 21–34). Washington, DC: NASPA-Student Affairs Administrators in Higher Education.

Baxter Magolda, M. B. (2011). The activity of meaning making: A holistic perspective on college student development. In M.E. Wilson & J. F. L. Jackson (Eds.), *College student development theory* (pp. 37–53). New York: Pearson Learning Solutions.

Balcazar, F. E., Taylor-Rizler, T., Dimpfli, S., Portillo-Pena, N., Guzman, A., Schiff, R., & Murvay, M. (2012). Improving the transition outcomes of low-income minority youth with disabilities. *Exceptionality, 20*, 114–132.

Charlton, J. (1998). *Nothing about us without us: Disability, oppression and empowerment.* Berkeley, CA: University of California Press.

Chickering, A. W., & Reisser, L. (1993). *Education and identity.* San Francisco: Jossey-Bass.

Cobb, W., Lehmann, J. Newman-Gonchar, R., Alwell, M. (2009). Self-determination for students with disabilities: A narrative meta-synthesis. *Career Development for Exceptional Individuals, 32*(2), 108–114.

Cory, R. C., White, J. M., and Stuckey, Z. (2010). Using disability studies theory to change disability services: A case study in student activism. *Journal of Postsecondary Education and Disability, 23*(1), 28–36.

Crudden, A. (2012). Transition to employment for students with visual impairments: Components for success. *Journal of Visual Impairment & Blindness, 106*(7), 389–398.

Evans, N. J., Forney, D. S., Guido, F. M., Patton, L. D., & Renn, K. A. (2010). *Student development in college: Theory, research and practice* (2nd ed.). San Francisco: Jossey-Bass.

Glennon, T. J., & Marks, A. (2010). Transitioning to college: Issues for students with an autism spectrum disorder. *Occupational Therapy Practice, 15*(11), 7–9.

Goodman, J., Schlossberg, N. K., & Anderson, M. L. (2006). *Counseling adults in transition* (3rd ed.). New York: Springer.

Greenfield, R. A., Mackey, M., & Nelson, G. (2016). Pre-service teachers' perceptions of students with learning disabilities: Using mixed methods to examine effectiveness of special education coursework. *The Qualitative Report, 21*(2), 330–351.

Guy, G. M., Cornick, J., Holt, R. J., & Russell, A. S. H. (2015). Accelerated developmental arithmetic using problem solving. *Journal of Developmental Education, 39*(1), 2–12.

Guzman, A., and Balcazar, F. (2010). Disability services' standards and the worldviews guiding their implementation. *Journal of Postsecondary Education and Disability, 23*(1), 50–61.

Hadley, W. M. (2009). Transition and adjustment of first-year students with specific learning disabilities: A longitudinal study. *Journal of College Orientation and Transition, 17*(1), 31–44.

Hadley, W. M., Twale, D. J., & Evans, J. H. (2003). First-year students with specific learning disabilities: Transition and adjustment to academic expectations. *Journal of College Orientation and Transition, 12*(1), 12–23.

Hamblet, E. C. (2014). Nine strategies to improve college transition planning for students with disabilities. *Teaching Exceptional Children, 46*(3), 53–59.

Hong, S. S. (2015). Qualitative analysis of the barriers college students with disabilities experience in higher education. *Journal of College Student Development, 56*(3), 209–227.

Hughes, C., Cosgriff, J. C., Argan, M., & Washington, B. H. (2013). Student self-determination: A preliminary investigation of the role of participation in inclusive settings. *Education and Training in Autism and Developmental Disabilities, 48*(1), 3–17.

Johnson, A. G. (2006). *Privilege, power and difference* (2nd ed.). New York: McGraw Hill.

Kraus, A. (2010). Professional perspective. *Journal of Postsecondary Education and Disability, 23*(1), 28.

Leake, D. W., Burgstahler, S., & Izzo, M. V. (2011). Promoting transition success for culturally and linguistically diverse students with disabilities: The value of mentoring. *Creative Education, 2*(2), 121–129.

Linton, S. (1998). *Claiming disability: Knowledge and identity*. New York: New York University Press.

Longmore, P. (2003). *Why I burned my book and other essays on disability*. Philadelphia, PA: Temple University Press.

Madaus, J. W. (2011). The history of disability services in higher education. In W. S. Harbour & J. W. Madaus (Eds.), *Disability services and campus dynamics: New directions for higher education*, no. 154 (pp. 5–17). San Francisco: Jossey-Bass

Mitchell, W. & Beresford, B. (2014). Young people with high-functioning autism and Asperger's syndrome planning for and anticipating the move to college: What supports a positive transition? *British Journal of Special Education, 41*(2) 151–169.

Morris, C. (September/2014). Beacon for learning disabled. *Diverse: Disability Issues in Higher Education, CMA publication*. Retrieved from http://www.diverseeducation.com.

National Center for Education Statistics (NCES) (2012). The Postsecondary Education Quick Information (PEQIS). Washington, DC. *U.S. Department of Education Institute System of Education Sciences.*

Nielsen, K. (2012). *As disability history of the United States*. Boston, MA: Beacon Press.

Novak, J. (2015). Raising expectations for U.S. youth with disabilities: Federal disability policy advances integrated employment. *Center for Educational Policy Studies Journal, 5*(1), 91–110.

Olkin, R. (1999). *What psychotherapists should know about disability*. New York: Guildford Press.

Plotner, A. J., & Marshall, K. J. (2015). Postsecondary education programs for students with an intellectual disability: Facilitators and barriers to implementation. *Intellectual and Developmental Disabilities, 53*(1), 58–69.

Reiff, H. B. (2007). *Self-advocacy skills for students with learning disabilities: Making it happen in college and beyond*. Port Chester: Dude Publishing.

Remy, C., & Seaman, P. (2014). Evolving from disability to diversity: How to better serve high-functioning autistic students. *Reference & User Services Quarterly 54*(1) 24–28.

Sparks, R. L., & Lovett, B. J. (2009). College students with learning disability diagnoses: Who are they and how do they perform? *Journal of Learning Disabilities, 42*(6) 494–510.

Thomas, C. (2004). How is disability understood? An examination of sociological approaches. *Disability and Society, 19*(6), 569–583.

Tucker, M.V. (2015). *(De)Constructing students of concern: How chief student affairs officers make meaning of concerning student behavior* (Unpublished doctoral dissertation). Northern Illinois University, De Kalb, IL.

VanBergeijk, E., Klin, A., & Volkmar, F. (2008). Supporting more able students on the autism spectrum: College and beyond. *Journal of Autism and Developmental Disorders, 38*, 1359–1370.

Vickers, M. Z. (2010). Accommodating college students with learning disabilities: ADD, ADHD, and dyslexia. *Pope Center Series on Higher Education*, 3–14.

Wernersbach, B. M., Crowley, S. L., Bates, S. C. & Rosenthal, C. (2014). Study skills course impact on academic self-efficacy. *Journal of Developmental Education, 37*(3), 14–23.

World Health Organization. (2011). *World report on disability*. Retrieved from http://whqlibdoc.who.int/hq/2011/WHO_NMH_VIP_11.01_eng.pdf.

7

USING A SPATIAL LENS TO EXAMINE DISABILITY AS DIVERSITY ON COLLEGE CAMPUSES

Holly Pearson and Michelle Samura

Disability cannot be ignored when addressing *diversity* in higher education. In 2011–2012, approximately 11% of students enrolled in higher education reported some type of disability (U.S. Department of Education, 2015). Of the reported students with disabilities, 43.7% were male and 56.3% were female, 58.0% were White, 17.6% were Black, 14.9% were Hispanic, 4.0% were Asian, 0.7% were Pacific Islander, 1.2% were American Indian/Alaskan Native, and 3.6% were two or more races. In spite of the incredible diversity within the category of disability, individuals with disabilities are often "thought of primarily in terms of their disability, just as sexual preference, gender, or ethnicity becomes the defining factor in perceiving another person" (Davis, 1995, p. 10). The absence of disability within the diversity conversation may be due to the dominant narrative of disability as medically deficient (Barnes & Mercer, 2010; Davis, 1995; Goodley, 2011). Conceptualizing disability as a medical impairment posits disability as merely an individual problem rather than a societal issue or a form of social difference (e.g., race, gender, class, age, or sexuality).

Utilizing disability studies' social model approach has elucidated how social institutions (e.g., political, economic, social, historic, educational, and cultural components) transcends disability from an individual issue to a societal issue (Barnes & Mercer, 2010; Davis, 1995; Gabel, 2005). This approach reflects the commonalities that disability has with social differences as they all are a social construction. However, due to the dominant narrative, it counters disability as diversity; thus, furthering removing disability from the diversity dialogue.

Similarly, space is often absent in the diversity dialogue. Intersecting space and human experiences resulted in recent efforts to explore the socio-spatial interaction among physical and social spaces and society (Cresswell, 2004; Tuan, 1977), which conveys different "way[s] of seeing, knowing and understanding the world"

(Cresswell, 2004, p. 11). Every setting is a form of social meaning as individuals engage with each other and space; therefore, the socio-spatial dynamics of disability may evince how disability is diversity. This raises the question: what can space contribute to the conversation of disability and diversity?

In this chapter, we make the case for (1) how a spatial approach to examining disability in higher education enables alternative insights, thus reflecting the importance of considering space in research, programs, and practice related to students with disabilities; and (2) the consideration of diversity of disabilities—that is, even within a larger category of "students with disabilities," there is a wide range of disabilities and subsequently a wide range of experiences of students with disabilities. We propose that a spatial approach to examining experiences of students with disabilities expands our understanding of diversity of and within disability.

Literature Review

There is a significant body of literature that asserts for a more authentic understanding of the issues that arise for students with disabilities on college campuses. Existing research indicates the need to understand both the barriers (e.g., transition, faculty attitudes, or perception of accommodations) and assets (e.g., developing awareness of one's disability and self-advocacy) that shape the students with disabilities' experiences within higher education (Cawthon & Cole, 2010; Garrison-Wade, 2012; Hadley, 2011; Barnard-Brak, Lechtenberger, & Lan, 2010; Mamiseishvili & Koch, 2011; Marshak, Wieren, Ferrell, Swiss, & Dugan, 2010; Quinlan, Bates, & Angell, 2012). While accessibility is a critical component in academic success and integration, many students with disabilities do not experience higher education solely from a disability standpoint. They also experience higher education from the standpoint of embodying, to various extents, a multitude of identities.

There is a growing body of literature intersecting disability with race (e.g., Annamma, 2015; Bell, 2012; Connor, 2008; Ferri & Connor, 2007; Stapleton, 2015), class (e.g., Jenkins, 1991), gender (e.g., Campling, 1981; Deegan & Brooks, 1985; Hall, 2011; Morris, 1992; Thomas, 1999), and sexuality (e.g., Gillespie-Sells, Hill & Robbins, 1998; Granite, 2013; Henry, Fuerth, & Figliozzi, 2010; McRuer & Mallow, 2012). While these studies complicate how disability is conceptualized and theorized (Barnes & Mercer, 2010; Davis, 1995; Freund, 2001; Gordon & Rosenblum, 2001), there is limited consideration of the role of space with the intersections of social differences and disability. Work done in the fields of geography, architecture, sociology, and anthropology reveals that space is not neutral (Harvey, 1996; Keith & Pile, 1993; Massey, 1993) and is more than merely a layout (Delaney, 2002; Tickamyer, 2000). Instead, space affects people just as people affect space.

In the disability and space literature, there has been exploration in how space(s) constructs and maintains hegemonic discourse of disability within architectural representation (e.g., Askew, 2011; Siebers, 2003); exclusion (e.g., Blackman et al., 2003; Imrie, 2001); temporal, movement, and speed (e.g., Freund, 2001;

Titchkosky, 2011); social space (e.g., Butler & Bowbly, 1997); inclusion (e.g., Bodaghi & Zainab, 2013; Dyment & Bell, 2008); and lived experiences (e.g., Dyck, 1995; Kruse, 2003). This research suggests that shifting towards a more enabling and inclusive society involves consideration of the socio-spatial dynamics of disability in addition to locating technological and accessible solutions (Butler & Bowlby, 1997; Freund, 2001; Imrie & Kumar, 1998; Kruse, 2003). However, there are limited insights about the intersections of social differences and disability in this research and great possibilities for considerations of space in research on disability and diversity.

Theoretical Framework

One particularly useful framework for examining the connections between space and various social identities—such as race, gender, sexuality, and even disability—is Neely and Samura's (2011) theory of racial space. Through tracing the parallel development of spatial and racial studies, Neely and Samura identified four key characteristics shared by both space and race. First, space and race are highly contested. Meanings of space and race should not be assumed, and they often are interwoven in the construction of each other's meanings. Second, both space and race are historical and fluid. Their meanings shift over time. Current meanings also are informed by past meanings. Third, space and race are interactional and relational. Meanings of space and race are not static, as they are created and recreated through interactions. And fourth, both space and race are defined by inequality and difference. Power relations are often inscribed into material spaces and even onto bodies. The analytical overlaps between space and race provide researchers ways to examine race and racial identity formation in ways that other approaches may overlook. According to Neely and Samura (2011), "a theory of racial space posits that space matters to race because, as the four characteristics are shared by both space and race, what is viewed as purely a matter of space is also a matter of race" (p. 14).

Although the primary intent of their article was to encourage race scholars to consider spatial dynamics in their racial research, Neely and Samura (2011) also proposed that theory of racial space would be useful for analyses of other types of inequality and difference. Since identities are negotiated in and through space, they suggest that examining other social identities and intersectionalities of identities with respect to spatial relationships may provide greater insight into complex social processes. In many ways, as with racial space, meanings of disability are contested, fluid, interactional, and infused with inequality; thus, we have chosen to use the theory of racial space to frame our analysis of the experiences of college students with disabilities.

Methodology

This study is part of a broader study on how racial/ethnic minorities with disabilities negotiate their identities and spaces in higher education.[1] The study used a purposive sampling technique to locate the individuals who fit the following criteria: (1) at least 18 years of age; (2) enrolled in an undergraduate, graduate, or doctoral program; (3) identify having a racial or ethnic minority background; and (4) identify having a disability. At two public and one private institutions, a letter of intent was sent by the disability services offices, student organizations, and student affairs offices. Various channels were utilized, as not all students disclose with disability services (Low, 1996; Prowse, 2009; Reid, 2014).

From three institutions, a total of 16 individuals—8 female and 8 males—agreed to participate in the study. There was a broad range of diversity within age, gender, racial/ethnic background, disability and their major. Participants ranged from 19 to 52 years old. Ten of the individuals self-identified as having a single racial or ethnic identity (e.g., Persian, Hispanic, or Jewish), while the remaining six self-identified as having two to five racial or ethnic identities (e.g., Mexican and Japanese, or Native American, Mexican, and French Canadian). One individual self-identified as having autism, while two individuals identified as having a mental disability. Three individuals self-identified as having a physical disability, and an additional three individuals self-identified having a sensory disability. Four individuals self-identified as having a learning disability. The remaining three individuals had multiple disabilities that fell into at least two different categories. The array of majors included business, education, biology, anthropology, drama, English, criminology, human services, political science, and sociology.[2]

Data was collected using PhotoVoice (Blinn & Harrist, 1991; Guillemin & Dew, 2010; Health & Cleaver, 2004; Lapenta, 2011; Wang, Cash, & Powers, 2000) and photo elicitation (Banks, 2008; Clark-Ibanez, 2007; Collier, 1957; Mitchell, 2011). PhotoVoice presented the opportunity for the individuals to create their own images of their social worlds, which enabled the researcher access insights that they may not have considered (Harper, 1987; Health & Cleaver, 2004; Pink, 2013; Wang et al., 2000). After the initial interview, the individuals received a shooting script that included a series of open-ended questions about their identities and experiences on campus (Samura, 2016; Suchar, 1997). The visual images taken based on the shooting script were used to structure and guide the interview process (Banks, 2008; Clark-Ibanez, 2007; Collier, 1957; Mitchell, 2011). Five individuals participated in one interview, four individuals participated in two interviews, and seven individuals participated in three interviews. The five individuals who completed only one interview did not capture images due to insufficient time to complete the following interviews. Two individuals opted to use descriptive narrative rather than capturing pictures due to various reasons. Eight individuals captured their own images, and with one individual, Holly assisted in capturing the images. The data collection occurred from February to July 2015.

All the interviews were transcribed and coded through multiple cycles of inductive open and selective coding (Charmaz, 2010; Creswell 2007). The visual images were examined individually and collectively in order to tease out selective codes (Collier, 2001; Collier & Collier, 1986; Pink 2013). Then the selected codes from the interviews and the visual images were contrasted and overlapped in order to triangulate themes between multiple sources (Pink, 2013). Finally, emergent themes were examined through the lens of racial space in order to analyze in-depth disability through a spatial lens. Themes and examples were organized under the four key characteristics of racial space: contested, fluid and historical, relational and interactional, and difference and inequality.

Findings

Disability and Space as Contested: In/Accessibility

When considering space as a political conflict over resources and access, there is a need to consider not only the impact of in/accessibility, but also the diverse array of interpretations of in/accessibility. For example, Wanda, who uses a motorized wheelchair, attends an institution where her department is a historical building that has an accessible ramp for the bottom floor, but the remaining floors are inaccessible due to absence of a lift or elevator. As she expressed frustration toward the inaccessibility, the notion of spontaneity and building relationships emerged. Wanda explained:

> [I feel] like a second class citizen. I always have to call Ben and ask him to come downstairs. . . . It's not the same when you want to start building a relationship with someone, but you can't just stop by and say hi.

While access is an issue, Wanda conveys how inaccessible spontaneity hinders her ability to build relationships.

Relatedly, Joe and Stephanie, who both have a visual impairment, emphasized how visual mediums (e.g., whiteboards, transparency, PowerPoint, Prezi) structure an inaccessible environment. Stephanie experiences difficulty with artificial lights such as PowerPoint, as the light worsens her double vision. When considering the specifics of what is accessible, Joe explained, "I usually work in very dark conditions, and *obviously* the real world is not like that." For him, the ideal light conditions take place 30 minutes before sunset. "If the conditions are ideal, which unfortunately *for me* [emphasized], it's only during a very small period of the day when people are active." Joe recognizes that his ideal environment is not part of the norm on campus, which triggers tension as he navigates a heavily light-oriented society.

Alternatively, Win illustrated how a space embodying multiple meanings structures tension between multiple parties within a single space. His institution previously allocated separate spaces for the Supportive Trustee Intellects, Academic Intellects, and Prospective Intellects. Due to budget cuts, all the Intellects presently share a location. While the institution emphasizes among the students that they are all Intellects, they counter that notion due to separate staff and events.

Furthermore, Win expressed the other Intellects are cold toward him and fellow Supportive Trustee Intellects. Win stated:

> I noticed a lot of weird looks from people. Almost like negative looks because we're Intellects, but we're not like them. We're not Academic Intellects. We're not super smart. We're hard workers, and we're not Prospective Intellects. We didn't do really well in high school, but we still got scholarships because we worked hard and we didn't have parents. We got scholarships based off of need, not based off of our intelligence. I don't think they like that.

The different conceptualization of how the space should be utilized creates further tension. The culture among the Supportive Trustee Intellects differed as they are sociable among each other, while the other Intellects appear to be quiet and focused on completing their work. This reflects how in/accessibility is an ongoing spatial contestation of meanings.

Reframing accessibility as an ongoing socio-spatial phenomenon reveals how accessibility as access is a loaded misconception, as disability consists of a broad spectrum of what constitutes in/accessibility. Seeing the diversity within disability, from a spatial standpoint, enables one to see the diversity within in/accessibility 1 (e.g., physical, social, cultural, energy, or time) and the emergence of ambiguity of access, inclusion, and exclusion (Titchkosky, 2011). The social-spatial lens raises two questions: For whom is the campus designed? (Titchkosky, 2011), and for whom are we making the campus accessible?

Disability and Space as Fluid and Historical: Majority-Minority

Meaning of disabilities and spaces are not only contested, but also fluid and historical as their meanings evolve temporally and in different contexts. When considering the fluidity of social differences, a spatial lens illuminates how certain identities may become more salient in different spaces. Across the individuals' experiences, there was awareness of the interexchange between being minority/majority.

For example, Joe's perception of his disability changed over time. When he was younger, he refuse to disclose his disability due to the stigma nature of disability. In K–12 and undergraduate schooling, he encountered teachers who said he would never be able to read. He also had teachers, some of whom had disabilities themselves, who refused to afford him accommodations such as writing with a black marker instead of a blue marker. This unsupportive environment discouraged him to self-identify and to perceive his disability negatively. Yet, in graduate school, Joe found an environment where he was willing to disclose his disability if needed. This may be due to developing close relationships with the faculty and staff, the advancement of technology that enables him to configure accordingly to his needs (e.g., large screen, large font, and negative colors), and emphasis on discussion based rather than PowerPoint lectures.

However, Joe pointed out that he feels like a minority all the time with his disability, as society is not built for individuals with visual impairments. "I'm constantly reminded of it because people don't even think about it.... I always feel like a minority, no question." His feeling of being a minority stems from simply not being able to see the building signs or the pervasive usage of PowerPoint at conferences, in a society that is built around light normativity. Therefore, while there is fluidity within one's perception of one's disability, disability continues to be salient as one continuously negotiates spaces.

Location wields considerable influences on the fluid meaning of disability and space. As an international student, Rachael commented on the flux in her majority-minority status. In her homeland, where she is the majority, her disability plays a greater role in being a minority. Rachael explained, "It's a different scale of identity, so *for me* [emphasized], in my daily life, if I put in balance the identity of my ethnic group through my disability identity, so I'm more aware of my disability than my identity." In the United States, both her racial and ethnic identity and disability reinforces a sense of being a minority, especially outside of her Jewish community. Within her classrooms, she recognizes being a foreigner whose native language is not English and her hearing loss mark her as different, as she struggles to grasp what is being said. However, within her Jewish community, she noted her disability becomes more salient; thus, reflecting the fluidity of majority and minority statuses.

Similarly, Alicia encountered a culture shock when she realized she was a minority due to her multiethnic heritage. Growing up in Hawaii, being multiethnic is viewed as being part of the majority and something to be celebrated. However, at her institution, she quickly realized that being multiethnic is not common. "I know when people are trying to figure me out. A lot of people just say, 'people like you.' I'm just like 'hmm, what does that mean? They just put me in a minority.'" The self-conceptualization of being a minority can be a location of tension due to the contradicting notion of one's self-perception. Conceptualization of one's social identities and surroundings is not only fluid temporally and contextually, but also influenced by one's past understanding of self and society.

Disability and Space as Relational and Interactional: Interactions with Social and Physical Spaces

To see how space and disability are fluid and historical, there is a need to consider how the two interconnected constructs are relational and interactional on both a macro and a micro level (Neely & Samura, 2011). This indicates that we consider the intersections between physical and social space to grasp how the meanings of space and disability are continuously constructing and perpetuating disabling environments (Gleeson, 1999; Hawkesworth, 2001; Imrie & Kumar, 1998). For someone with an invisible disability, Hilda noted that her disability becomes salient entering into a classroom, while determining her seating location. She commented:

> It's [seating] got to be at least one or two rows away from the door, can't be too far, and it's got to be at the edge of the seat because I have to be able to have an evacuation plan if I'm completely losing it or I have to be able to be very subtle and discreet if I'm able to just take my medicine there. I think about it constantly in class.

The seating location influences whether she will go to class or not, as a undesirable seating position interferes with her learning. She remarked:

> Because when you're panicking or when you have tons of anxiety, just waves of it hitting you, you can't concentrate . . . I'm not going to put myself through that if I don't have to. It is frustrating. Then sometimes I'm like, "Why can't I just tell people, 'Hey, I have a disability. Can you move somewhere?'"

Therefore, the intersections of physical location and society's skeptical view of invisible disabilities contribute to her resistance in disclosing, by containing her disability by where she sits or by choosing not to attend class as an attempt to control her peers' perception of her. Hilda's experiences also demonstrate how the individuals can use spaces themselves as a means of upholding a sense of normalcy.

Alternatively, Wanda illustrated the intersection of social/cultural spaces and disability when discussing the difference between being simply a Palestinian young woman and being a young woman with a disability. Encountering individuals who encouraged her to be more independent by living on her own, Wanda feels her disability flips the script by assuming that there is something wrong with her for wanting to live at home with her parents, or that there is a dysfunctional pathological relationship. However, as a Palestinian young woman, there may be no afterthought, since it is a common tradition that young Palestinian women live at home until they get married. As a result of this social and cultural inaccessibility, Wanda has sought out locations such as a local coffee shop. While the venture is physically accessible, she expressed appreciation of the social and cultural nature. "I don't feel like I'm always having to explain or apologize [that] I need help because they've gotten to know me so well by now." This conveys a sense of not having to defend or justify herself. Thus at the coffee shop, she is able not necessarily to forget about her disability, but at least to momentarily put it to the side.

Reapproaching disability from a socio-spatial lens highlights how the relationships among physical and social spaces, disability, attitudes, cultures, and ideologies continuously construct one another through everyday routines and patterns (Cresswell, 2004; Hawkesworth, 2001; Napolitano, 1996). Framing disability in the context of accessibility reflects not only the need to address technical issues such as access into a building, but also the need to consider the socio-cultural accessibility of the space (Kitchin, 2000; Napolitano, 1996, Neumann & Uhlenkueken, 2001).

Disability and Space Defined by Difference and Inequality: Campuses that Separate

Disability and spaces are both shaped by inequality and difference. Conceptualizing spaces as social and cultural sites offer a means of teasing out dominant ideologies of power, inequality, disability, and citizenship (Hawkesworth, 2001; Imrie, 1996; Imrie & Kumar, 1998; Kitchin, 1998). Noah reflected on his experience of how differences and inequality are embedded on multiple levels such as desk style, class routes, and the physical terrain of the campus. For example, in class, there are single desks with a flip table attached to the side of the chair. With a manual wheelchair, this style of desk is difficult to use, and he prefers not to transfer himself. In response, he has to request an accessible desk from disability services. The accessible desk is a huge four-legged desk that stands in stark contrast to the other desks in the classroom. "At UOL for some reason they always put these big, ugly desks that sets you apart from everybody and it was huge ... and you feel like a red M&M in a bowl of green M&M's, you're like sticking out." Being situated separately from his peers hinders not only his ability to interact with his peers organically, but also his ability to build social connections: according to Noah, "everybody can see you. You're part of the show."

Locating classrooms' entrances uses up extra energy as he searches for access. Noah expressed that accessible entrances feel like "the service entrance," and there is a sense of "this is your path, this is my path." One form of building social connection is walking to class, but for Noah, it is a reminder of how he is different. He explained:

> It sets you apart from a crowd, so if you're walking with a friend or you meet a friend and you're like, "Let's go to class," and then they start walking out this way, "Oh, no, I've got to go this way," so you're isolated ... They just stay acquaintances instead of becoming friends because there's that separation.

The absence of the spontaneity of casual interactions interferes with Noah's building relationships with his peers. Moreover, as the hilly layout of the campus impacts his ability to maneuver his wheelchair to different parts of campus, he has to go to his car, put his wheelchair in the car, locate parking lots that are close to the area that he is traveling to, park, get his wheelchair out, and return back onto campus. As a result, he misses opportunities to build social relationships, which impacts his experience on campus. On multiple levels, there continues to be a discrepancy of differences and inequality within everyday space, in spite of the Americans with Disabilities Act and Section 504 in effect.

Reexamining the campus from an aerial point of view offers further insights into how differences and inequality are interwoven into the campus layout. As Rachael discussed where she goes on campus, she mentioned the Office of International Students, Disability Services, Religious and Spiritual Center, "Center of Holocaust", and a flag of her homeland. With each location, she deals with specific concerns: for example, if she has legal and financial issues, she goes to the Office of International Students. If she has disability issues, she visits the Disability Services. From an aerial standpoint, these offices are situated in separate locations on campus.

Yet, at South State University, these student resources (e.g., academic services, disability services, multicultural office) are located in a single building, while the University of Luminton has a central area where the students can access food, study spaces, ATMs, coffee, clubs, organizations, and student meetings. Surrounding this area is also the majority of the student resources—with the exception of Disability Services, which is located on the opposite side of campus. Thus, considering the socio-spatiality of disability from an individual and institutional standpoint highlights how power is embodied in material and social spaces, which in turn organize and segregate bodies and identities. The layout of the campus thus conveys insights regarding the dominant ideologies about difference and diversity as well as upholds the disconnect between disability and diversity.

Conclusions and Implications

This chapter aimed to demonstrate to scholars of disability and diversity the importance of considering space when researching experiences of students with disabilities. Through the examples discussed above, we can more clearly see how students with disabilities' experiences in different campus spaces revealed complexities of their identities. This research can broaden the field of disability research by continuing to build upon the current literature that intersects disability with other social differences. The field of disability studies could benefit from continuing not only to build upon the dynamics of space and disability, but also to see how the spatial lens can stretch the imaginations of disability as diversity.

The field of disability studies also would benefit from employing unconventional methodologies, particularly visual methods, to examine the wide range of perspectives of individuals with disabilities. Although an in-depth discussion of our methodology was outside the scope of this chapter, we do want to draw attention to the utility of visual methodologies to examine students' experiences in spaces on college campuses. Using visual methods enabled us to better understand the nuances of specific spaces such as the multiple forms of in/accessibility that the students with disabilities had to negotiate within everyday settings; thus accessibility is not merely a physical issue.

Researchers can ask a number of questions that builds upon, extends, and even tests this work. For example, what further alternative nuances can be gained by expanding the study to multiple institutions (e.g., private, state, land grant, public, 2-year)? Additionally, future research should continue to focus on the diversity within individuals with disabilities as a means of continuing not only to disrupt the dominant narrative of disability, but also to expand our understanding of these individuals' experiences and needs. This will enable insights into how to improve their experiences in college and universities both academically and socially. Future research could investigate how the uses and meanings of space overlap or vary among students with different types of disabilities.

Finally, when thinking about policies and practices that would enhance student success among those with disabilities, there is a need to consider the role of space. For university staff, faculty, and administration, using a spatial lens reflects the need to understand the needs of students with disabilities as multidimensional, as these students are continuously negotiating their multiple identities in everyday spaces. While certain forms of disability may be more readily apparent, all forms of disability intersect with other identities, which in turn impact these students' everyday experiences. Recognizing the complexity in their experiences may enable university staff, faculty, and administration to structure campus spaces that help them to thrive academically and socially. Campus planners and designers also need to consider the importance of user experiences when designing campuses. Only when institutions of higher education consider the experiences and perceptions of students with disabilities, as well as the broad diversity within the disability category, will the needs of all students be better met.

Notes

1   Pearson, H. (2016). Spatiality of racial and ethnic minorities with disabilities in higher education. (Ph.D. Dissertation), Chapman University, Orange, CA.
2   All names, institutions, and any other personally identifying information have been replaced with pseudonyms to ensure confidentiality.

References

Annamma, S. A. (2015). "It was just like a piece of gum": Using an intersectional approach to understanding criminalizing young women of color with disabilities in the school-to-prison pipeline. In D. J. Connor, J. W. Valle, & C. Hale (Eds.), *Practicing disability studies in education: Acting towards social change* (pp. 83–102). New York, NY: Peter Lang.

Askew, E. (2011). (Re)creating a world in seven days: Place, disability and salvation in *Extreme Makeover: Home Edition. Disability Studies Quarterly, 31*(2). Retrieved from http://dsqsds.org/article/view/1590/1558.

Banks, M. (2008). *Using visual data in qualitative research.* Thousand Oaks, CA: SAGE Publications.

Barnard-Bark, L., Lechtenberger, D., & Lan, W. Y. (2010). Accommodation strategies of college students with disabilities. *The Qualitative Report, 15*(2), 411–429. Retrieved from http://www.nova.edu/ssss/QR/QR15-2/barnard-brak.pdf.

Barnes, C., & Mercer, G. (2010). *Exploring disability: A sociological introduction* (2nd ed.). Cambridge, UK: Polity Press.

Bell, C. (Ed.). (2012). *Blackness and disability: Critical examination and cultural interventions.* East Lansing, MI: Michigan State University Press.

Blackman, T., Mitchell, L., Burton, E., Jenks, M., Parsons, M., Raman, S., & Williams, K. (2003). The accessibility of public spaces for people with dementia: A new priority for the "'open city.'" *Disability & Society, 18*(3), 357–371. doi:10.1080/0968759032000052914.

Blinn, L., & Harrist, A. W. (1991). Combining native instant photography and photo-elicitation. *Visual Anthropology, 4*(2), 175–192. doi:10.1080/08949468.1991.9966559.

Bodaghi, N. B., & Zainab, A. N. (2013). My carrel, my second home: Inclusion and the sense of belonging among visually impaired students in an academic library. *Malaysian Journal of Library & Information Sciences, 18*(1), 39–54. Retrieved from http://e-journal.um.edu.my/filebank/published_article/4683/1337.pdf.

Butler, R., & Bowlby, S. (1997). Bodies and spaces: An exploration of disabled people's experiences of public space. *Environment and Planning D: Society and Space 1997, 15*(14), 411–433. doi:10.1068/d150411.

Campling, J. (Ed.). (1981). *Images of ourselves: Women with disabilities talking.* London, UK: Routledge & Kegan Paul.

Cawthon, S. W., & Cole, E. V. (2010). Postsecondary students who have a learning disability: Student perspectives on accommodation access and obstacles. *Journal of Postsecondary Education and Disability, 23*(2), 112–128. Retrieved from http://www.eric.ed.gov/PDFS/EJ906696.pdf.

Charmaz, K. (2010). Grounded theory: Objectivist and constructivist methods. In W. Luttrell (Ed.), *Qualitative educational research: Readings in reflexive methodology and transformative practice* (pp. 183–207). New York, NY: Routledge.

Clark-Ibanez, M. (2007). Inner-city children in sharper focus: Sociology of childhood and photo elicitation interviews. In G. C. Stanczak (Ed.), *Visual research methods: Image, society, and representation* (pp. 167–196). Thousand Oaks, CA: SAGE Publications.

Collier, J., Jr. (1957). Photography in anthropology: A report on two experiments. *American Anthropologist, 59*(5), 843–859. Retrieved from http://www.jstor.org/stable/665849.

Collier, M. (2001). Approaches to analysis in visual anthropology. In T. van Leeuwen & C. Jewitt (Eds.), *Handbook of visual analysis* (pp. 35–60). Thousand Oaks, CA: SAGE Publications.

Collier, J., Jr., & Collier, M. (1986). *Visual anthropology: Photography as a research method.* Albuquerque, NM: University of New Mexico Press.

Connor, D. J. (2008). *Urban narratives portraits in progress: Life at the intersections of learning disability, race, & social class.* New York, NY: Peter Lang.

Creswell, J. W. (2007). *Qualitative inquiry & research design: Choosing among five approaches* (2nd ed.). Thousand Oaks, CA: SAGE Publications.

Cresswell, T. (2004). *Place: A short introduction.* Oxford, UK: Blackwell Publishing Ltd.

Davis, L. J. (1995). *Enforcing normalcy: Disability, deafness, and the body.* New York, NY: Verso.

Deegan, M. J., & Brooks, N. A. (Eds.) (1985). *Women with disability: The double handicap.* New Brunswick, NJ: Transaction.

Delaney, D. (2002). The space that race makes. *Professional Geographer, 54*(1).

Dyck, I. (1995). Hidden geographies: The changing lifeworlds of women with multiple sclerosis. *Social Science & Medicine, 40*(3), 307–320. Retrieved from http://www.ncbi.nlm.nih.gov/pubmed/7899943.

Dyment, J. E., & Bell, A. C. (2008). "Our garden is colour blind, inclusive and warm": Reflections on green school grounds and social inclusion. *International Journal of Inclusive Education, 12*(2), 169–183. doi:10.1080/13603110600855671.

Ferri, B., & Connor, D. J. (2007). *Reading resistance: Discourses of exclusion in desegregated & inclusion debates.* New York, NY: Peter Lang Publishing.

Freund, P. (2001). Bodies, disability and spaces: The social model and disabling spatial organizations. *Disability & Society, 16*(5), 689–706. Retrieved from http://dx.doi.org/10.1080/09687590120070079.

Gabel, S. L. (Ed.). (2005). *Disability studies in education: Reading in theory and method.* New York, NY: Peter Lang Publishing.

Garrison-Wade, D. F. (2012). Listening to their voices: Factors that inhibit or enhance postsecondary outcomes for students' with disabilities. *International Journal of Special Education, 27*(2), 113–125. Retrieved from http://www.eric.ed.gov/PDFS/EJ982866.pdf.

Gillespie-Sells, K., Hill, M., & Robins, B. (1998). *She dances to different drums: Research into disabled women's sexuality.* London: UK: King's Fund.

Gleeson, B. (1999). *Geographies of disability,* New York, NY: Routledge.

Goodley, D. (2011). *Disability studies: An interdisciplinary introduction.* Thousand Oaks, CA: SAGE Publications.

Gordon, B. O., & Rosenblum, K. E. (2001). Bringing disability into the sociological frame: A comparison of disability with race, sex, and sexual orientation statuses. *Disability and Society, 16*(1), 5–19. doi:10.1080/713662032.

Granite, A. C. (2013). "Run whatcha brung"—Of passengers and pigeonholes: A phenomenological study on the gender construction of men with intellectual disabilities (Unpublished dissertation). Chapman University, Orange, CA.

Guillemin, M., & Dew, S. (2010). Questions of process in participant-generated methodologies. *Visual Studies, 25*(2), 175–188. doi:10.1080/1472586X.2010.502676.

Hadley, W. M. (2011). College students with disabilities: A student development perspective. *New Directions for Higher Education, 2011*(154), 77–81. doi:10.1002/he.436.

Hall, K. Q. (Ed.). (2011). *Feminist disability studies.* Bloomington, IN: Indiana University Press.

Harper, D. (1987). The visual ethnographic narrative. *Visual Anthropology, 1*(1), 1–19. doi:10.1080/08949468.1987.9966457.

Harvey, D. (1996). *Justice, nature, and the geography of difference.* Oxford: Blackwell Publishing.

Hawkesworth, M. (2001). Disabling spatialities and the regulation of a visible secret. *Urban Space, 38*(2), 299–318. doi:10.1080/00420980124535.

Health, S., & Cleaver, E. (2004). Mapping the spatial in shared household life: A missed opportunity. In C. Knowles & P. Sweetman (Eds.), *Picturing the social landscape: Visual methods and the sociological imagination* (pp. 65–78). New York, NY: Routledge.

Henry, W. J., Fuerth, K., & Figliozzi, J. (2010). Gay with a disability: A college student's multiple cultural journey. *College Student Journal, 44*(2), 377–388. Retrieved from http://www.freepatentsonline.com/article/College-Student-Journal/228428423.html\.

Imrie, R. (1996). *Disability and the city: International perspectives.* London, UK: Paul Chapman Publishing.

Imrie, R. (2001). Barriered and bounded places and the spatialities of disability. *Urban Studies, 18,* 231–237. doi:10.1080/00420980124639.

Imrie, R., & Kumar, M. (1998). Focusing on disability and access in the built environment, *Disability & Society, 13,* 357–374. doi:10.1080/09687599826687.

Jenkins, R. (1991). Disability and social stratification. *British Journal of Sociology,* 42(4), 557–580. Retrieved from http://www.jstor.org/stable/591447.

Keith, M. & Pile, S. (Eds.). (1993). *Place and the politics of identity.* New York, NY: Routledge.

Kitchin, R. (1998). 'Out of place,' 'knowing one's place': Space, power and the exclusion of disabled people. *Disability & Society, 13*(3), 343–356. Retrieved from http://dx.doi .org/10.1080/09687599826678.

Kitchin, R. (2000). *Disability, space and society.* Sheffield, Ireland: Geographical Association.

Kruse, R. J. (2003). Narrating intersections of gender and dwarfism in everyday spaces. *The Canadian Geographer, 47*(4), 494–508. doi:10.1111/j.0008-3658.2003.00038.x

Lapenta, F. (2011). Some theoretical and methodological views on photo-elicitation. In E. Margolis & L. Pauwels (Eds.), *The SAGE handbook of visual research methods* (pp. 201–213). Thousand Oaks, CA: SAGE Publications.

Low, J. (1996). Negotiating identities, negotiating environment: An interpretation of experiences of students with disabilities. *Disability & Society, 11*(2), 235–248. Retrieved from http://dx.doi.org/10.1080/09687599650023254.

Mamiseishvili, K.. & Koch, L. C. (2011). First-to-second-year persistence of students with disabilities in postsecondary institutions in the United States. *Rehabilitation Counseling Bulletin, 54*(2), 93–105. doi: 10.1177/0034355210382580.

Marshak, L., Wieren, T.V., Ferrell, D. R., Swiss, L., & Dugan, C. (2010). Exploring barriers to college student use of disability services and accommodations. *Journal of Postsecondary Education and Disability, 22*(3), 151–165. Retrieved from http://www.eric.ed.gov/ PDFS/EJ906688.pdf.

Massey, D. (1993). Politics and space/time. In M. Keith & S. Pile (Eds.), *Place and the politics of identity* (pp. 141–161). New York, NY: Routledge.

McRuer, R., & Mallow, A. (Eds.). (2012). *Sex and disability.* Durham, NC: Duke University Press.

Mitchell, C. (2011). *Doing visual research.* Thousand Oaks, CA: SAGE Publications.

Morris, J. (1992). Personal and political: A feminist perspective in researching physical disability. *Disability, Handicap & Society, 7*(2), 157–166.

Napolitano, S. (1996). Mobility impairment. In G. Hales (Ed.), *Beyond disability: Towards an enabling society* (pp. 30–35). Thousand Oaks, CA: SAGE Publications.

Neely, B., & Samura, M. (2011). Social geographies of race: Connecting race and space. *Ethnic and Racial Studies, 28*(4), 1–20. doi:10.1080/01419870.2011.559262.

Neumann, P., & Uhlenkueken, C. (2001). Assistive technology and the barrier-free city: A case study from Germany. *Urban Studies, 38*(2), 367–376. doi:10.1080/00420980123806

Pink, S. (2013). *Doing visual ethnography* (3rd ed.). Thousand Oaks, CA: SAGE Publications.

Prowse, S. (2009). Institutional construction of disabled students. *Journal of Higher Education Policy and Management, 31*(1), 89–96. doi:10.1080/13600800802559302.

Quinlan, M. M., Bates, B. R., & Angell, M. E. (2012). 'What can I do to help?': Postsecondary students with learning disabilities' perceptions of instructors' classroom accommodations. *Journal of Research in Special Educational Needs, 12*(4), 224–233. doi:10.1111/j.1471-3802.2011.01225.x.

Reid, D. P. (2014). *Stuck between a rock and a hard place: Exploring the lived experiences of college students who do not request accommodations.* Dissertation, Chapman University. ProQuest, UMI Dissertation Publishing, #3665093.

Samura, M. (2016). Remaking selves, repositioning selves, or remaking space: An examination of Asian American college students' processes of "belonging." *Journal of College Student Development, 57*(2), 135–150.

Siebers, T. (2003). What can disability studies learn from the culture wars? *Cultural Critique*, *55*, 182–216. Retrieved from http://www.jstor.org/stable/1354652.

Stapleton, L. (2015). When being deaf is centered: d/Deaf women of color experiences with racial/ethnic and d/Deaf identities in college. *Journal of College Student Development*, *56*(6), 570–586. doi:10.1353/csd.2015.0061.

Suchar, C. (1997). Grounding visual sociology in shooting scripts. *Qualitative Sociology*, *20*(1), 33–55.

Thomas, C. (1999). *Female forms: Experiencing and understanding disability*. Buckingham, UK: Open University Press.

Tickamyer, A. (2000). Space matters! Spatial inequality in future sociology. *Contemporary Sociology*, *29*.

Titchkosky, T. (2011). *The question of access: Disability, space, meaning*. Toronto, Canada: University of Toronto Press.

Tuan, Y. F. (1977). *Space and place: The perspective of experience*. Minneapolis, MN: University of Minnesota Press.

U.S. Department of Education, National Center for Education Statistics. (2015). *Digest of Education Statistics, 2013* (2015-011), Chapter 3. Retrieved from http://nces.ed.gov/fastfacts/display.asp?id=60.

Wang, C. C., Cash, J. L., & Powers, L. S. (2000). Who knows the streets as well as the homeless? Promoting personal and community action through PhotoVoice. *Health Promotion Practice*, *1*(1), 81–89. doi:10.1177/152483990000100113.

PART III

Perspectives of Faculty and Higher Education Administration

8

FACULTY AND ADMINISTRATOR KNOWLEDGE AND ATTITUDES REGARDING DISABILITY

Allison R. Lombardi and Adam R. Lalor

In the last fifty years access to higher education has increased for students with disabilities due to the disability rights movement, legal changes, and successful policy initiatives within the K-12 education system (Madaus, 2011). Despite the increased enrollment of students with disabilities in American colleges and universities, graduation rates for this student population remain low. According to Newman and colleagues (2011), 66% of students with disabilities do not persist to graduation, a rate 17% higher than their peers without disabilities. As college completion is associated with more work experience, higher employment rates, higher hourly wages, and more flexible work hours for students with disabilities, successful completion of a college degree is particularly important for this student population (Bureau of Labor Statistics, 2013; Newman et al., 2011).

Research suggests that higher education faculty and administrators can play a role in improving the experiences of students with disabilities (Fichten et al., 2014; Hartman-Hall & Haaga, 2002; Salzer, 2012; Stumbo, Hedrick, Weisman, & Martin, 2010; Wilson, Getzel, & Brown, 2000). In particular, faculty and administrators can play important roles in developing a campus climate that welcomes, supports, and offers full access to students with disabilities. However, in order to best support students with disabilities, faculty and administrators must possess some degree of disability-related knowledge and nondiscriminatory, disability-related attitudes toward this student population. Thus, the purpose of this chapter is to review the literature on the knowledge and attitudes of higher education faculty and administrators, including professional development efforts, and to advocate for additional research and training on disability-related topics.

Disability-Related Knowledge and Attitudes

Competencies refer to "knowledge, skills, mind-sets, thought patterns, and the like—that when used whether singularly or in various combinations, result in successful performance" (Dubois, 1998, p. v). As such, the development of knowledge and attitudes used in the workplace are components of an overall competency approach to successful work performance. For the purposes of this chapter, disability-related knowledge includes the facts and information that are learned by an individual. Such knowledge includes, but is not limited to, disability law, the history of discrimination against individuals of disabilities, and the range of disability types. Likewise, disability-related attitudes are defined as the way in which an individual thinks or feels about people with disabilities. Disability-related attitudes include, but are not limited to, a desire to learn about individuals with disabilities, a willingness to provide accommodations and support for individuals with disabilities, and a willingness to advocate for the needs and rights of individuals with disabilities.

Knowledge and Attitudes of Higher Education Faculty

Currently, there are no formal training requirements for faculty with regard to teaching students with disabilities in higher education settings. For years, college faculty have relied on institutional resources (e.g., institutional Office for Disability Services) to provide additional supports to students with disabilities. In fact, many faculty may have been unaware they have students with disabilities enrolled in their classes. However, given the steady increase in the population of college students with disabilities and the lack of funding to bolster supports for such institutional personnel, faculty now must provide academic accommodations to exams and assignments in their courses. Requests for accommodations come from students with *and* without disabilities. Examples of such requests might include (but are not limited to) extended deadlines and alternate exam formats and assignments. Even though more faculty are directly supporting students with disabilities, at most universities there is no professional development or training to ensure faculty are aware of their legal obligations (Raue & Lewis, 2011). Further, the majority of faculty receive little to no training in effective teaching practices that will benefit diverse learners, including students with disabilities.

Prior efforts to understand faculty attitudes toward students with disabilities in postsecondary settings have focused on knowledge about disability, disability-related laws, and knowledge of disability support services and other campus resources (Murray, Wren, & Keys, 2008; Vogel, Holt, Sligar, & Leake, 2008). The results of these investigations suggest that faculty generally endorse positive attitudes toward students with disabilities including a willingness to provide accommodations but often report feeling underprepared to provide such supports. Other researchers have examined similar issues but from the perspectives of college students with disabilities (Barnard-Brak, Sulak, Tate, & Lechtenberger, 2010; Madaus et al., 2003). Findings from this body of research suggest that college students with disabilities experience barriers in requesting accommodations from faculty, and adequate supports vary considerably according to an instructor's willingness to make individual accommodations (Lombardi, Gerdes, & Murray, 2011).

Knowledge and Attitudes of Higher Education Administrators

Higher education administration is comprised of a diverse group of professionals working in an array of functional areas and divisions within a college or university. For example, administrators hold positions in academic affairs, communication and advancement, enrollment and retention, and student affairs, to name just a few. For the purpose of this chapter, the knowledge and attitudes of disability services professionals and student affairs professionals will be discussed. Although disability services offices are often part of student affairs, this is not always the case (Shaw & Dukes, 2001). Furthermore, given that disability services professionals deal with disability-related issues on a daily basis, the knowledge and attitudes of this group of administrators are likely qualitatively different than those of students affairs professionals who engage disability-related issues with less frequency.

Disability Services Professionals

With increasing numbers of students with disabilities pursuing higher education, the number of professionals dedicated to serving them has also increased. These professionals are referred to by a number of titles (e.g., Disability Services Coordinator, Director of Accessibility Services, Assistant Dean of Disability Services), but, for the sake of brevity, they will henceforth be referred to as disability services professionals (DSPs). The primary roles of DSPs are to review and coordinate the provision of disability-related services and accommodations and to ensure access for students with disabilities on campus. Thus, with some exceptions (e.g., special education faculty), DSPs likely have the greatest knowledge of disability and among the most positive attitudes toward individuals with disabilities. However, not all DSPs possess the same levels of knowledge and skills (Dukes & Shaw, 2004), nor do they share identical attitudes toward their work (Guzman & Balcazar, 2010).

Complicating the issue of providing effective and consistent services is a dearth of evidence-based practices. Presently, the profession lacks an understanding of which practices and interventions are effective in meeting the needs of students with disabilities (Shaw & Dukes, 2013). Although a number of promising practices exist (e.g., assistive technology, coaching, universal design for instruction), empirical support for these practices is still emerging. Lacking evidence-based practices, guidance from professional associations becomes more important.

In response to concerns about the professionalization and preparation of DSPs, the Association on Higher Education and Disability (AHEAD) adopted the *AHEAD Professional Standards* and the *AHEAD Code of Ethics* to guide DSPs in the development of essential knowledge and attitudes (Madaus, 1997).

Student Affairs Administrators

Researchers suggest that student affairs professionals lack disability-related knowledge (Murray, Flannery, & Wren, 2008; Myers, 2008a). Considering disability-related topics (e.g., disability identity development, statistics and characteristics about students with disabilities) are generally omitted from student affairs preparation program curricula (Evans, Herriott, & Myers, 2009) and mainstream higher education journals rarely publish articles on disability (Peña, 2014), this lack of knowledge is understandable.

Fortunately, lack of disability-related knowledge has not gone unnoticed. Research indicates that administrators, including student affairs professionals, not only have recognized their lack of disability-related knowledge, but also have expressed desire to learn more about disability (Murray, Flannery, & Wren, 2008; Murray, Lombardi, & Wren, 2011; Murray, Wren, Stevens, & Keys, 2009). Additionally, student affairs and disability scholars have expressed that student affairs professionals need to be ready to serve and support students with disabilities (Evans, Herriot, & Myers, 2009; Hall & Belch, 2000; Myers, 2008a, 2008b; Myers & Bastian, 2010).

Disability-related knowledge is essential for student affairs administrators. It is the responsibility of the student affairs professional to ensure equal access to the co-curriculum. The co-curriculum is the student-affairs coordinated, out-of-class activities that enrich, extend, and complement the academic curriculum (Dalton & Crosby, 2012). Examples of such activities are service learning trips, diversity speakers and programing, and health and wellness programing. Although student affairs professionals, other than those in disability services (and sometimes health and counseling centers), are not required to review disability-related documentation to determine accommodations, they are the administrators frequently tasked with enacting accommodations and should proactively address barriers to services. For example, ensuring that housing accommodations are enacted is traditionally the responsibility of housing or residential life offices, and ensuring that student union programming is accessible to students with orthopedic impairments is the responsibility of student union and/or student activities offices. Failure to enact specified accommodations or consider access is discriminatory, and potentially opens opportunity for litigation (McCabe, 2014). Furthermore, these failures violate the principle of egalitarianism shared by the student affairs profession (ACPA, 2006; Council for the Advancement of Standards in Higher Education, 2006).

In terms of attitudes regarding disability, researchers indicate that student affairs professionals generally hold positive views of students with disabilities

(Murray, Flannery, & Wren, 2008). Despite these positive views, student affairs professionals who have engaged in disability-focused training have more positive disability-related attitudes and perceptions than professionals who have not engaged in disability-focused training (Murray, Lombardi, & Wren, 2011; Murray et al., 2009). Essentially, opportunity exists to improve the attitudes and perceptions that student affairs professionals hold regarding disability. Although more intensive training (e.g., enrolling in a disability-related course or workshop) is related to higher levels of positive attitudes and perceptions than less intensive training (e.g., reading disability-related books or articles, visiting a disability related website), less intensive training on disability is related to higher levels of positive attitudes and perceptions than is having received no training (Murray, Lombardi, & Wren, 2011). In other words, any training is better than no training when it comes to improving attitudes of student affairs professionals. However, the more intensive the better.

Faculty Professional Development

Evidence-based faculty development programs exist, but they remain the exception rather than the rule. Research findings show that faculty who participate in some type of institutional training or workshop report greater awareness of students with disabilities and greater provision of accommodations (Murray et al., 2009; Lombardi & Murray, 2011; Lombardi, Murray, & Gerdes, 2011). These findings are promising and support institutional initiatives to fund and provide such training opportunities to faculty and staff. However, a recent national survey of 29 public four-year institutions found that the greatest barrier (reported by 70% of respondents) to faculty training was limited staff resources and faculty time (Raue & Lewis, 2011). At a time when a growing number of students with disabilities are gaining access to postsecondary settings, federal funds to support training initiatives are declining and many colleges and universities lack sufficient resources to deliver training opportunities without external support (Newman et al., 2011). This lack of funding may stifle campus efforts to promote inclusion and expand the definition of diversity, which would be unfortunate for students with and without disabilities.

Faculty Teaching Practices

Efforts to promote inclusive teaching practices began with several research groups promoting instructional frameworks based on Universal Design (UD) (Connell et al., 1997), a framework that originated in the field of architecture and was later adapted to fit instruction. Universal Design for Learning (UDL) (Rose et al., 2006) and Universal Design for Instruction (UDI) (Scott, McGuire, & Shaw, 2003) are two frameworks that were developed to encourage college faculty to be inclusive in the planning, delivery, and evaluation stages of instruction. Ultimately, the various UD frameworks promote *inclusive* instructional practices.

While UD frameworks are promising in helping faculty create more accessible and equitable learning environments, the literature base remains very much in development. In fact, very few empirical studies on the effectiveness of UD on student outcomes exist (McGuire, 2014; Roberts et al., 2011). This is understandable considering that there has not been a standardized way to assess UD practices across different UD models. Yet, the conceptual value of UD frameworks is promising and was recognized by the Higher Education Opportunity Act of 2008 (Edyburn, 2010). Thus, while UD is not evidence-based, it is endorsed in federal legislation and a promising practice. Efforts to study the effects of UD-based instruction on student learning are needed, but may be scarce due to limited federal funding.

Research findings on college faculty using inclusive teaching practices have focused on the development and testing of climate survey instruments and professional development training packages (Murray et al., 2009; 2014). Disability services personnel and administrators use such instruments to measure faculty knowledge of disability and inclusive teaching practices. Two examples are the Inclusive Teaching Strategies Inventory (ITSI) (Lombardi, Murray, & Gerdes, 2011) and the Assessment of Campus Climate to Enhance Student Success (ACCESS) (Vogel et al., 2008). Both these tools are intended for faculty and measure knowledge and perceptions of disability, including legal mandates and the provision of accommodations. The ITSI also measures faculty knowledge and use of inclusive teaching practices. Use of these measures by administrators can aid in the planning of faculty professional development topics. For example, the survey results may show that most faculty understand the process of requesting accommodations, but many do not know how to design an inclusive assessment. With this information, disability services personnel and higher education administrators may prioritize faculty training topics.

Administrator Professional Development

Training administrators is important if they are to develop the needed knowledge and attitudes to adequately support students with disabilities. The following sections discuss the training of DSPs and student affairs professionals.

Training DSPs

A dearth of preparation programs exist to prepare administrators to serve as DSPs. Though a handful of programs dedicated to preparing DSPs have existed, the only program that remains as of the year 2015 is the Online Graduate Certificate Program in Postsecondary Disability Services offered by the University of Connecticut (http://pds-certificate.uconn.edu/). Thus, few DSPs have received extensive training in postsecondary disability services work (Dukes & Shaw, 1999). As such, DSPs vary in terms of educational and professional background

(Kasnitz, 2013). In a report published by AHEAD, it is noted that the professional backgrounds of DSP range from working in the medical profession to K–12 education to teaching in higher education (Kasnitz, 2013). Given such varied backgrounds, it is not surprising that researchers have promoted ongoing professional development of DSPs in order to ensure that students with disabilities are appropriately served (Dukes & Shaw, 1999, 2004).

Given the lack of available professional preparation programs for DSPs and the need for knowledge and attitudes necessary for a career in postsecondary disability services, DSPs must seek out opportunities for professional development. Fortunately, a variety of avenues for professional development are available to DSPs, which range from reviewing the primary journal for the field, the *Journal of Postsecondary Education and Disability*, to attending conferences. Through these opportunities, DSPs can develop knowledge and cultivate attitudes expected of professionals working in disability services.

Training Student Affairs Professionals

Opportunities for student affairs professionals to develop disability-related knowledge and skills are less readily accessible than for DSPs. As previously discussed, disability is seldom included in the curricula of student affairs preparation programs (Evans et al., 2009), and articles about disability rarely appear in mainstream higher education journals, much less student affairs journals (Peña, 2014). As such, student affairs professionals must be more intentional about seeking opportunities for additional professional training. For example, due to the limited inclusion of disability-related content, student affairs professionals interested in reading articles about disability-related topics will need to search journals beyond those published by the primary student affairs generalist professional associations (i.e., the American College Personnel Association [ACPA] and the National Association of Student Personnel Administrators [NASPA]).

The ACPA Coalition for (Dis)Ability and the NASPA Disability Knowledge Community have advanced disability as a facet of diversity within their respective associations (ACPA, 2013; NASPA, 2015). Efforts of these committees have focused on increasing knowledge and awareness of individuals with disabilities and disability-related issues among their respective memberships (ACPA, 2013; NASPA, 2015). However, most student affairs professionals continue to show limited knowledge of disability-related topics (Murray, Flannery, & Wren, 2008; Myers, 2008a; Myers & Bastian, 2010). As such, more explicit and focused effort to integrate disability-related content into the ACPA and NASPA organizations is needed. The Coalition for (Dis)Ability and the Disability Knowledge Community must, through advocacy, persuasion, and collaboration, identify ways to encourage their association membership to develop the knowledge and attitudes to support individuals with disabilities.

TABLE 8.1 Disability-Related Practices for Student Affairs Professionals

Practice
Collaborate with disability/accessibility offices to improve your programs/services for students with disabilities.
Evaluate and challenge your own attitudes, comfort, and understanding of disability.
Include disability in your understanding of diversity and actively include it in your discussions, trainings, and marketing of diversity.
Know about campus resources that may benefit students with disabilities (e.g., disability services, academic support centers, counseling center, etc.), and make referrals as needed.
Know and understand disability law and what it requires of you.
Learn the definitions of common types of disabilities.
Learn the principles of Universal Design and apply them to your development of programs, services, instruction, and supervision.
Learn to identify and remove barriers to access.
Look for areas of strength in students prior to looking for areas of deficit.
Promote a campus climate that acknowledges and respects differences in ability.

Source: The National Association of Student Personnel Administrators Region I Annual Conference, Manchester, NH.

There is sparse evidence in the literature on effective and evidence-based practices for working with and supporting college students with disabilities (Faggella-Luby et al., 2014; Shaw & Dukes, 2013). Despite the lack of empirical evidence, some practices for supporting students with disabilities have been suggested in the student affairs and disability literature and are worthy of note. Examples of these disability-related practices are included in Table 8.1. Additionally, guidance on practices specific to the needs of disability services offices and DSPs is available from AHEAD and the Council for the Advancement of Standards in Higher Education.

Decision-Making Tools for Use by Higher Education Faculty, Administrators, and Staff

Assessment and the resulting data use and interpretation play important and varied roles for students with disabilities in higher education, both academically and non-academically. At the program level, data can help to identify the unique needs of subgroups of students (e.g., first generation college students with disabilities) and to develop programs to address such needs. For DSPs or any other relevant institutional personnel, data can be used to make decisions about resource allocation and to prioritize student skill development. However, a necessary initial step is to identify effective and useful instruments. It is often challenging to obtain rigorous instruments; there is no single comprehensive resource that catalogues measured constructs or the psychometric properties of instruments that have been published over time.

Through a systematic review of the research literature, Lombardi and colleagues (in press) identified and analyzed published studies that focused on the development or evaluation of instruments that assess a range of topics concerning higher education and students with disabilities. The goal of this research was to promote use of the instruments by student affairs professionals and, potentially, other relevant higher education personnel, including researchers.

The findings revealed that available instruments are designed for two populations: (1) professionals, or (2) students. "Professionals" includes higher education administrators, staff (including DSPs), or faculty. For administrators and staff, subscales include service quality, infrastructure, responsiveness, professional development, office evaluation, and office policies and procedures. For instruments designed for faculty, subscales include attitudes and perceptions toward accommodations, knowledge of disability and legislation, characteristics, opinions or assumptions about student performance, and professional development (Lombardi et al., in press). Tables 8.2 and 8.3 provide listings of instruments identified in the research literature that are available to higher education professionals and faculty respectively.

TABLE 8.2 Measures Intended for Higher Education Professionals (Non-Faculty)

Measure name	Subscales	Citation
The Accessibility of Campus Computing for Students with Disabilities Scale (ACCSDS)	1. Access to Adaptive Computers 2. Infrastructure and Collaboration 3. Academic Inclusion 4. Adaptive Technology Competence	Fossey et al., 2005
ARCHSECRET	1. Access 2. Responsiveness 3. Communication 4. Humaneness 5. Competence 6. Reliability	Vaughan & Woodruffe-Burton, 2011
iEvaluate	1. Campus and Community Collaboration 2. Information Dissemination 3. Office Administration 4. Office Policies and Procedures 5. Office Evaluation 6. Self Determination 7. Universal Design 8. Educational Access 9. Educational Preparation and Professional Development	Dukes, 2011

(continued)

TABLE 8.2 *(continued)*

Measure name	Subscales	Citation
National Center for the Study of Postsecondary Education Supports (NCSPES) Survey	1. Strategies 2. Assistive Technology 3. Accommodations 4. Vocation/Work Support	Christ & Stodden, 2005
SERVQUAL	Service quality	Vaughan & Woodruffe-Burton, 2011

Importantly, the instruments for faculty tend to focus on measuring attitudes and actions toward inclusive instruction in classroom settings. The instruments intended for administrators and staff focus on the quality of service to students in non-instructional settings. With respect to student characteristics, instruments included academic, nonacademic, and disability-specific traits. By using a combination of instruments to measure attitudes and knowledge of professionals working in instructional and non-instructional settings, as well as student characteristics, assessment of comprehensive campus climate can be evaluated. The work of Lombardi and colleagues (in press) catalogued available instruments for higher education students, faculty, and administrators that could be used to assess campus climate. Data-based decision-making practices that incorporate use of these instruments are encouraged. Partnerships between administrators, student affairs, DSPs, faculty, and researchers is greatly needed to push these efforts forward. In the current landscape, these partnerships remain few and far between.

TABLE 8.3 Measures Intended for Faculty

Measure name	Subscales	Citation
Accommodation of University Students with Disabilities Inventory (AUSDI)	1. Willingness to accommodate students with LD 2. Willingness to accommodate students with deafness or blindness 3. Willingness to accommodate students with emotional problems 4. Willingness to accommodate students with physical disabilities 5. Assumptions about students with disabilities 6. Professional development provided by the college 7. Friendship with persons with disabilities	Wolman, McCrink, Rodriguez, & Harris-Looby, 2004

Measure name	Subscales	Citation
Assessment of Campus Climate to Enhance Student Success (ACCESS): Faculty Questionnaire	1. Faculty Knowledge 2. Fair Accommodations 3. Fair Modifications 4. Faculty Needs and Interests	Vogel, Holt, Sligar, & Leake, 2008
Expanding Cultural Awareness of Exceptional Learners (ExCEL) survey	1. Fairness in Providing Accommodations 2. Knowledge of Disability Law 3. Adjustment of Course Assignments and Requirements 4. Minimizing Barriers 5. Campus Resources 6. Willingness to Invest Time 7. Accessibility of Course Materials 8. Performance Expectations	Lombardi & Murray, 2011
A Campus Survey of Faculty and Student Perceptions of Persons with Disabilities (Faculty version)	1. Overall climate for students with disabilities 2. Beliefs about students with disabilities 3. Inclusion in the classroom 4. Capabilities 5. Reactions 6. Familiarity with Disabled Persons 7. Willingness to Accommodate Students 8. Knowledge about Disabilities 9. Self-identification 10. Disclosure and Treatment 11. Opinion and beliefs of disabled students	Baker, Boland, & Nowik, 2012

Conclusion

In this chapter, we addressed what is known in the literature about faculty and administrators' knowledge and attitudes toward students with disabilities on college campuses. Additionally, we present progress thus far in identifying effective professional development opportunities. Ultimately, we presented promising practices and strategies (shown in Table 8.1) that could be utilized by faculty and administrators to support college students with disabilities. However, more coordinated efforts from higher education professionals—faculty and administrators alike—will be necessary in order to effect change.

Specifically, these coordinated efforts must include training on disability awareness and inclusive instructional practices. Misunderstandings about the various disability types remain prevalent, particularly with regard to invisible disabilities such as learning disabilities, and mental health disorders (Burgstahler & Moore, 2009). Second, training must be effective and useful, and designed to fit the needs of higher educational professionals who are already quite busy. Online, interactive modules are an ideal platform for delivering such trainings, as they allow for flexibility of time and availability of the content anytime, anywhere. Finally, disability-related content must be explicitly integrated into existing professional standards in a broad range of higher education professional organizations, including ACPA and NASPA. Currently, AHEAD offers useful and applicable standards, but these standards are specific to DSPs and must be altered to fit a broader range of higher education professionals. Prioritization of this content across the various professional organizations must occur first.

Importantly, while the number of students with disabilities has continued to grow in more recent years, it is grossly underestimated (Newman & Madaus, 2015). Many students who received special education services in high school do not disclose their disability in college (Newman & Madaus, 2015), and potentially many more students are unaware they qualify as a person with a disability. Thus, these adjustments to the higher education culture are worthwhile and will not necessarily benefit only 11% of the population, but a far larger number. Ultimately, higher education allows for potential upward mobility and long-term improvement of quality of life. By our creating a more accessible and inclusive environment, more people with disabilities will be afforded these same opportunities for a college education and beyond.

References

ACPA (American College Personnel Association) (2006). *Statement of ethical principles and standards.* Retrieved from http://www.myacpa.org/sites/default/files/Ethical_Principles_Standards.pdf.

ACPA (American College Personnel Association) (2013). *History of the ACPA Standing Committee for Disability.* Retrieved from http://www.myacpa.org/sites/default/files/SCD%20History.pdf.

Baker, K. Q., Boland, K., & Nowik, C. M. (2012). A campus survey of faculty and student perceptions of persons with disabilities. *Journal of Postsecondary Education and Disability, 25,* 309–329.

Barnard-Brak, L., Sulak, T., Tate, A., & Lechtenberger, D. (2010). Measuring college students' attitudes toward requesting accommodations: A national multi-institutional study. *Assessment for Effective Intervention, 35,* 141–147.

Bureau of Labor Statistics. (2013). *Persons with a disability: Barriers to employment, types of assistance, and other labor-related issues—May 2012.* (Department of Labor Publication No. 13-0729).

Burgstahler, S., & Moore, E. (2009). Making student services welcoming and accessible through accommodations and Universal Design. *Journal of Postsecondary Education and Disability, 21*(3), 155–174.

Christ, T. W., & Stodden, R. (2005). Advantages of developing survey constructs when comparing educational supports offered to students with disabilities in postsecondary education. *Journal of Vocational Rehabilitation, 22,* 23–31.

Connell, B. R., Jones, M., Mace, R., Mueller, J., Mullick, A., & Ostroff, E. (1997). *The principles of universal design*. Retrieved from http://www.ncsu.edu/www/ncsu/design/sod5/cud/.

Council for the Advancement of Standards in Higher Education (2006). CAS statement of shared ethical principles. In Council for the Advancement of Higher Education (Ed.), *CAS professional standards for higher education* (6th ed.). Washington, DC: Author. Retrieved from http://www.cas.edu/ethics.

Dalton, J. C., & Crosby, P. C. (2012). Reinventing the extracurriculum: The educational and moral purposes of college student activities and experiences. *Journal of College and Character, 13*(3), 1–7.

Dubois, D. D. (1998). *The competency casebook*. Amherst, MA: HRD.

Dukes, L. (2011). The iEvaluate OSD guidelines and exemplars: A disability services evaluation tool. *Journal of Postsecondary Education and Disability, 24*(2), 71–97.

Dukes, L. L., & Shaw, S. F. (1999). Postsecondary disability personnel: Professional standards and staff development. *Journal of Developmental Education, 23*(1), 26–30.

Dukes, L. L., & Shaw, S. F. (2004). Perceived personnel development needs of postsecondary disabilities services professionals. *Teacher Education and Special Education, 27*(2), 134–145.

Edyburn, D. L. (2010). Would you recognize Universal Design for Learning if you saw it? Ten propositions for the second decade of UDL. *Learning Disability Quarterly, 33*, 1–41.

Evans, N. J., Herriott, T. K., & Myers, K. A. (2009). Integrating disability into the diversity framework in the training of student affairs professionals. In J. L. Higbee & A. A. Mitchell (Eds.), *Making good on the promise: Student affairs professionals with disabilities* (pp. 111–128). Lanham, MD: University Press of America.

Faggella-Luby, M., Lombardi, A., Lalor, A., & Dukes III, L. L. (2014). Methodological trends in disability and higher education research: Historical analysis of the *Journal of Postsecondary Education and Disability. Journal of Postsecondary Education and Disability, 27*(4), 357–368.

Fichten, C. S., Nguyen, M. N., Amsel, R., Jorgensen, S., Budd, J., Jorgensen, M., & Barile, M. (2014). How well does the theory of planned behavior predict graduation among college and university students with disabilities? *Social Psychology of Education, 17*, 657–685.

Fossey, M. E., Asuncion, J. V., Fichten, C., Robillard, C., Barile, M., Amsel, R., Prezant, F., & Morabito, S. (2005). Development and validation of the accessibility of campus computing for students with disabilities scale: Service providers' perspective. *Journal of Postsecondary Education and Disability, 18*, 23–33.

Guzman, A., & Balcazar, F. E. (2010). Disability service's standards and the worldviews guiding their implementation. *Journal of Postsecondary Education and Disability, 23*(1), 50–64.

Hall, L. M., & Belch, H. A. (2000). Setting the context: Reconsidering the principles of full participation and meaningful access for students with disabilities. In H. A. Belch (Ed.), *New directions for student services*, No. 91 (pp. 5–17). San Francisco, CA: Jossey-Bass.

Hartman-Hall, H. M., & Haaga, D. A. (2002). College students' willingness to seek help for their learning disabilities. *Learning Disability Quarterly, 25*(4), 263–274.

Kasnitz, D. (2013). *The 2012 Biennial AHEAD survey of disability service and resource professionals in higher education: Employment and compensation*. Huntersville, NC: Association on Higher Education and Disability. Retrieved from http://www.ahead.org/uploads/docs/members/AHEAD_2012_%202013_Biennial_Report_Employment_and_Compensation.pdf.

Lalor, A. R., & Lalor, G. M. (2015, November). *RAs with LDs: Training and supervision using Universal Design for Instruction*. Concurrent session at the National Association of Student Personnel Administrators Region I Annual Conference, Manchester, NH.

Lombardi, A., Gelbar, N., Dukes, L. L., Kowitt, J., Wei, Y., Madaus, J. W., Lalor, A., & Faggella-Luby, M. N. (in press). Higher education and disability: A systematic review of assessment instruments designed for students, faculty, and staff. *Journal of Diversity in Higher Education*. Online first publication, http://dx.doi.org/10.1037/dhe0000027.

Lombardi, A. R., Gerdes, H., & Murray, C. (2011). Validating an assessment of individual actions, postsecondary supports, and social supports of college students with disabilities. *Journal of Student Affairs Research and Practice, 48*(1), 107–126.

Lombardi, A. R., & Murray, C. (2011). Measuring university faculty attitudes toward disability: Willingness to accommodate and adopt Universal Design principles. *Journal of Vocational Rehabilitation, 34*(1), 43–56.

Lombardi, A. R., Murray, C., & Gerdes, H. (2011). College faculty and inclusive instruction: Self-reported attitudes and actions pertaining to Universal Design. *Journal of Diversity in Higher Education, 4*(4), 250–261.

Madaus, J. W. (1997). The process: Development of AHEAD Professional Standards. *Journal of Postsecondary Education and Disability, 12*(3), 8–25.

Madaus, J. W. (2011). The history of disability services in higher education. In W. S. Harbour & J. W. Madaus (Eds.), *Disability services and campus dynamics* (New Directions for Higher Education No. 154, pp. 5–15). San Francisco, CA: Jossey-Bass.

Madaus, J. W., Scott, S., & McGuire, J. (2003). *Barriers and bridges to learning as perceived by postsecondary students with learning disabilities* (Technical Report No. 01). Retrieved from: http://www.facultyware.uconn.edu/TechnicalReports.cfm.

McCabe, K. A. (2014). Create awareness of how disability laws apply to sports, extracurricular activities. *Disability Compliance for Higher Education, 20*(5), 1–4.

McGuire, J. M. (2014). Universally accessible instruction: Oxymoron or opportunity? *Journal of Postsecondary Education and Disability, 27*(4), 387–398.

Murray, C., Flannery, B. K., & Wren, C. (2008). University staff members' attitudes and knowledge about learning disabilities and disability support services. *Journal of Postsecondary Education and Disability, 21*(2), 73–90.

Murray, C., Lombardi, A., Seeley, J., & Gerdes, H. (2014). Effects of an intensive disability-focused training experience on university faculty self-efficacy. *Journal of Postsecondary Education and Disability, 27*(2), 179–193.

Murray, C., Lombardi, A., & Wren, C. T. (2011). The effects of disability-focused training on the attitudes and perceptions of university staff. *Remedial and Special Education, 32*, 290–300.

Murray, C., Wren, C. T., & Keys, C. (2008). University faculty perceptions of students with learning disabilities: Correlates and group differences. *Learning Disability Quarterly, 31*, 95–113.

Murray, C., Wren, C. T., Stevens, E. B., & Keys, C. (2009). Promoting university faculty and staff awareness of students with learning disabilities: An overview of the Productive Learning u Strategies (PLuS) Project. *Journal of Postsecondary Education and Disability, 22*, 117–129.

Myers, K. A. (2008a). Infusing Universal Instructional Design into student personnel graduate programs. In J. L. Higbee & E. Goff (Eds.), *Pedagogy and student services for institutional transformation: Implementing Universal Design in higher education* (pp. 291–304). Minneapolis, MN: College of Education and Human Development, University of Minneapolis. Retrieved from http://cehd.umn.edu/passit/docs/PASS-IT-BOOK.pdf.

Myers, K. A. (2008b). Using learning reconsidered to reinvent disability education. *About Campus, 13*, 2–9.

Myers, K. A., & Bastian, J. J. (2010). Understanding communication preferences of college students with visual disabilities. *Journal of College Student Development, 51*, 265–278.

NASPA (National Association of Student Personnel Administrators) (2015). *Disability Knowledge Community: About.* Retrieved from https://www.naspa.org/constituent-groups/kcs/disability.

Newman, L. A., & Madaus, J. W. (2015). Reported accommodations and supports provided to secondary and postsecondary students with disabilities: National perspective. *Career Development and Transition for Exceptional Individuals, 38*, 173–181.

Newman, L., Wagner, M., Knokey, A., Marder, C., Nagle, K., Shaver, D., & Wei, X. (2011). *The post–high school outcomes of young adults with disabilities up to 8 years after high school: A report from the National Longitudinal Transition Study-2.* (NCSER 2011-3005). Menlo Park, CA: SRI International.

Peña, E. V. (2014). Marginalization of published scholarship on students with disabilities. *Journal of College Student Development, 55*, 30–40.

Raue, K., & Lewis, L. (2011). *Students with Disabilities at Degree-Granting Postsecondary Institutions* (NCES 2011–018). U.S. Department of Education, National Center for Education Statistics. Washington, DC: U.S. Government Printing Office.

Roberts, K. D., Pak, H. J., Brown, S., & Cook, B. (2011). Universal design for instruction in postsecondary education: A systematic review of empirically based articles. *Journal of Postsecondary Education and Disability, 24*(1), 5–15.

Rose, D., Harbour, W., Johnston, S., Daley, S., & Abarbanell, L. (2006). Universal Design for Learning in postsecondary education: Reflections on principles and their application. *Journal of Postsecondary Education and Disability, 19* (2), 135–151.

Salzer, M. S. (2012). A comparative study of campus experiences of college students with mental illnesses versus a general college sample. *Journal of American College Health, 60*, 1–7.

Scott, S. T., McGuire, J. M., & Shaw, S. F. (2003). Universal design of instruction: A new paradigm for adult instruction in postsecondary education. *Remedial and Special Education, 24*, 369–379.

Shaw, S. F., & Dukes, L. L. (2001). Program standards for disability services in higher education. *Journal of Postsecondary Education and Disability, 14*, 81–90.

Shaw, S. F., & Dukes, L. L. (2013). Transition to postsecondary education: A call for evidence-based practice. *Career Development and Transition for Exceptional Individuals, 36*, 51–57.

Stumbo, N. J., Hedrick, B. N., Weisman, C., & Martin, J. K. (2010). An exploration into the barriers and facilitators experienced by university graduates with disabilities requiring personal assistance services. *Journal of Science Education for Students with Disabilities, 14*, 1–24.

Vaughan, E., & Woodruffe-Burton, H. (2011). The disabled student experience: Does the SERVQUAL Scale measure up? *Quality Assurance in Education: An International Perspective, 19*, 28–49.

Vogel, S. A., Holt, J. K., Sligar, S., & Leake, E. (2008). Assessment of campus climate to enhance student success. *Journal of Postsecondary Education and Disability, 21*, 15–31.

Wilson, K., Getzel, E., & Brown, T. (2000). Enhancing the post-secondary campus climate for students with disabilities. *Journal of Vocational Rehabilitation, 14*(1), 37–50.

Wolman, C., McCrink, C. S., Rodriquez, S. F., & Harris-Looby, J. (2004). The Accommodation of University Students with Disabilities Inventory (AUSDI): Assessing American and Mexican faculty attitudes towards students with disabilities. *Journal of Hispanic Higher Education, 3*, 284–295.

9

WORKING IT BACKWARD

Student Success through Faculty Professional Development

Cali Anicha, Chris M. Ray, and Canan Bilen-Green

Introduction

In this chapter we take a series of steps backward to explore key influences on our outcome of interest—student success. Student success is linked to faculty professional development (PD) via a somewhat circuitous route: because faculty are pivotal in the production and performance of education programs, and because their responsibilities extend beyond teaching to include research, service, and participation in university governance, faculty play central roles in the (re)production of campus culture and are uniquely positioned to influence student success from multiple directions. We trace a path on which student classroom experiences, faculty workplace experiences, and campus climate intersect and overlap. These way stations are then connected with a broadly conceptualized approach to PD designed to leverage faculty roles and responsibilities in service to institutional transformation.

After reviewing demographic disparities in education access and attainment we highlight the growing recognition of disability as an important though underattended facet of diversity. We explore the claim that assumptions about disability are foundational to discriminatory beliefs and behaviors in general and consider a number of critical emancipatory narratives of disability that invoke more fully inclusive concepts of diversity. With this understanding of diversity as inclusive of disability, we review evidence that a diverse student body brings substantive benefits for all students. Next, we link the presence of a diverse faculty with academic success for all students and make the case for a welcoming workplace as a prerequisite for recruiting and retaining a diverse professorate. Coming full circle, we find that student success is enhanced when a welcoming campus climate is generated through inclusive classroom and academic workplace practices that explicitly value social equity. Finally, we link a welcoming campus climate with a critical and intersectional faculty PD approach designed to advance institutional transformation for social justice from a disability studies vantage point.

In brief, the three components of this PD approach, the ACT (Accessibility, Climate, Tenure) Framework, focus on classroom and workplace practices that (1) promote a broadly conceptualized view of *accessibility*, (2) establish a welcoming and inclusive campus *climate*, and (3) leverage faculty roles in university governance to alter *tenure* policies. This model is fashioned after the faculty gender parity work of National Science Foundation ADVANCE initiatives and primarily addresses tenure; however, other tactical policy adjustments are relevant for all campus organizational change efforts.

Descriptions of Student Success

Acquisition of skills and degree completion are two self-evident aspects of student success. A third aspect comes into view when degree attainment is disaggregated by demographics such as race, gender, disability. From here we immediately see what Nieto (2010) has identified as an advantage gap: students from dominant/majority sociocultural backgrounds continue to be overrepresented while students from marginalized sociocultural backgrounds continue to be underrepresented in recruitment and retention figures in undergraduate as well as graduate programs (Baldwin, 2010; Fleming & Fairweather, 2012; Kena et al., 2015). Such advantage gaps have profound and long-term consequences because considerable benefits in socioeconomic opportunities arise from increased educational attainment, and this is especially so for those who may not have otherwise attended college (Erisman & Looney, 2007). One clear benefit concerns lifetime earning potential. Bachelor's degree recipients may earn up to 75% more than the income of persons with a high school diploma (Day & Newburger, 2002), translating to approximately $1000/week in 2014 dollars (BLS, 2014). College graduates report increased financial savings, greater personal and professional mobility, expanded leisure activities, better overall health, and improved quality of life for themselves and their families (IHEP, 1998).

Chronic educational disparities are clearly at odds with the mission of higher education (APLU, 2012). How do we understand this state of affairs when postsecondary education promotes socioeconomic successes for individuals and communities (Baum, Ma, & Payea, 2013) and benefits our economic standing in the world (Eberly & Martin, 2012)? Data regarding education disparities offer compelling evidence to suggest that conventional college practices may thwart efforts to recruit and retain a diverse student body. To increase the rates of matriculation and degree completion for all learners we need to look at student experiences within programs.

Employers increasingly plead for workers with proficiency in communication, collaboration, complex problem-solving, and critical thinking. When student success is gauged through performance in the workforce, programs that garner reputations for academic excellence are those with graduates who apply a strong fund of knowledge while working collaboratively in diverse team settings (AAC&U, 2013). Developing those skills requires practice through active learning opportunities (Bellanca & Brandt, 2010). Popularized as 21st century skills, these proficiencies are also associated with education experienced in the context of a diverse student body, a finding we will explore later in this chapter.

For now, our definition of student success compels the question: How can academic institutions cultivate a welcoming climate that permeates classroom and campus spaces and encourages *all* students to persist to degree completion? Before moving further in this inquiry, we briefly review the evolution of disability as a protected demographic and take note of its growing recognition as an important facet of diversity.

Brief Contemporary History of Disability

Individual differences that are currently perceived as disabilities have always been present. In large measures, the idea of disability as understood today in the United States has roots in the Industrial Revolution and the concomitant standardization of labor/laborers, as well as unsafe factory conditions that produced impairments and then disbarred impaired workers (Nielsen, 2012). Industrialization also spawned urbanization with dense neighborhoods of immigrants often unknown to one another. During this period the infamous "ugly laws" were enacted, criminalizing the public appearance of persons with physical, health, or cognitive atypicalities (Schweik, 2009). Notably, discriminatory beliefs about race and gender have applied the same standards of normativity that characterize notions of disability. For example, sexist and racist ideologies have asserted that the bodies and minds of women and men of color and of white women were deficient relative to white men (Baynton, 2008).

Persistent creative campaigns by disability activists have established disability as a minority demographic warranting broadened legal protections with the passage of the Americans with Disabilities Act of 1990 (Davis, 2015). Disability as a positive dimension of diversity continues to evolve; disability as civil and human rights concerns are gaining international recognition as well. The United Nations Convention on the Rights of Persons with Disabilities was adopted in 2006 and a recent report on the global status of disability included recommendations for community-wide actions to create "enabling environments" (Officer & Posarac, 2011, p. xi). Bickenbach (2011) asserted that the report represented disability as simultaneously a social construction and individually embodied, resulting in a portrayal of disability as "a complex, dynamic, multidimensional concept [including] features of the physical, human-built, social, and attitudinal environments" (p. 656).

These developments reflect a consequential shift in the focus of accountability, from individuals perceived as disabled to the beliefs, policies, and practices that create and maintain social and physical barriers to access and participation. Many scholars contend that such analyses do not go far enough to interrupt notions of disability as always negative (Price, 2011). Nonetheless, views of disability as simultaneously a function of a disabling society and as a positive aspect of human diversity are increasingly common. In the following section we explore disability from a spectrum of perspectives in order to develop a foundation for our PD framework.

Contours of Disability: Ground of Discrimination and Foundation for Social Justice

As discussed later in this chapter, it is well established that myriad benefits are associated with diversity, and that these benefits are a function of the multiple perspectives brought by individuals with varying beliefs, experiences, and sociocultural identities (Page, 2007). Even so, disability is frequently missing from diversity discourses (Davis, 2011). The burgeoning transdisciplinary field of disability studies (DS) seeks to resolve this absence through explorations of "social, political, cultural, and economic" facets of disability (SDS, n.d., p. para. 2). Grounded in critical theory (Burghardt, 2011; Guess, 1981), DS calls us to question dominant cultural narratives for the purpose of guiding actions toward emancipatory democratic ends. Next we consider the paradox of disability as a belief central to all systemic discrimination and as a positive identity-marker with profound implications for social justice.

Similar to critical theorizing in race and gender discourses, critical disability theory has given rise to myriad models that reveal, and thereby resist, inherently discriminatory paradigms. The social model birthed in the United Kingdom characterizes disability as that which is superimposed upon impairments, disabling individuals via social structures (Finkelstein, 2007). Disability activism in the United States has centered on the civil rights of individuals perceived as having a disability (Davis, 2015). Intersectional investigations explore disability through the lenses of racialized (Ferri & Connor, 2005), classed (Barnes & Sheldon, 2010), and gendered identities (Arenas Conejo, 2011; McRuer, 2006). Scholars are increasingly exploring experiences of disability in local through global contexts (Campbell, 2009; Erevelles, 2011). Contemporary scholars and activists offer nuanced analyses of overlapping personal and political implications of disability from spatial (Kitchin, 1998), identity (Putnam, 2005), social-relational (Thomas, 2004), linguistic (Harpur, 2012), psychological (Watermeyer, 2012), and academic perspectives (Price, 2011). Each of these approaches provides meaningful illumination of the multifaceted networks of beliefs, experiences, and social behaviors that co-create notions of disability.

Yee (2007) identifies crucial conceptual shifts reflected in these critical investigations—a move from social or civil rights toward human rights and a step beyond mere "normalizing" of disability to a more radical recognition that normality itself is a pivotal myth. The premise that disability discrimination is foundational to the construction of difference-as-deviance is found in a number of scholarly analyses (among many others see Dudley-Marling & Gurn, 2010), which brings us to the next theoretical bend in our inquiry. Rather than diminishing Lorde's (2009) assertion that there is no hierarchy of oppression, this framing suggests that there is much to be gained in diversity and justice work by beginning with a critical intersectional analysis of perceptions of disability and disability discrimination. Burch (2003) captures this insight in her review of Davis (2002) when she notes that because cultural notions of normalcy are built on mutable assumptions of non-normalcy, it is "paradoxically the most marginalized group—people with disabilities—who can provide the broadest way of understanding contemporary systems of oppression" (Burch, 2003, pp. 1, quoting Davis, 2002). Mingus (2011) similarly dares us to move toward an "understanding of disability justice . . . that embraces difference, confronts privilege and challenges what is considered 'normal' on every front" (para. 5). These critical and intersectional models of disability offer vantage points from which we can build more broadly inclusive approaches for transforming our classrooms, workplaces, campuses, and communities. With this inclusive framing of diversity we turn next to an exploration of benefits for all students.

Academic Benefits of a Diverse Student Body

Relatively few studies documenting the benefits associated with diversity (e.g., innovative performance, constructive problem-solving, effective collaborations) examine disability directly. Nonetheless it is well established that the gains associated with diverse groups arise from variations in perspectives brought by individuals with a range of experiences and beliefs rather than by demographics per se (Page, 2012). A robust body of research has established that a diverse student body is associated with educational, psychological, and financial benefits (Milem, 2003). These benefits accrue to all students, whether they hail from dominant/majority or underrepresented groups (Zirkel, 2008).

Theories and empirical work concerning the development and socialization of college students indicate that interaction with diverse peers results in numerous positive inter- and intra-personal outcomes such as self-confidence, empathy, and even enhanced cognitive development (Antonio et al., 2004; Williams, Berger, & McClendon, 2005). In a study exploring peer interaction during college, Astin (1993) found that frequent interaction with peers diverse from oneself was connected to increased cultural awareness and commitment to understanding others' perspectives. These peer interactions were also related to increased knowledge, analytical and writing skills, and satisfaction with the college experience. When exploring the impact of a diverse campus environment, Chang (1996) found that increased racial diversity on college campuses resulted in greater socialization across race, which ultimately led to increased discussions of racial issues and enhanced racial understanding. In the same year, Pascarella and colleagues reported that interactions with diverse others promoted critical thinking skills (Pascarella, Edison, Nora, Hagedorn, & Terenzini, 1996). A 2005 study of college students revealed that those who reported more diversity experiences also showed higher scores on measures of academic self-confidence, social agency, and dispositional critical thinking (Nelson Laird).

More recently, in a series of six studies undertaken in four countries (Israel, Singapore, China, and the United States), repeated diversity experiences were shown to reduce discrimination and to lead to enduring attitude and behavior change *when existing preconceptions were simultaneously recognized and questioned* [emphasis added], a process identified as "epistemic unfreezing" (Tadmor, Hong, Chao, Wiruchnipawan, & Wang, 2012). Moreover, anti-discriminatory influences were observed to apply to "cultural groups not involved in the initial exposure" (Tadmor et al., 2012, p. 753). In the following section we link success for all students with faculty diversity, then identify a welcoming workplace as a prerequisite for recruiting and retaining a diverse professorate.

Campus-Wide Benefits of a Diverse Faculty

A commitment to equity and diversity has been identified as "critical to the health and functioning of colleges and universities" (Worthington, Stanley, & Lewis, 2014, p. 227). Whereas student diversity is increasing on many campuses, university faculty remain remarkably demographically homogeneous (Moody, 2012). Given the above-detailed beneficial influences of a diverse student body on learning as well as on the development of workplace and interpersonal skills, it is reasonable to expect that a diverse faculty, inclusive of faculty with disabilities, may also support student successes. Indeed, an abundance of research shows that a diverse faculty promotes academic excellence (Xu, 2012). As Smith (2004) notes, faculty diversity is valuable for its "contributions to the diversity of the scholarship and curriculum available" (p. 8) and a diverse faculty may reach a broadened range of learners. Additionally, substantial scholarship indicates that the presence of role models with similar identities (in-group members) offers positive support for non-majority individuals (Knapp, 2008).

Student success does not, of course, rest on the presence of in-group faculty role models for every form of diversity—nor is that even possible when intersectional and intra-group diversity are taken into account. Indeed, simply adding token faculty who appear diverse from dominant norms may do little to benefit students. Taylor and colleagues (2011) found that when individuals felt at risk for confirming negative stereotypes about their own demographic group, known as stereotype threat, in-group members who were believed to have gained success by luck rather than by skill did not elicit positive influences. However, when in-group role models were perceived as deserving of their successes, their presence reduced stereotype threat and was associated with improved academic performance (Taylor, et al., 2011). Taken together, these findings affirm that a diverse faculty promotes student success in a number of ways and indicate the need to prioritize the recruitment and retention of a diverse faculty.

Not only do benefits accrue for students—a diverse faculty engenders significant beneficial influences on overall workplace satisfaction, research productivity, and teaching quality (Major, Fletcher, Streets, & Sanchez-Hucles, 2014). The recruitment and retention of a diverse faculty depends on a host of factors. Influences include cumulative advantaging or disadvantaging resulting from subtle biases in selection for training or promotion opportunities, availability of effective mentorship, and a welcoming or chilly climate for diversity (Weinberg, 2008).

Certainly a diverse faculty does not guarantee that any given faculty member will be prepared to meet the needs of all learners. Although faculty are expected to provide accessible, relevant, and cutting-edge educations for all learners, their own education regarding systemic inequities, culturally responsive pedagogies, and/or instructional design may be quite limited (Edyburn, 2010; Tierney & Sallee, 2008). Thus, there is a clear need for ongoing PD that supports educators in broadening their repertoire of instructional strategies and skills regarding bias-based discrimination (McIntosh, 2012). Moreover, those PD opportunities will be most productive when approached within a comprehensive strategic *culture plan* that includes campus-wide engagement in the co-creation of, and thus co-accountability for, institutional transformation (Leigh, 2013).

Given the above findings, we posit that student success can fruitfully be addressed by first attending to workplace climate and equity concerns related to a diverse faculty. We acknowledge the crucial roles of Student Affairs and anticipate that professional development opportunities that include all campus staff will be most productive. Though our PD framework focuses on faculty roles, the approach is flexibly designed to support the institutional transformations necessary for postsecondary education to fulfill its mission for the public good.

Professional Development in Service to Institutional Transformation

Most US postsecondary faculty continue to be overrepresented relative to the general population by white cisgender heterosexual men who are not perceived to be disabled (Bilimoria & Stewart, 2009; NCES, 2013). Although dominant/majority members may adopt ally identities and intervene to promote equity (Stoudt, Fox, & Fine, 2012), many are unaware of systemic over-advantaging that accrues for them (Pratto & Stewart, 2012). Given that faculty are pivotal in the production and performance of education programs, and consequently in the (re)production of campus culture, an unwelcoming campus climate is a frequent result (Acker, 2012). Dominant/majority individuals may resist diversity trainings, perhaps especially so when trainings do not adequately address the painful emotional aspects of long-standing privileging and oppressing (Bishop, 2005).

Postsecondary faculty have numerous responsibilities beyond the traditional role of teaching, such as research and service, including participation in university governance. The ACT Framework focuses on PD that leverages those aspects of faculty positions. Applying a critical DS lens, we adopt the perspective that dominant cultural norms around disability may be foundational to multiple systems of privileging and oppressing (Campbell, 2009). Discrimination manifests similarly yet uniquely across academic workplaces and addressing disability discrimination through an intersectional approach simultaneously tackles multiple forms of over-privileging and/or discrimination.

Disability discrimination occurs when there are structural or functional *accessibility* problems such as inaccessible classrooms or technologies, or when a chilly *climate* is reflected in unabashed use of pejorative terms such as lame or idiot, or when *tenure* policies and practices (including promotion, annual evaluation, and post-tenure review) ignore or perpetuate systemic advantaging and disadvantaging based on perceived disability status. Notably, these three interdependent elements are relevant for all faculty: the ability to meaningfully access workplace resources contributes to a sense of belonging and a welcoming climate, experiences which are profoundly influenced by tenure policies and practices that promote equity. Thus addressing accessibility, climate, and tenure from the perspective of disability can aid in the successful recruitment and retention of underrepresented faculty in general, thereby contributing to a productive and welcoming workplace for all faculty and simultaneously providing a stronger foundation for student success.

Figure 9.1 depicts the ACT Framework as operating within day-to-day micro level environments via PD focused on Accessibility, Climate, and Tenure, components which simultaneously arise from and influence campus climate at the

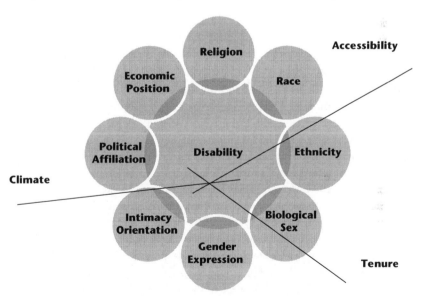

FIGURE 9.1 Toward a Norm of Difference-as-Normative. The ACT Framework: Faculty Professional Development focused on Accessibility, Climate, and Tenure in service to institutional transformation for social justice via a critical and intersectional disability studies approach.

macro level with an ultimate goal of fostering a norm through which differences are expected and embraced. In the following section, we describe an anticipatory social imaginary in which each element is effectively manifested.

Accessibility, Climate, and Tenure: A Framework for ACTion

The ACT Frameworks identifies Accessibility, Climate, and Tenure as essential components of a successful program serving the retention and recruitment of underrepresented faculty through the establishment of a welcoming workplace for diversity, inclusive of disability. Taken together the three elements provide faculty-relevant avenues for positively addressing equity from multiple vantage points across the university and sustaining those efforts over the long haul. Each element overlaps with the others representing unique aspects of a comprehensive strategic culture plan, one that intentionally builds a unified organizational culture through explicitly valuing diverse perspectives. Inspiration for this approach comes in large measure from the gender parity work developed through a recent ADVANCE initiative (NSF_HRD_0811239, 2008). An intersectional critical DS perspective ensures that multiple aspects of diversity are also addressed within each element with the intention of exposing and amending beliefs and practices that perpetuate biases. In the following section, we describe an anticipatory social imaginary in which each element is effectively manifested.

Accessibility

The first element, accessibility, includes architectural spaces, materials such as curricula, the digital commons of the Internet and wi-fi technologies, as well as social spaces in classrooms and campus gathering spaces. Meaningful and functional accessibility is considered across all contexts and is grounded in the tenets of Universal Design (UD) and Universal Design for Learning (UD/L). That is, products, environments, learning materials, and instructional approaches are usable by all people to the greatest extent possible, without the need for modifications or adaptation (Salmen, 2011).

On campuses where accessibility is actively valued, offices, classrooms, and student unions are physically as well as technologically available. Event planners recognize that gatherings are constituted by physical, cyber/online, and social spaces and each of these aspects are addressed in manners that promote accessibility. During professional workshops or conferences adequate transition time is scheduled for persons with mobility concerns and quiet spaces are identified for attendees who need reprieve from the conference pace or the social demands of day (Price, 2009).

Discourses that unfold in classrooms, administrative meetings, lounges, or the faculty senate are critiqued to reveal potential avenues for dismantling access barriers across communities of difference. In accessible and inclusive environments where UD/L considerations have been centralized, the vast majority of workplace and academic adjustments (accommodations) are simply available as needed. In such genuinely accessible contexts procedural requirements emblematic of the inherently discriminatory medical model of disability, such as documentation of impairment provided by a licensed practitioner (Huger, 2011), will eventually fade from institutional practice and cultural memory.

Climate

The second element of the ACT Framework concerns workplace and campus climate. Campus climate arises from a complex social web of relationships within and outside academic institutions (Rankin & Reason, 2008). This concise definition of campus climate was offered by a University of California diversity study group: "a measure—real or perceived—of the campus environment as it relates to interpersonal, academic, and professional interactions. In a healthy climate, individuals and groups generally feel welcomed, respected, and valued" (SGUD, 2007, p. 1). Climate has been identified as central to the recruitment and retention of a diverse faculty (Moreno et al., 2006).

When educational institutions actively value a welcoming climate, common practices include the intentional and ongoing promotion of awareness regarding what constitutes discrimination while simultaneously cultivating a generalized attitude of cultural humility (Duntley-Matos, 2014). PD opportunities impart culture-general interpersonal skill building and culture-specific information (Roybal Rose, 1996). Campus-community alliances are fostered in order to develop increasingly successful solutions (Warren & Mapp, 2011); for example, formal ties to Centers for Independent Living support the recruitment of faculty and students with disabilities and offer avenues for timely information exchange. Ally relationships create multi-directional pathways for access to resources, mentoring, and other forms of support (Tierney, 1993; Wilcox, 2009) and establish networks of professional and personal relationships that facilitate the ongoing (re)education needs of us all.

Tenure

The third element concerns institutional practices related to tenure and promotion policies that perpetuate unearned advantaging and disadvantaging (Moody, 2012). Policies originally developed with women faculty in mind—such as longer probationary periods, tenure-clock-stopping options, working less than full-time while remaining in tenure-track positions, and modifications of duties—also provide flexible benefits for all faculty, inclusive of faculty with disabilities (Fox, Schwartz, & Hart, 2006; Thornton, 2005). Implementing these policies without additional institutional changes potentially allows for an accumulation of disadvantage such as a career-long deflated salary due to delayed time to tenure (Valian, 2000), thus additional tenure policy changes are enacted to address those issues.

University tenure policies designed to recruit and retain a diverse faculty begin with the recognition that outstanding faculty members with disability are already present in the institution. Policies that support faculty in accessing needed resources and accommodations are clearly stated and well known to faculty and administrators. Social stigma associated with disability (Knapp, 2008) is more and more rare since avenues for advocacy and collective voice have been established for faculty experiencing disability, including faculty in contingent and non-tenured positions such as clinical faculty, full and part-time instructors, and adjuncts (Beretz, 2003).

Conclusion

Diverse learning environments are well established as effective means to enhance educational and lifetime outcomes of all students. Meaningful access for a wide diversity of students to a high quality postsecondary education is a democratic ideal that continues to be greatly valued for its individual as well as collective benefits. Although diversity discourses have emphasized categories of race, gender, or socioeconomic status, disability is increasingly included as one among many diverse attributes. Just as it is important to diversify the student body according to other areas of individual difference, including diverse perspectives associated with experience of what we have come to call disability will enhance the capacity of all students to participate in workplace and social spheres through meaningful interactions with others.

An important route to diversifying the student body inclusive of students with disabilities is through supporting not only students with disabilities, but also faculty and staff with disabilities. A critical focus on disability may not directly address the unique needs of every underrepresented group; however, the cross-cutting nature of disability provides fertile ground from which to cultivate critical examinations of our social responses to a broad range of diversity. Situated within a strategic culture plan, the ACT Framework provides a comprehensive scheme for student success by addressing the multilayered and multi-faceted forms of discrimination and injustice present today on college campuses.

References

Association of American Colleges and Universities (AAC&U). (2013). It takes more than a major: Employer priorities for college learning and student success. In H. R. Associates (Ed.), *Online Survey among Employers*. Washington, D.C.: Association of American Colleges and Universities.http://www.aacu.org/leap/presidentstrust/compact/2013SurveySummary.

Acker, J. (2012). Gendered organizations and intersectionality: Problems and possibilities. *Equality, Diversity and Inclusion: An International Journal, 31*(3), 214–224. doi: 10.1108/02610151211209072.

Antonio, A. L., Chang, M. J., Hakuta, K., Kenny, D., Levin, S., & Milem, J. F. (2004). Effects of racial diversity on complex thinking in college students. *Psychological Science, 15*(8), 507–510. doi: 10.1111/j.0956-7976.2004.00710.x

Association of Public and Land-Grant Universities (APLU). (2012). *The land-grant tradition.* Washington, D.C.: Association of Public and Land-Grant Universities.

Arenas Conejo, M. (2011). Disabled women and transnational feminisms: Shifting boundaries and frontiers. *Disability & Society*, *26*(5), 597–609. doi: 10.1080/09687599.2011.589193.

Astin, A. W. (1993). How are students affected? *Change, 25*(2), 44–50.

Baldwin, C. P. (2010). *Situatedness: The interrelation of factors impacting the educational pathway to degree attainment among Black and White doctoral students*. PhD Dissertation, College of William and Mary, Williamsburg, VA.

Barnes, C., & Sheldon, A. (2010). Disability, politics and poverty in a majority world context. *Disability & Society, 25*(7), 771–782. doi: 10.1080/09687599.2010.520889.

Baum, S., Ma, J., & Payea, K. (2013). *Education pays 2013: The benefits of higher education for individuals and society*. New York, NY: College Board.

Baynton, D. C. (2008). Disability in history. *Disability Studies Quarterly, 28*(3). Retrieved from http://dsq-sds.org/article/view/108/108.

Bellanca, J. A., & Brandt, R. S. (Eds.). (2010). *21st century skills: Rethinking how students learn*. Bloomington, IN: Solution Tree Press.

Beretz, E. M. (2003). Hidden disability and an academic career. *Academe, July-August*. Retrieved from http://www.aaup.org.

Bickenbach, J. (2011). The World Report on Disability. *Disability & Society, 26*(5), 655–658. doi: 10.1080/09687599.2011.589198.

Bilimoria, D., & Stewart, A. J. (2009). "Don't ask, don't tell": The academic climate for lesbian, gay, bisexual, and transgender faculty in science and engineering. *National Women's Studies Association Journal, 21*(2), 85–103.

Bishop, A. (2005). *Beyond token change: Breaking the cycle of oppression in institutions*. Halifax, NS: Fernwood.

BLS. (2014). Earnings and unemployment rate by educational attainment. *Employment Projections*. Retrieved from http://www.bls.gov/emp/ep_chart_001.htm.

Burch, S. (2003). Review article: Bending over backwards: Disability, dismodernism, and other difficult positions. *H-Net Reviews in the Humanities and Social Sciences*. Retrieved from http://www.h-net.org/reviews/home.php.

Burghardt, M. (2011). The human bottom of non-human things: On critical theory and its contributions to critical disability studies. *Critical Disability Discourse, 3*, 1–16. Retrieved from https://pi.library.yorku.ca/ojs/index.php/cdd/article/view/31560.

Campbell, F. K. (2009). *Contours of ableism: The production of disability and abledness*. New York, NY: Palgrave Macmillan.

Chang, M. J. (1996) Racial diversity in higher education: Does a racially mixed student population affect educational outcomes?, Unpublished Doctoral Dissertation. University of California.

Davis, L. J. (2002). *Bending over backwards: Disability, dismodernism, and other difficult positions*. New York, NY: New York University Press.

Davis, L. J. (2011). Why is disability missing rrom the discourse on diversity? *Chronicle of Higher Education, 58*(6), B38–B40. Retrieved from http://proxy.library.ndsu.edu/login?url=http://search.ebscohost.com/login.aspx?direct=true&db=aph&AN=66540041&site=ehost-live&scope=site.

Davis, L. J. (2015). *Enabling acts: The hidden story of how the Americans with Disabilities Act gave the largest US minority its rights*. Boston, MA: Beacon Press.

Day, J. C., & Newburger, E. C. (2002). The big payoff: Educational attainment and synthetic estimates of work-life earnings. *Current Population Reports, Special Studies, P23–210*. Washington, D.C.: Commerce Dept., Economics and Statistics Administration, Census Bureau.

Dudley-Marling, C., & Gurn, A. (Eds.). (2010). *The myth of the normal curve* (Vol. 11). New York, NY: Peter Lang Publishing.

Duntley-Matos, R. (2014). Transformative complicity and cultural humility: De- and re-constructing higher education mentorship for under-represented groups. *Qualitative Sociology*, *37*(4), 443–466. doi: 10.1007/s11133-014-9289-5.

Eberly, J., & Martin, C. (2012). *The economic case for higher education*. Washington, D.C.: U.S. Treasury Department.

Edyburn, D. L. (2010). Would you recognize Universal Design if you saw it? Ten propositions for new directions for the second decade of UDL. *Learning Disability Quarterly*, *33*(1), 33–41. doi: 10.1177/073194871003300103.

Erevelles, N. (2011). *Disability and difference in global contexts: Enabling a transformative body politic*. New York, NY: Palgrave Macmillan.

Erisman, W., & Looney, S. (2007). *Opening the door to the American dream: Increasing higher education access and success for immigrants*. Retrieved from http://www.ihep.org/assets/files/publications/m-r/OpeningTheDoor.pdf.

Ferri, B. A., & Connor, D. J. (2005). Tools of exclusion: Race, disability, and (re)segregated education. *Teachers College Record*, *107*(3), 453–474. doi: 0161-4681

Finkelstein, V. (2007). The "social model of disability" and the disability movement. *The Disability Studies Archive UK*, 1-15. Retrieved from http://disability-studies.leeds.ac.uk/files/library/finkelstein-The-Social-Model-of-Disability-and-the-Disability-Movement.pdf.

Fleming, A. R., & Fairweather, J. S. (2012). The role of postsecondary education in the path from high school to work for youth with disabilities. *Rehabilitation Counseling Bulletin*, *55*(2), 71–81. doi: 10.1177/0034355211423303.

Fox, G., Schwartz, A., & Hart, K. M. (2006). Work-family balance and academic advancement in medical schools. *Academic Psychiatry*, *30*(3), 227–234. doi: 10.1176/appi.ap.30.3.227.

Guess, R. (1981). *The idea of a critical theory: Habermas and the Frankfurt school*. New York, NY: Press Syndicate of the Cambridge University Press.

Harpur, P. (2012). From disability to ability: Changing the phrasing of the debate. *Disability & Society*, *27*(3), 325–337. doi: 10.1080/09687599.2012.654985.

Huger, M. S. (2011). Fostering a disability-friendly institutional climate. *New Directions for Student Services* (134), 3–11. doi: 10.1002/ss.390.

Institute for Higher Education Policy (IHEP). (1998). Reaping the benefits: Defining the public and private value of going to college. *The new millennium project on higher education costs, pricing, and productivity*. Washington, D.C.: Institute for Higher Education Policy.

Kena, G., Musu-Gillette, L., Robinson, J., Wang, X., Rathbun, A., Zhang, J., et al. (2015). *The condition of education*. Washington, D.C.: National Center for Education Statistics.

Kitchin, R. O. B. (1998). "Out of Place," "Knowing One's Place": Space, power and the exclusion of disabled people. *Disability & Society*, *13*(3), 343–356. doi: 10.1080/09687599826678.

Knapp, S. D. (2008). Why "diversity" should include "disability" with practical suggestions for academic unions. *American Academic*, *4*, 105–130.

Leigh, A. (2013). *Ethical leadership: Creating and sustaining an ethical business culture*. Retrieved from http://common.books24x7.com/toc.aspx?bookid=57777.

Lorde, A. (2009). *I am your sister: Collected and unpublished writings of Audre Lorde*. New York, NY: Oxford University Press.

Major, D. A., Fletcher, T. D., Streets, V., & Sanchez-Hucles, J. (2014). One is the loneliest number: Comparing ethnic minority solos and non-solos. *Journal of Women and*

Minorities in Science and Engineering, 20(4), 341–358. doi: 10.1615/JWomenMinor ScienEng.2014008210.

McIntosh, P. (2012). Reflections and future directions for privilege studies. *Journal of Social Issues, 68*(1), 194–206. doi: 10.1111/j.1540-4560.2011.01744.x.

McRuer, R. (2006). *Crip theory: Cultural signs of queerness and disability.* New York, NY: New York University Press.

Milem, J. F. (2003). The educational benefits of diversity: Evidence from multiple sectors. In M. Chang, D. Witt, J. Jones & K. Hakuta (Eds.), *Compelling interest: Examining the evidence on racial dynamics in higher education* (pp. 126–169). Palo Alto, CA: Stanford University Press.

Mingus, M. (2011). Changing the framework: Disability justice: How our communities can move beyond access to wholeness. *Leaving evidence—a blog by Mia Mingus.* Retrieved from https://leavingevidence.wordpress.com/2011/02/12/changing-the-framework-disability-justice/.

Moody, J. (2012). *Faculty diversity: Removing the barriers.* New York, NY: Routledge.

Moreno, J., Smith, D., Parker, S., Clayton-Pedersen, A., Parker, S., & Hiroyuki-Teraguchi, D. (2006). The revolving door for under-represented minority faculty in higher education: An analysis from the Campus Diversity Initiative. *The James Irvine Foundation Campus Diversity Initiative.* Washington D.C: Association of American Colleges and Universities.

NCES. (2013). Digest of education statistics. *National Center for Education Statistics.* Retrieved February 28, 2016, from https://nces.ed.gov/programs/digest/.

Nelson Laird, T. F. (2005). College students' experiences with diversity and their effects on academic self-confidence, social agency, and disposition toward critical thinking. *Research in Higher Education, 46*(4), 365–387. doi: 10.1007/s11162-005-2966-1.

Nielsen, K. E. (2012). *A disability history of the United States.* Boston, MA: Beacon Press.

Nieto, S. (2010). *The light in their Eyes: Creating multicultural learning communities* (10th Anniversary Edition). New York, NY: Teachers College Press.

NSF_HRD_0811239. (2008). *NDSU Advance FORWARD: Transforming a gendered institution.* Grant Proposal. NSF ADVANCE Institutional Transformation proposal, North Dakota State University, Fargo, ND. Retrieved from http://www.nsf.gov/awardsearch/showAward?AWD_ID=0811239.

Officer, A., & Posarac, A. (2011). World Report on Disability. Retrieved from http://www.who.int/disabilities/world_report/2011/en/index.html.

Page, S. E. (2007). *The difference: How the power of diversity creates better groups, firms, schools, and societies.* Princeton, NJ: Princeton University Press.

Page, S. E. (2012). *The hidden factor: Why thinking differently is your greatest asset.* Chantilly, VA: The Teaching Company.

Pascarella, E. T., Edison, M., Nora, A., Hagedorn, L. S., & Terenzini, P. T. (1996). Influences on students' openness to diversity and challenge in the first year of college. *Journal of Higher Education, 67*(2), 174–222.

Pratto, F., & Stewart, A. L. (2012). Group dominance and the half-blindness of privilege. *Journal of Social Issues, 68*(1), 28–45. doi: 10.1111/j.1540-4560.2011.01734.x.

Price, M. (2009). Access imagined: The construction of disability in conference policy documents. *Disability Studies Quarterly, 29*(1). Retrieved from www.dsq-sds.org.

Price, M. (2011). *Mad at school: Rhetorics of mental disability and academic life.* Ann Arbor, MI: University of Michigan Press.

Putnam, M. (2005). Conceptualizing disability: Developing a framework for political disability identity. *Journal of Disability Policy Studies, 16*(3), 188–198. doi: 10.1016/0277-9536(94)90295-x.

Rankin, S., & Reason, R. (2008). Transformational tapestry model: A comprehensive approach to transforming campus climate. *Journal of Diversity in Higher Education, 1*, 262–274. doi: 10.1037/a0014018.

Roybal Rose, L. (1996). White identity and counseling White allies about racism. In R. G. Hunt & B. P. Bowser (Eds.), *Impacts of racism on White Americans* (2nd ed.). Thousand Oaks, CA: SAGE Publications.

Salmen, J. P. S. (2011). Universal design for academic facilities. *New Directions for Student Services, 134*, 13–20. doi: 10.1002/ss.391.

Schweik, S. M. (2009). *The ugly laws: Disability in public.* New York, NY: New York University Press.

SDS. (nd). *What is Disability Studies?* Retrieved from http://www.disstudies.org/about/what_is_ds.

SGUD. (2007). Study group on university diversity campus climate report. Oakland, CA: University of California.

Smith, D. G. (2004). The campus diversity Initiative: Current Status, Anticipating the Future. Association of American College & Universities commissioned report, March 2004, 1–19. Retrieved from https://folio.iupui.edu/handle/10244/43.

Stoudt, B. G., Fox, M., & Fine, M. (2012). Contesting privilege with critical participatory action research. *Journal of Social Issues, 68*(1), 178–193. doi: 10.1111/j.1540-4560.2011.01743.x.

Tadmor, C. T., Hong, Y.-Y., Chao, M. M., Wiruchnipawan, F., & Wang, W. (2012). Multicultural experiences reduce intergroup bias through epistemic unfreezing. *Journal of Personality and Social Psychology, 103*(5), 750–772. doi: 10.1037/a0029719.

Taylor, C.A., Lord, C. G., McIntyre, R. B., & Paulson, R. M. (2011). The Hillary Clinton effect. *Group Processes & Intergroup Relations, 14*(4), 447–459. doi: 10.1177/1368430210382680.

Thomas, C. (2004). How is disability understood? An examination of sociological approaches. *Disability & Society, 19*(6), 569–583. doi: 10.1080/0968759042000252506.

Thornton, S. (2005). Implementing flexible tenure clock policies. *New Directions for Higher Education* (130), 81–90. doi: 10.1002/he.180.

Tierney, W. G. (1993). *Building communities of difference: Higher education in the twenty-first century.* Westport, CT: Bergin & Garvy.

Tierney, W. G., & Sallee, M. W. (2008). Do organizational structures and strategies increase faculty diversity? A cultural analysis. *American Academic, 4*, 159–184.

Valian, V. (2000). *Why so slow?: The advancement of women.* Cambridge, MA: MIT Press.

Warren, M. R., & Mapp, K. L. (2011). *A match on dry grass: Community organizing as a catalyst for school reform.* New York, NY: Oxford University Press.

Watermeyer, B. (2012). Is it possible to create a politically engaged, contextual psychology of disability? *Disability & Society, 27*(2), 161–174. doi: 10.1080/09687599.2011.644928.

Weinberg, S. L. (2008). Monitoring faculty diversity: The need for a more granular approach. *Journal of Higher Education, 79*(4), 365–387. doi: 10.1353/jhe.0.0014.

Wilcox, H. N. (2009). Embodied ways of knowing, pedagogies, and social justice: Inclusive science and beyond. *NWSA Journal, 21*(2), 104–120. doi: 10.1353/nwsa.0.0084

Williams, D. A., Berger, J. B., & McClendon, S. A. (2005). *Toward a model of inclusive excellence and change in postsecondary institutions.* Washington, D.C.: Association of American Colleges and Universities.

Worthington, R. L., Stanley, C. A., & Lewis, W. T., Sr. (2014). National Association of Diversity Officers in Higher Education standards of professional practice for chief diversity officers. *Journal of Diversity in Higher Education, 7*(4), 227–234. doi: 10.1037/a0038391.

Xu, Y. J. (2012). Lessons from the past and directions for the future. *New Directions for Institutional Research, 2012*(155), 99–104. doi: 10.1002/ir.20024.

Yee, S. (2007). From civil rights to human rights: 30th anniversary of the 504 sit-in. Retrieved from http://dredf.org/publications/Civil_rights_to_human_rights.pdf.

Zirkel, S. (2008). The influence of multicultural educational practices on student outcomes and intergroup relations. *Teachers College Record, 110*(6), 1147–1181. Retrieved from http://www.tcrecord.org.

10

"IT'S A VERY DEEP, LAYERED TOPIC"

Student Affairs Professionals on the Marginality and Intersectionality of Disability

Annemarie Vaccaro and Ezekiel Kimball

The two major professional associations for the student affairs field, College Student Educators International (ACPA) and Student Affairs Administrators in Higher Education (NASPA), have made it clear that student affairs professionals should actively support diversity, social justice, and inclusion on campus as part of their holistic commitment to student growth and development (ACPA/NASPA, 2015). Yet, little research has documented how support for students with disabilities is infused into student affairs practice (Kimball, Vaccaro, & Vargas, 2016; Peña, 2014; Vaccaro, Kimball, Wells & Ostiguy, 2015). In this chapter, we address this gap using findings from an action-based grounded theory study of 31 entry-, mid-, and senior-level student affairs professionals about their perceptions of, and experiences working with, students with disabilities on campus.

This chapter begins with a summary of the competencies for student affairs educators—focusing specifically on those related to disability topics. We then describe our study methods and key findings. Our findings demonstrate that disability is a complex phenomenon involving diverse diagnoses, accommodations, self-advocacy levels and strategies, and intersections with other social identities. This remarkable range of manifestations makes it clear that disability is a form of diversity. Findings also reveal training that addresses disability as a complex diversity topic is needed in the field of student affairs. The chapter concludes with implications for practice.

Literature

Competencies for Student Affairs Educators: Through the Lens of Disability

For decades, scholars and supervisors have wrestled with the question, "What does it mean to be an effective student affairs professional?" Since scholars, practitioners, and faculty often hold different perspectives about which student affairs competencies are most important, the two major student affairs professional associations, ACPA and NASPA created a joint task force in 2010 to develop one set of professional competencies for the field. The task force drafted an initial competency report which identified ten major professional competency areas for the field. Five years later, another joint task force revised and updated the competency areas, levels, and associated outcomes. The new document, *Professional Competency Areas for Student Affairs Educators*, summarizes "essential knowledge, skills, and dispositions expected of all student affairs educators, regardless of functional area or specialization within the field" (ACPA/NASPA, 2015, p. 7). Student affairs professional competencies are categorized into ten areas that are further divided into foundational, intermediate, and advanced outcomes. As practitioners progress through their careers, they are expected to continuously improve their competence. In this short chapter, it is not possible to discuss every competency area. Instead, we briefly highlight three competency areas (Student Learning and Development; Social Justice and Inclusion; Law, Policy, and Governance) and selected outcomes therein to show how imperative disability-related competencies are to effective student affairs practice.

Student affairs educators are often referred to as student development professionals because they work (typically outside the classroom) to develop the whole college student using a variety of learning and developmental theories. A foundational outcome in the Student Learning and Development competency area states that all professionals need to be able to "articulate how race, ethnicity, nationality, class, gender, age, sexual orientation, gender identity, dis/ability, and religious belief can influence development during the college years" (ACPA/NASPA, 2015, p. 32). An intermediate Student Learning and Development competency outcome includes the ability to "build and support inclusive, socially-just, and welcoming campus communities that promote deep learning and foster student success" (ACPA/NASPA, 2015, p. 32).

Student affairs educators must also possess a variety of competencies in the Social Justice and Inclusion competency area, which "includes the knowledge, skills, and dispositions needed to create learning environments that foster equitable participation of all groups" (ACPA/NASPA, 2015, p. 30). While *all* the Social Justice and Inclusion competencies can be applied to students with disabilities, one foundational competency is especially relevant to this chapter: "[the capacity to] connect and build meaningful relationships with others while recognizing the multiple, intersecting identities, perspectives, and developmental differences people hold" (ACPA/NASPA, 2015, p. 30). Students are more than their disability. Every student with a disability possesses multiple social identities (e.g., race, gender, class, sexual orientation), that intersect in unique ways to shape their worldviews and experiences. Intersectionality is the notion that privileged and minoritized social identities "serve as organizing features of social relations [and] mutually constitute, reinforce, and naturalize one another" (Shields, 2008, p. 302). Intersectionality uniquely shapes people's personal, educational, and social realities (Crenshaw, 1989; Collins, 2000). For instance, students with multiple marginalized identities (e.g., queer students with disabilities, women of color with disabilities) may experience college differently than students with disabilities with privileged social identities (e.g., heterosexual, white men with disabilities).

Another relevant intermediate competency in the Social Justice and Inclusion area requires professionals to have the capability to "design programs and events that are inclusive" (ACPA/NASPA, 2015, p. 31) for all students. To do so, practitioners must be aware of the many types of disabilities and the multitude of accommodation strategies to support students with diverse intersecting identities.

The final competency area with clear relevance to disability is the Law, Policy, and Government competency area. In order to engage in competent practice, educators must understand the laws, policies, and judicial decisions that impact university operations and student life. According to a foundational ACPA/NASPA (2015) Law, Policy, and Government competency, professionals must "act in accordance with national, state/provincial, and local laws and with institutional policies regarding non-discrimination" (ACPA/NASPA, 2015, p. 22). Some of those laws include the Americans with Disabilities Act of 1990 and ADA Amendments Act of 2008.

This snapshot of some of the many connections between competent student affairs practice and support for students with disabilities demonstrates that student affairs professionals need awareness, knowledge, and skills regarding the diverse and complex topic of disability in order to do their work effectively. Unfortunately, very little attention has been paid to if, and how, professionals actually gain these competencies, with only two, slightly dated studies having examined the extent to which student affairs professionals were prepared to respond to the needs of students with disabilities (Preece, Roberts, Beecher, Rash, Shwalb, & Martinelli, 2007; Belch & Marshak, 2006).

Methods

This chapter is based upon data derived from an action-based, constructivist-grounded theory study (Charmaz, 2006) of 31 student affairs professionals. The main research question was, "What are the perceptions and experiences of student affairs professionals working with college students with disabilities?"

Participants were employed at 21 different colleges and universities in the Northeastern United States. They held positions at all levels of the student affairs hierarchy, including graduate students, entry-level professionals, middle managers, and senior student affairs officers. Three participants (Jayden, Ajani, Tashi) were employees of campus disability services offices, where they had daily contact with students with disabilities. The remaining participants represented almost every student affairs functional area (e.g., housing, advising, student activities, student conduct, Greek life) and typically had less frequent interactions with students with disabilities due to their work with a more general student population. To safeguard participant identities, we refer to them by pseudonyms in this chapter.

As scholar-practitioners, we seek to do non-exploitative research based upon reciprocity and beneficence (Guillemin & Gillam, 2004). These are also central concepts in action-based qualitative research. Through our project, we aimed for reciprocity and beneficence whereby participants would contribute to the research project while also gaining new knowledge and skills regarding our methods (focus groups) and topic (students with disabilities).

Procedure

Most data collection for this project took place at a regional conference for student affairs professionals. Our purposive selection of the conference collection site afforded us access to student affairs professionals from a wide range of backgrounds and the structure to deliver professional development. Participants from the conference self-selected into the study, based upon our conference program description. We used an introductory conference session to provide an overview of our action research project. In that session, we also conducted a brief professional development session about focus groups in education. On the second and third days of the conference, we conducted six focus groups—including participants who had, and had not, attended the introductory session. With beneficence in mind, we closed each focus group with time for debriefing about both the process and content of the focus group conversations and allotted time for participants to exchange ideas, best practices, and contact information. On the final day of the conference, we presented preliminary findings, compared those findings to literature, and invited attendees to discuss how preliminary findings might inform their work with students with disabilities.

After the conference, we used grounded theory purposive sampling to increase the diversity of institutional types where study participants worked. Participants for the seventh focus group were recruited via e-mails sent to the student affairs division at a mid-sized public institution. This institution was purposefully selected because a large portion of the conference participants came from private institutions. As with the conference site, we collected data and conducted a professional development session with student affairs professionals at the university.

The seven focus groups varied in size from two to nine participants. We utilized a loosely structured protocol that allowed the facilitator to listen for, and respond to, emergent group interests (Morgan, 1996). While the precise phrasing and order varied from focus group to focus group, questions typically included: (1) How do you define disability? (2) What role does thinking about people with disabilities play in your work? (3) Tell us about your experiences with disability or with people with disabilities; (4) What people and offices provide support for students with disabilities or leadership on disability-related issues? (5) What obstacles exist on your campus in working with students with disabilities? As one facilitator managed the conversation, the other recorded recurring emergent ideas and posed follow-up questions as needed. We audio recorded all sessions.

We conducted constant comparative grounded theory data analysis (Charmaz, 2006). Immediately following each focus group, we conducted a preliminary analysis of the emergent codes and themes. Using questions in our protocol as the framework, we sorted responses into a grid consisting of positive and negative phenomena (Morgan, 1996). After all focus groups were completed, we then examined variations within each focus group, across focus groups, within each question, and across questions. We included these analyses in our professional development presentations about preliminary findings at the conference and large public institution. Once transcriptions of all seven focus groups were complete, we conducted a more thorough analysis of the transcribed data. Using the meanings generated by participants, we generated open codes that were compared and contrasted with the preliminary codes developed at the conference. Next, we generated focused codes by combining similar open codes into larger categories. Finally, we looked for interconnections among the categories and generated axial codes. This paper reflects our axial codes related to disability diversity as understood by student affairs professionals and their reflections on preparedness to support this diverse population.

Limitations

Our study has several limitations. First, our conversations quickly moved toward consensus. Pressure to conform to group perspectives is always a potential limitation of focus groups. Second, participants in our study were drawn from one geographic region in the United States. Third, while the lack of racial and ethnic diversity in our sample is consistent with the region, the representation of few perspectives from people of color is certainly a limitation.

The Many Layers of Disability Diversity

In the opening sections of this chapter, we argued that student affairs professionals need to possess a variety of competencies to effectively support students with disabilities. As one participant said of disability: "It's a very deep, layered topic." This quote, which gives our chapter its title, highlights the complicated nature of disability. Reflecting this complexity, our analysis revealed four themes related to the connection between diversity and disability: (1) diversity of diagnoses, (2) diversity of accommodation needs, (3) diversity of self-advocacy skills, and (4) diversity of social identities and intersectionality. In the following sections, narratives from student affairs professionals show they were often overwhelmed by, and unprepared to effectively navigate, the diversity *within* disability.

The findings section concludes with participant perspectives about the need for comprehensive training regarding disability topics in order to achieve professional competence.

Diversity within *Disability*

Diversity of Diagnoses

One of the first layers of disability diversity includes the diversity of diagnoses. There are a multitude of diagnoses as well as a plethora of ways to categorize disability (Raue & Lewis, 2011; Vaccaro, Kimball, Wells & Ostiguy, 2015). One common myth among educators is that students with disabilities are largely comprised of students with mobility restrictions. However, only 7% of students enrolled in two- and four-year degree-granting postsecondary institutions are categorized as having a mobility limitation or orthopedic impairment (Raue & Lewis, 2011). Morris explicated how pervasive the myth is: "You obviously think of the physical disabilities as the main [type of disability, but] . . . there *are* invisible disabilities." Noting his increased awareness of students with autism spectrum disorders, Logan described a recent shift in his understanding of the diversity among people with different disabilities. He explained:

> I think I've been a lot more cognizant lately of students on the spectrum . . . It's definitely something I want to be *more* cognizant of. When I think of ability in my day-to-day work I think a lot about how mental disability works as opposed to physical disability.

Similarly, Tabitha shared, "It's not just about the person who may have that physical disability and can't walk. But we're talking about Aspergers. We're talking about mental health. We're talking about eating disorders. I just think it just makes it more complex." In sum, professionals in our study recognized how the umbrella term "disability" encompassed a variety of diagnoses.

Diversity of Accommodation Needs

A second form of diversity regarding disability relates to accommodation needs. Students with different disabilities required vastly different types of accommodations, based on the interplay between their diagnosis and the institutional environment (Banerjee, Madaus, & Gelbar, 2014). One residence life professional explained how, despite preparedness for students with some types of disabilities, campus residence halls were not equipped to accommodate students with other types of disabilities. For instance, a residence hall with a ramp and elevator that accommodated a student in a wheelchair might not be accommodating for a blind student who needed signs in braille. Or a residence hall with braille signage would not be accommodating for a deaf student who needed an adapted fire alarm. Tabitha lamented that "one hall might have some [accommodation] one time and another hall might have some [accommodation] another time."

Our participants talked about how students who needed similar accommodations might have quite diverse disabilities. For instance, students with a host of disabilities required extended testing time or single residence hall rooms. Fabio and his colleagues were caught off guard when they assumed a comfort animal was a service dog for a student with a visual impairment. "That really threw people in our community because they thought, 'Oh I see this dog. [The student] must clearly need it because of a physical disability or their vision.' It was not and so people really were thrown by that." Through their campus interactions with students, practitioners learned that students with diverse disabilities often needed similar accommodations.

They also discussed how students with the *same* disability diagnosis might need different accommodations and levels of support. Ajani explained,

> It's trying to figure out individually what that student's difficulties are, because students can have the same diagnosis, come from the same situation, but they really respond to the social environment and also academics differently. So for me it's trying to figure out in interacting with the student— What are their weaknesses? What are their strengths? And trying to figure out the resources and places we can plug them in and what we can do.

Chloe explained how complicated and individualized accommodations needed to be. As an academic advisor, she worked with a student with obsessive compulsive disorder (OCD) and anxiety on low academic performance. Chloe realized concentration and study strategies were not the only types of support the student needed. The hold on this particular student's registration stemmed from not only academic but also financial issues. Therefore, Chloe's typical advising strategies were not sufficient.

> She was referred to me almost at the end of the academic year. She had already had a rocky road . . . That was because, [it was not just] academic-related. It was related to financial aid, it was related [to] the registration processes. . . . She had about one a week until she would no longer be able to acquire a loan . . . I just made a suggestion: "Would it be helpful for [me] to at least to go into this meeting and hear what's being said? Maybe we can translate together and come up with some meaningful next steps of what can happen and make sure you get this done on time?" She agreed to have me come along. [At the meeting, I saw firsthand] how this student was interacting with the [financial] office. She would literally walk in and her anxiety prohibited her from even listening to what was going on. She would walk in and start choking and [the office staff] really weren't equipped to know how to help this student.

Chloe recognized she could not support this student by relying on "typical" accommodation strategies for students with OCD or anxiety. This student had unique needs, and Chloe's support strategies had to honor this form of disability diversity. Accompanying the student to the financial aid office was well beyond the scope of Chloe's academic support job functions, but a strategy necessary for the student's success.

In addition to considering accommodation needs associated with an individual's unique disability and diagnosis, practitioners also wrestled with how to fairly and confidentially provide accommodations to individuals within group settings such as classrooms and residence halls. Aiden felt unprepared to support a student with a disability in his first-year seminar class. He stated,

> It was like, "Oh god. I am not ready for this." I had to really go back and think, "How I am going to teach this topic to a whole group? And also do it so that I'm not outing someone, I'm not sort of making the student uncomfortable." So I felt less prepared.

Because it is unlawful to disclose a student's disability, educators had to walk a fine line of honoring confidentiality while providing unique accommodations to students with disabilities who lived and learned among a community of peers. Penny explained this challenge: "The resident has a disability, but that doesn't mean you need to single them out and make them feel singled out. It's complex." As Penny and Aiden's quotes suggest even practitioners who felt confident providing accommodations in individualized settings, felt less prepared when students with disabilities were part of a larger group (e.g., classes, residence hall communities). In sum, practitioners described the challenges of providing appropriate support, in diverse settings, to students with very different accommodation needs.

Diversity of Self-Advocacy Skills

Various levels of self-advocacy skills provided an additional layer of disability diversity and another hurdle for effective student affairs practice. Self-advocacy, the ability to make decisions about the supports needed to achieve goals and communicate those decisions to others, relies on knowledge of self, knowledge of rights, ability to communicate, and ability to be a leader (Test et al., 2005). Once a student reaches post-secondary education, they are fully responsible for testing, documentation, and requesting accommodations. As such, self-advocacy skills are a necessity for success in higher education (Daly-Cano, Vaccaro & Newman, 2015; Vaccaro, Daly-Cano & Newman, 2015).

The range of self-advocacy skills among college students necessitated diverse actions by practitioners in our study. Sometimes professionals had to remind students how important it was to self-advocate while in college. They encouraged students to use basic skills like time management, test taking, study methods, and negotiation. For students presenting with less developed self-advocacy skills, discussions revolved around the importance of knowing oneself and accommodation needs and finding the courage to ask for what they needed. For instance, student affairs professionals coached students about negotiating with faculty members who were not providing adequate accommodations or confronting peers who were being exclusionary. Lelah explained: "It's a matter of help[ing] them with advocating for themselves—especially in the classroom." Abby recalled a conversation about self-advocacy with a student who had a peanut allergy. She told the student,

> You have to advocate for yourself and have a conversation with your roommate about why it's not okay for them to have peanut butter in that room with you. . . . You need to be able to walk into a dining hall, residence hall, your future work place and advocate, say this is what I [need].

For some students, self-advocacy interventions were important because they arrived at college with limited self-advocacy skills. Other students came to college with strong self-advocacy skills, but still needed to learn how to utilize them in a higher education setting. Tabitha explained:

> [Students] get to the college and university level and . . . don't have those systems in place necessarily, and . . . I don't know that we're quite able to accommodate all of the things that were done K–12. And so that's a challenge, helping a student navigate through that [new environment].

In other cases, students possessed strong self-advocacy skills and regularly advocated for themselves. These students did not need the same kinds of interventions from professionals. Karma described how a student with severe allergies self-advocated and engaged in a form of activism by educating peers and the residence life staff about her disability and accommodation needs.

> She would talk about [her disability]. She got to know people [and educated them about] things they just didn't even consider. She helps to educate Resident Assistants. She came into a staff meeting. That was helpful because she felt comfortable opening up about those things [while we were] being educated.

In sum, supporting students with various levels of self-advocacy skills required different approaches by professionals. Autumn explained: "[One] student was very independent and was very good at advocating for herself. It was a good experience for me to figure out how best to work with the student. But, she did make it easy for me because I know, in general, 18, 19-year-olds, advocating for themselves isn't always a strength."

Diversity of Social Identities and Intersectionality

Students with disabilities arrive at university with a range of awareness, understanding, and acceptance of or pride in their disability (Riddell & Weedon, 2014). They also engage in diverse patterns of meaning-making regarding the ways their disability identity intersects with their other social identities (e.g., race, class, gender, sexual orientation). These variations comprised yet another layer of diversity among students with disabilities.

The societal stigma about disability and people with disabilities is ever present (e.g., Charlton, 2006; Lombardi & Murray, 2011). College students with disabilities make meaning of their self and identity in the context of these messages. The results of those meaning making processes are incredibly diverse, with some students feeling ashamed while others exude identity pride as a people with disabilities. For instance, Laleh described how students with mental health diagnoses often experience denial and or shame regarding their disability: "Some students don't want to be labeled, especially . . . with mental health . . . . The students are struggling with accepting their diagnosis . . . the pathology of it." Along a similar vein, Autumn estimated that roughly 70% of students with disabilities that she interacts with have not disclosed their disability to anyone at the college—including the disability services office. She believed lack of disclosure was related to shame and stigma. By contrast, other students (like the one Karma described earlier), were not only open about their disabilities, but also expressed identity pride through activism (Daly-Cano et al., 2015; Pasque & Vargas, 2014). Another participant described how students with visual impairments at his college hosted a "dark dinner" where attendees dined with the lights off so that they could learn what life was like for students with sight impairments.

Some practitioners noted that identity intersectionality added to the diversity among students with disabilities. Students with disabilities possess a variety of other social identities (e.g., national origin, race, gender, religion, sexual orientation) that contribute their unique social realities. For instance, Teshi explained how cultural norms for international students intersected with their disabilities and shaped their expectations and experiences of academic success:

> Dealing with the intersections of culture and disability are huge. This semester in particular . . . we have a pretty high international student population and I've been having more students from China and Japan come and talk to me. Because even though we're from very different cultures the stigma around having a non-physical disability and what that means for their functioning as a student is huge. [Students express concerns such as] "I need to do better so that I can transfer to a more prestigious university and I can't even function in a state school. What's wrong with me?" We've been having to have those conversations a lot. That is a really difficult conversation to have with someone who's been told all of their life even when they're

struggling with major issues that [those issues] are not legitimate. And that you better figure this out because now you are an adult and you don't get accommodations in the real world. So those are really problematic.

Talking about disability as a diversity topic without considering intersectionality of other social identities is overly simplistic and ignores people's lived realities. In fact, a number of scholars who have studied Black deaf students (Stapleton, 2016), queer students with disabilities (Miller, Wynn & Webb, this volume), and women with disabilities (Banks & Kaschak, 2014) have affirmed that inter-sectionality of multiple social identities adds complexity to the lived realities of people with disabilities. It also offers a layer of complexity for student affairs professionals as they strive to competently educate, teach, advise, and support students on campus.

Disability Competency and the Need for "Multifocal" Competency Development

Given the vast diversity within disability, student affairs educators in our study often felt unprepared to effectively support students with disabilities. Practitioners at all levels—graduate students to vice presidents—described a lack of knowledge and preparedness to navigate the "very deep, layered topic" of disability. Anna stated "For me, [disability] doesn't seem very clear all the time—at all." Karma responded, "I don't know that many of my colleagues would have any idea even where to start [either]." Without adequate training, Penny found it challenging to support students with disabilities with diverse diagnoses, divergent accommo-dation needs, and different self-identities.

> We know our students are coming in with a lot of . . . unique characteris-tics and background experiences. It's just being able to accommodate and empower them to be ready to handle those things. I think that that's a challenge.

Like Penny, most of our participants experienced this challenge because they had little formal preparation (i.e., courses, workshops) about disability topics. Only one-third of participants had any formal education about disability topics. Most of that education came in the form of one class session in a semester-long course on diversity, student development, or law.

Most participants acknowledged basic diversity training was standard for university employees and student paraprofessionals. Unfortunately, those trainings rarely included disability as a diversity topic. Fabio expressed, "As far as inclusivity, we do a lot of education with our faculty [staff and] with our stu-dents I would say we don't do as much education with or around [disability]." Karma lamented how students with disabilities were often overlooked in campus

Banerjee, M., Madaus, J. W., & Gelbar, N. (2014). Applying LD documentation guidelines at the postsecondary level: Decision making with sparse or missing data. *Learning Disability Quarterly, 38*(1), 27–39.

Banks, M., & Kaschak, E. (Eds.). (2014). *Women with visible and invisible disabilities: Multiple intersections, multiple issues, multiple therapies.* New York, NY: Routledge.

Belch, H. A., & Marshak, L. E. (2006). Critical incidents involving students with psychiatric disabilities: The gap between state of the art and campus practice. *Journal of Student Affairs Research and Practice, 43*(3), 840–859.

Charlton, J. I. (2006). The dimensions of disability oppression: An overview. In L. J. Davis (Ed.), *The disability studies reader* (2nd ed.) (pp. 217–227). New York, NY: Routledge.

Charmaz, K. (2006). *Constructing grounded theory: A practical guide through qualitative analysis.* Los Angeles, CA: SAGE Publications.

Collins, P. H. (2000). *Black feminist thought: Knowledge, consciousness, and the politics of empowerment.* New York, NY: Routledge.

Crenshaw, K. (1989). Demarginalizing the intersection of race and sex: A black feminist critique of antidiscrimination doctrine, feminist theory, and antiracist politics. *University of Chicago Legal Forum, (1),* 139–168.

Daly-Cano, M., Vaccaro, A., & Newman, B. M. (2015). College student narratives about learning and using self-advocacy skills. *Journal of Postsecondary Education and Disability 28*(2), 209–223.

Evans, N. J., Assadi, J. L., & Herriott, T. K. (2005). Encouraging the development of disability allies. *New Directions for Student Services, 2005 (110),* 67–79.

Guillemin, M., & Gillam, L. (2004). Ethics, reflexivity, and "ethically important moments" in research. *Qualitative Inquiry, 10*(2), 261–280.

Kimball, E., Vaccaro, A. & Vargas, N. (2016). Student affairs professionals supporting students with disabilities: A grounded theory model. *Journal of Student Affairs Research & Practice, 53*(2), 1–14.

Lombardi, A. R., & Murray, C. (2011). Measuring university faculty attitudes toward disability: Willingness to accommodate and adopt universal design principles. *Journal of Vocational Rehabilitation, 34*(1), 43–56.

Miller, R. A., Wynn, R. D., & Webb, K. W. Queering disability in higher education: Views from the intersections. In E. Kim & K. C. Aquino (Eds.), *Disability as diversity in higher education: Policies and practices to enhance student success.* New York, NY: Routledge.

Morgan, D. L. (1996). *Focus Groups as Qualitative Research* (2nd ed.). Thousand Oaks, CA: SAGE.

Raue, K., and Lewis, L. (2011). *Students with disabilities at degree-granting postsecondary institutions* (NCES 2011–018). U.S. Department of Education, National Center for Education Statistics. Washington, DC: U.S. Government Printing Office.

Pasque, P. A. & Vargas, J. G. (2014). Performances of student activism: Sound, silence, gender, and dis/ability. In C. J. Broadhurst & G. L. Martin (Eds.), *New Directions for Higher Education,* "Radical Academia"? Understanding the Climates for Campus Activists" *24*(167), 59–71.

Peña, E. V. (2014). Marginalization of published scholarship on students with disabilities in higher education journals. *Journal of College Student Development, 55*(1), 30–40.

Preece, J. E., Roberts, N. L., Beecher, M. E., Rash, P. D., Shwalb, D. A., & Martinelli, E. A. (2007). Academic advisors and students with disabilities: A national survey of advisors' experiences and needs. *NACADA Journal, 27*(2), 57–72.

Riddell, S., & Weedon, E. (2014). Disabled students in higher education: Discourses of disability and the negotiation of identity. *International Journal of Educational Research, 63,* 38–46.

Shields, S. A. (2008). Gender: An intersectionality perspective. *Sex Roles, 59*, 301–311.

Stapleton, L. D. (2016, in press). When deafness is centered: Deaf students of color navigating deaf and racial identity in college. *Journal of College Student Development*.

Test, D. W., Fowler, C. H., Wood, W., Brewer, D. M., & Eddy, S. (2005). A conceptual framework of self-advocacy for students with disabilities. *Remedial and Special Education, 26*(1) 43–54.

Vaccaro, A., Daly-Cano, M., & Newman, B. (2015). A sense of belonging among college students with disabilities: An emergent theoretical model. *Journal of College Student Development, 56*(7), 670–686.

Vaccaro, A., Kimball, E. W., Wells, R. S., & Ostiguy, B. J. (2015). Researching students with disabilities: The importance of critical perspectives. *New Directions for Institutional Research, 163*, 25–41.

Vance, M. L., Parks, K., & Lipsitz, N. (Eds.). (2014). *Beyond the Americans with disabilities act: Inclusive policy and practice for higher education*. Washington, DC: NASPA.

11

TOOLS FOR MOVING THE INSTITUTIONAL ICEBERG

Policies and Practices for Students with Disabilities

Jacalyn Griffen and Tenisha Tevis

The numbers of students with disabilities in postsecondary education is on the rise (Brown & Broido, 2015; National Center for Learning Disabilities [NCLD], 2013; Steinmetz, 2002). For most students, their transition to college is challenging, especially for students with disabilities, because they often "lack the self-advocacy skills necessary to survive in college" (Eckes & Ochoa, 2005, p. 6). "Students with disabilities stand at a crossroads when transitioning from high school to college or career, and are absent from the dominant discourse regarding underserved populations in higher education" (Tevis & Griffen, 2014, p. 239). Yet, there is a dearth of literature that explores the intersectionality of students with disabilities and how university administrators provide support at the postsecondary level. Moreover, the perspective of the disability services administrator is minimally explored within the dominant discourse that focuses on underrepresented groups in higher education (Tevis & Griffen, 2014). Research confirms that information plays a critical role in disadvantaged students' college access, preparation, and graduation process; and yet students with disabilities are overlooked by this body of research (Vargas, 2004). Thus, these students could be unaware of what they need to know to ensure their successful transition to and through college. In this chapter, we discuss challenges faced by students with disabilities when transitioning to college; shed light on the complexities faced by both students and disability services administrators when seeking and providing support services; and lastly, we discuss strategies, recommendations, and implications for policy and practice to move what we call the *institutional iceberg* in order help students with any or multiple disabilities transition to college and gain the self-advocacy skills required for academic success. We define institutional iceberg as a metaphor for the slow-to-change higher education system, disengaged policymakers, and disconnected secondary and postsecondary education systems.

Having a disability can cut across ethnic, economic, and cultural lines. Thus, akin to labels used to describe students from communities of color, the label of disability is a socially constructed stigma rooted in the idea of lacking a normative way to function (Brown & Broido, 2015). Changes to section 504 of the Americans with Disabilities Act Amendment of 2008 (United States Equal Opportunity Employment Commission [EEOC], 2015) broadened how the term "disability" is interpreted. Although students labeled as *disabled* may have an impairment, not all students with impairments are disabled nor are eligible to receive services as an impairment must severely limit a major life function (Brown & Broido, 2015). In contrast to their underserved peers, for students with disabilities whose impairments may or may not be obvious, the transition to college may need to be much more than specialized programming (e.g., summer bridge; focused orientations) and geared to helping students to become self-advocates. We find that the shift from secondary to postsecondary institutions for students with disabilities warrants an unarticulated two-faceted process. While these students are transitioning from one educational context to another, the responsibility for obtaining services shifts from K-12 institutional support to the individual(s) requiring or requesting services. Therefore, common transitional problems—time management, study skills, and developing new relationships—are compounded as students with disabilities must become owners of their education plan and accountable for their own reasonable accommodations. Grappling with this two-dimensional transition to college process can create frustration and anxiety, leading to higher dropout rates (Quaye & Harper, 2015).

Federal mandates such as the American Disabilities Act (ADA) and Individuals with Disabilities Education Act (IDEA) ensure that K-12 students are supported by multiple adults in various roles: parents, teachers, and counselors (US Department of Education Office of Special Needs & Rehabilitative Services [OSERS], 2006). Hence, K-12 schools are required to identify, create a support team, and provide services to a student with disabilities. Unfortunately, this often produces students who are not empowered to be self-advocates and creates a gap in understanding that they not only *can* request services but are responsible *for* requesting services when they enter higher education (Eckes & Ochoa, 2005; Fitchen, Goodrick, Tagalakis, Amsel, & Libman, 1990; Getzel & Thoma, 2008; Gliedman & Roth, 1980; Test, Fowler, Wood, Brewer, & Eddy, 2005). Further, it is fair to assume that when K-12 students with disabilities graduate from high school, the institutions of higher education they transition to should be prepared to fully support them. However, ingrained systemic barriers imposed by the Family Educational Rights and Privacy Act (FERPA) and the loss of mandated K-12 support can impact the transition of these students and ultimately their persistence to degree attainment (Higbee, Katz, & Schultz, 2010; Getzel & Thoma, 2008). Further, it is difficult to identify a transitioning student who wishes to leave the label of *disabled* behind upon entering postsecondary education, but once enrolled may find themselves in need of services (Cooper, 2012).

Thus, the question becomes, who advocates for this marginalized group of students once they transition to college? Whether students realize it or not, once they enter the postsecondary world, disability services administrators become the sole provider of all supports and services, a task that was once the responsibility of multiple K-12 stakeholders. The disability services administrators in institutions of higher education are responsible for providing support services and ensuring that these students develop the skills to advocate on their own behalf (Cooper, 2012; Fiedler & Danneker, 2007). Disability services administrators play a vital role in students with disabilities' two-dimensional transition to college—a process that requires the administrators to assist the student in moving from a state dependency to self-advocacy. Thus, disability services administrators assume multiple roles to bridge the gap between the K-12 and postsecondary contexts.

Our Research

Before proceeding we present specifics of the larger study that undergirds this chapter and define a few key concepts that frame our discussion. This chapter explores the role disability services administrators play in facilitating inclusion, which was rooted in the larger study and focused on how academically successful college students with physical disabilities transition to and navigate higher education from a strengths-based perspective of intersectionality. The overarching study took place in a mid-size private institution on the West Coast, located in a metropolitan area. This institution serves over 5,000 undergraduate and graduate students across three city campuses. In the larger study, we utilized a comparative case study approach to understand how students with disabilities successfully navigated the postsecondary landscape. While interviewing the student participants about their transition to and through college, we found that administrators had played a familial role, across all three cases. Thus, we were led to interview administrators Virginia and Cy (pseudonyms) from the Disability Services Office. In the first phase of data collection from the administrators, we provided the protocol prior to the interview, and they were given the option to bring typed responses to the interview and/or submit them via e-mail. Following the initial 45-minute interview, we reviewed the audio and created individual reflections. We transcribed the interview session and developed follow-up questions. We e-mailed each administrator to delve deeper into their initial responses. Cy submitted his follow-up responses via e-mail, and Virginia preferred to provide her responses via one-on-one interview. We employed member checking by having each administrator read their transcribed data. Data were triangulated through the use of two researchers, analysis of interview transcriptions, document analysis, and creating field notes, and audit trails to record our decisions (Yin, 2016).

During the administrative interviews we found that the many roles they must fill included making changes to physical buildings, creating inclusive campus policies, and altering faculty perceptions leave them feeling as if they are "moving an iceberg through frozen waters" (Virginia, personal communication, August, 2013). As the number of students with disabilities who transition to college increases, it is imperative that university administrators are equipped with the tools and strategies to help each student succeed. Each administrator in our study emphasized the need for students to recognize that "mom is not here for them any longer; their success is up to them" (Virginia personal communication, August, 2013). However, just as parents act as *advocates* and *liaisons* to meet students' needs, we learned that these disability services administrators also *assumed* this role of *parent* as they assisted each student to move the institutional iceberg to reach academic success.

Our administrative participants emphasized that helping students with disabilities to develop self-advocacy skills were key to moving the institutional iceberg. Virginia and Cy not only viewed the student's ability to self-advocate as crucial to their academic success but were champions as well. When first assessing a student's needs, each asks, "How do I help them advocate for themselves? How do I advocate for them" (Cy, personal communication, August, 2013). Virginia stated that the Disability Services Office is "intentionally focused on helping the student become a stronger self-advocate" (Cy, personal communication, August, 2013). However, Cy stated that it starts with "[telling] somebody that there's a need." Both Virginia and Cy believe that "Self-advocacy [helps the individual] to articulate strengths and challenges" (Cy, personal communication, August, 2013). Fiedler and Danneker (2007) found the ability to self-advocate is essential to the academic success of students with disabilities. Thus, it is imperative that college administrators be equipped with the tools necessary to help these students find their voice.

Typically, in the K–12 system the voices of parents, educators, and administrators often outweigh the voice of the individual student (Cooper, 2012). Thus, when the student arrives at a postsecondary institution, the accommodations that were necessary in K–12 now become optional. Administrators in our study found that it is crucial to shift students' perspective from one of outsider to one of insider-participant—empowering each student to acquire knowledge and become engaged in the process of his or her own individual success. This then makes the disability services administrators the liaison and mediator between students and faculty members, on-campus service providers, and outside vendors and agencies. This requires a shift in thinking in order to further move the iceberg.

Lastly, we learned that disability services administrators are resourceful. Virginia and Cy explained that a majority of their time was spent collaborating, searching for resources to meet the unique needs of each student, and meeting the challenge of being responsive to student needs with short staff and/or with minimal budgets. They agreed, "The biggest challenge continues to be resources, both financial and human" (Virginia, personal communication, August 2013). Cy partnered with a state prison who connected him with an inmate who was certified in braille; and Virginia made sure that textbooks were re-bound to make them more accessible, so that students could better interact with their course materials. Such acts are crucial when creating a "comprehensive college experience" (Cooper, 2012, p. 13).

Drawing from our research, academic success refers to the process of "obtaining a bachelor's degree or higher from a degree granting institution" (Tevis & Griffen, 2014, p. 69). For this chapter we expand this definition by adding the ability to advocate for one's self. Self-advocacy, in an educational setting, has been conceptualized as developing a set of "skills, knowledge, and beliefs that enable a person to engage in a goal-directed, self-regulated, autonomous behavior" (Field, Martin, Miller, Ward, & Wehmeyer, 1988, p. 2). Self-advocacy is important for framing academic success of students with disabilities, since upon transitioning to college, they are responsible for their own accommodations, seeking support services, and working with faculty to ensure their support is implemented (Eckes & Ochoa, 2005; Getzel & Thoma, 2008; Test et al., 2005). Due to federal protections, developing the skill for self-advocacy falls by the wayside in many K-12 schools (Fiedler & Danneker, 2007; Gliedman & Roth, 1980). Therefore, upon transition to postsecondary education, it becomes the responsibility of disability services administrators to assist students with disabilities to develop this skill in order for them to achieve academic success, and progress through college.

Framing the Issues

Being classified as having a disability can encompass a number of medical, behavioral, or developmental impairments (US Department of Education OSERS, 2006), and can range from mild to severe. According to the Americans with Disabilities Act, "a person with a disability [is] a person who has a physical or mental impairment that substantially limits one or more major life activity" (Americans with Disabilities Act National Network, FAQ page, 2015). Like other marginalized and underserved populations, in the past postsecondary institutions often did not make provisions for students with disabilities to enroll. Paul (2000) explains it was not until the 1970s that such students were granted admission and access to colleges and universities in the United States. For students with disabilities, access means something very different than how it is framed for other underrepresented students. Generally, speaking, access within the transition to college literature refers to having the opportunity to engage with or exposure to information, social networks, and/or programming. However, for students with disabilities, access means to ensure accessibility, and is functional. Students with visual and/or physical impairments expressed the "need for architectural accommodations . . . ramps, handrailings, and curbcuts" (p. 4). Further, functionality for students with non-ambulatory disabilities are related to other supports and accommodations (e.g., notetakers or extended time on tests). Due to the fact that students with disabilities have to request services, they continue to be marginalized or altogether excluded from having a positive collegiate experience, further impeding their ability to be self-advocates. This barrier is just one of several a student with disabilities must navigate in order to persist to graduation. Thus, the complexities of the college access landscape for this underserved population requires them to develop an extra layer of knowledge and sense of self.

Though it is beyond the scope of this chapter to provide an in-depth literature review on students with disabilities as an underrepresented group, it is fitting to highlight the gaps in three areas of college access research: college knowledge, transition to college, and persistence to degree attainment. We seek to share the implications in these three areas as it pertains to the administrators' role to empower students with disabilities to become self-advocates. Yet there is a paucity of literature on the college knowledge necessary for such students' successful transition to college, as well as college administrators and the role they play in these students' transition to and their persistence through college. Though these bodies of research provide an understanding of both the individual and institutional characteristics that impede student college access, college preparation, and degree attainment, they omit students with disabilities, and neglect what these themes mean for them. Moreover, the research does not take into account students with disabilities' intersectionality, their two-dimensional transition process, or the dependence on the K–12 system.

Transition to College

Transition to college research highlights the myriad factors that influence students' move from secondary to postsecondary institutions. These prior inquires contribute to our understanding of how race/ethnicity, gender, academic preparation, financial aid, and socioeconomic status (SES), to name a few, can act as barriers to students' degree attainment; and yet, having a disability is overlooked. Although "the term disability . . . cuts across all of the traditionally mentioned identification categories" (Tevis & Griffen, 2014, p. 242), it is not referenced as a theme within the broader college transitions discourse. Yet, according to Paul (2000), "students with disabilities represent one of the groups . . . more active in their pursuit of advanced learning opportunities" (p. 2). Again, access for some means accessibility of institutional structures, both physical and virtual, and requires institutional players to take an inclusive approach to support. Within the transition to college research, college preparation focused on underserved populations is rooted heavily in academic achievement. In the case of students with disabilities, it is related to their IEP and eligibility for special education, which is not in the student's control. And it is clear that degree completion is the goal for most students who matriculate at the college/university level. Complicating degree completion rates for students with disabilities is the impasse many of them reach when their individual attributes intersect with institutional characteristics. Even if they successfully transition to college, degree completion will be difficult to attain if students with disabilities do not persist in their academic pursuits.

College Persistence

Literature related to college persistence explains that there are a variety of individual characteristics, external forces, and institutional attributes that impede a college students' ability to socially and academically integrate, and to reach degree attainment. However, similar to the literature on college transitions, students with disabilities are missing and voiceless. Persistence is "a student's postsecondary education continuation behavior that leads to graduation" (Texas Guaranteed Student Loan Corporation, 1999, p. 5). Our research illustrates for students with disabilities that such behavior is predicated on institutional support. Cy and Virginia indicated that having "The appropriate tools or accommodations in place to have equal access to the environment is so critical" (Cy, personal communication, August, 2013). Further, Virginia stated that "the idea of student success is the responsibility of multiple parties at the institution" (Cy, personal communication, August, 2013). However, just as students with disabilities are absent from the literature, we find that they absent from the institutional academic success discourse and policies (Tevis & Griffen, 2014).

Tinto's seminal model of student integration (1975) and college student departure theory (1993) provided a rationale for why students integrate, commit, graduate, and/or leave institutions of higher education. These and subsequent studies denote why particular underrepresented populations have persistence issues. Such related research has advanced our understanding of how higher education administrators can better support diverse populations. However, despite its contribution, criticism, and revisions, it continues to omit students with disabilities and their ability to persist in postsecondary institutions. Although many factors (e.g., commitment and social and academic integration) are foundational for student persistence, they are also conceptually different for students with disabilities. In our larger study, we found that both college administrators and students with disabilities are more committed to meeting federal mandates such as FERPA and inspiring self-advocacy, and less committed to the institutional policies. Students are engaged in the college campus as much as the environment allows them to function. Administrators are committed to pushing against the institutional barriers in order to foster an inclusive setting that allows for such students to be their own advocates, leading to academic success. We also found that in order to facilitate both social and academic integration, students with disabilities need to be their own advocate, and the institutional community needs to do more than simply oblige the law or understand how to *accommodate* students (Fitchen et al., 1990; Higbee et al., 2010). Students with disabilities "are still not fully integrated in college life" (Higbee et al., 2010, p. 8) and remain unrepresented in the literature. For students with disabilities to fully integrate and persist requires all institutional players to understand that there are both educational and pecuniary implications for ensuring this success. For instance, institutions of higher education are not obliged to pay for any accommodations that are not available to every student—thus placing an additional financial burden on the student with disabilities, which can negatively impact persistence to degree attainment.

Administrators are called upon to ensure students with disabilities have access to a "comprehensive college experience" (Cooper, 2012, p. 13); however, the void in the scholarly discourse does not allow for this. Unfortunately, prior research does not provide disability services administrators with the scholarly knowledge, theoretical frameworks, nor best practices for inspiring self-advocacy and ensuring the academic success of students with disabilities.

Self-Advocacy

The federal government has legislated that preparing students with disabilities to become *self-determined adults* as a mandatory goal for K-12 schools (Fielder, 2007). Yet, self-advocacy is an important tenet of self-determination (Field et al., 1988; Test et al., 2005). Based on Test and colleagues' (2005) literature review of self-advocacy for students with disabilities, Wehmeyer and Berkobien (as cited in Test et al., 2005) provide the most relevant definition of self-advocacy for understanding the implications for higher education administrators: "Self-advocacy is to request or petition for oneself . . . represented as a group or organization directed by individuals with . . . disabilities . . . Self-advocacy is a component of self-determination . . . a visible manifestation of self-regulation and, to a latter extent, autonomy" (p. 47). However, since the educational planning process for providing special education services in the K-12 system excludes students from being partners or responsible for their academic career, students with disabilities lack the ability to advocate for themselves. The ability to self-advocate is a necessary skill as these students transition to higher education (Fielder & Danneker, 2007). The administrators from our study explained that developing this skill is critical to students with disabilities' academic journey. The disability services administrators we interviewed expressed that they inspire such skill development through "understanding the individual circumstances of each student" and empower the student to "be invested in their own success" (Cy, personal communication, August, 2013). Virginia ensures that each student is aware that "you are now the person in the driver's seat of your own education" (Virginia, personal communication, August, 2013). Thus, we found that the disability services administrators view the student as an equal partner in the accommodations process, thereby co-constructing knowledge to empower the student to advocate on their own behalf while creating understanding that there is an institutional administrator who will be there to provide support.

Challenges: Moving the Institutional Iceberg

The reception and response of major stakeholders at institutions of higher education for students with disabilities are analogous to the reception and response for students of color and *other* marginalized groups. Advocating for changes to physical buildings, campus policies, and faculty perceptions is only a portion of what is *required* of disability services administrators. Thus, we liken their multiple responsibilities to moving an iceberg through frozen waters. The Americans with Disabilities Act of Amendments Act of 2008 expanded the definition of disability to broaden the scope of individuals protected under this legislative umbrella. As the number of students who qualify for disability services increases, it is imperative that university administrators are equipped with tools to help each student succeed. Our findings indicated that administrators are the ones who can shape and mold the academic trajectory for each student, as well as influence how the postsecondary community will engage in the process. Each administrator in our study emphasized the need for students to recognize that "Mom is not here for them any longer, their success is up to them" (Cy, personal communication, August, 2013). However, just as families, educators, and counselors act as advocates, to creatively find resources for student needs; we found that these administrators also *assumed* these roles as they assisted each student to *move the iceberg* to reach academic success.

The systemic disconnect between the K-12 and higher education systems creates barriers to degree attainment. Access to postsecondary education means more than merely admission or absence of physical barriers; students with disabilities need to know how to navigate this new terrain. When students do not understand the landscape, they can become alienated from the environment, turning their disability into a handicap (Fitchen et al., 1990; Gliedman & Roth, 1980; Higbee et al., 2010). The K-12 team support system and the federal policies that inform them can create a state of systemic dependency for the student. This leaves them unprepared to advocate for themselves upon entering higher educational contexts.

Fiedler and colleagues (2007) found the ability to self-advocate is essential to the academic success of students with disabilities, but many students are leaving the K-12 system woefully unprepared. It is not enough for K-12 teachers to inspire student self-advocacy (Fiedler & Danneker, 2007); we found that it is equally important that university disability service administrators do the same for students with disabilities. Prior to interviewing students about what factors influence their academic success, we were not aware of the integral role disability service administrators play in students' academic success. As the number of students with disabilities in postsecondary education rises, disability services administrators are required to adapt as new needs emerge. Thus, it is imperative that college administrators be equipped with the tools and strategies necessary to help these students find their voice.

In the K-12 system the voices of parents, educators, and administrators often outweigh the voice of the individual student (Cooper, 2012). Thus, when the student arrives at a postsecondary institution the accommodations that were necessary in K-12 now become a *choice*. The administrators in our study found that it was crucial to move their own thought process from one of providing accommodations to engaging students with disabilities and empowering them to succeed. Facilitating meetings with faculty members, on-campus service providers, and outside agencies were among the many tools they used to empower each student to acquire knowledge and become engaged in the process of their own individual success. Studies show supports are crucial for students with disabilities to be able to finish school, become employed, and gain economic independence (Gliedman & Roth, 1980; Harry, Kalyanpur, & Day 1999; Heiman, 2002; NCLD, 2013; US Department of Education National Longitudinal Transitional Study 2 [NLTS2], 2005). Our larger study found that disability services administrators are most often the initial resource that students would go to for assistance (Tevis & Griffen, 2014). However, we also found that these administrators act as the liaison between the student and the faculty, other administrative personnel, and the institution itself. Disability services administrators thereby have the power to shape the culture of the institution and the climate of the atmosphere to foster an environment of inclusion and support. Therefore, we offer a few recommendations and implications for policy and practice. Although Brown and Broido (2015) found that disability services offices are contextual to each institution, there are strategies that all disability services administrators can consider regardless of the site. Hence, our focus is on how disability services administrators facilitate academic success for students with disabilities and build on the strengths of each individual student, to empower them to become self-advocates.

Implications for Students and Families, Practitioners, and Policymakers

We found that in order to develop effective practices, students with disabilities must first be made aware of their two-dimensional transition to college process. Though the number of these students transitioning from secondary to postsecondary is increasing, many of them are unaware that the responsibility for seeking and obtaining services shifts from their many K-12 constituents to their individual shoulders. To transition to and persist through college, students with disabilities must take the initial step in facilitating a partnership with disability services administrators who provide support and services. These students may lack some of the knowledge necessary to assume responsibility for their own education due to a fostered dependent state of mind. Thus, they may lack the ability to be their own advocate. The disability services administrators we interviewed expressed that it is now up to them to thwart systemic dependency by providing self-advocacy skill development through their support services for students with disabilities. For example, ADA requires organizations to provide reasonable accommodations for students with disabilities, but the advocating for one's self and developing collaborative partnerships with postsecondary administrators is not a consequence of this federal mandate. Because disability services administrators are aware of the needs of their student body, they are the ones who can shape and mold the institutional climate and foster academic success for each student.

Implications for Practitioners

By practitioner, we mean all who are actively involved in the Individual Education Plan (IEP) of K-12 students, and we include higher education disability services administrators in this definition. Our research highlights the obvious and impactful disconnect between secondary and postsecondary systems when working with students with disabilities. When partnerships are developed between educational systems, disenfranchised students and families are better supported (Epstein et. al, 2002; NLTS 2, 2005). Thus, we contend that if the siloed efforts of these systems unite for the purpose of assuaging some of the challenges faced by students with disabilities, then navigating this two-dimensional transition process becomes less complex.

In our study, we found that the parental role of the disability services administrators was key to creating partnerships with students in successfully supporting their transition to college. Virginia and Cy collaborated and partnered with faculty and other university personnel, state prisons, and the local community. By expanding their partnership-network to include the appropriate K-12 administrators, disability services administrators can create a pipeline to institutions of higher education for this population and provide the opportunity for students to develop self-advocacy skills well before college. Thus, we recommend the following concrete strategies:

- Disability services administrators receive professional training to understand how to reach out, partner with, and collaborate with secondary support personnel (e.g., school counselors, administrators).
- Disability services administrators should collaborate with K-12 districts to hold professional development workshops for practitioners.
- Disability services administrators should develop partnerships with secondary school counselors to identify and arrange family and student information nights while students are still in high school.
- Disability services administrators need to be a visible and integral part of high school recruitment events, university-wide events, and orientation activities. Office contact information needs to be located on the front page of the university website.
- Disability services administrators should reach out to local community service agencies to hold information sessions.

In these environments disability services administrators could meet with students with disabilities and their families to empower them with the knowledge they need to succeed in higher education. This would be a stepping stone to self-advocacy for the student. It would bridge the college knowledge gap experienced by students with disabilities and the K-12 educators who serve them. Creating understanding by bridging the metaphorical systemic divides could begin to increase postsecondary access rates for this group of students. Understanding the challenges faced by secondary school counselors will assist university administrators in determining how to best transition students from secondary to postsecondary education.

Implications for Students and Families

K–12 educators should act as a guide to help students and families understand the changes to regulations and impacts once their child transitions to higher education. To counter systematic dependency families should assist their student in building skills for self-advocacy by including them in decisions regarding their K–12 education. Thus, we recommend:

- Families should begin college visits in middle school to understand how and where to navigate for services. Collecting contact information and building a *college knowledge* reference binder can help ease transition. Thus, even if the student desires to leave the label of disabled behind once they transition to college, they will still have the knowledge of who to seek out if they require services. Virginia told us that she encourages families to "contact her directly" during campus visits (Virginia, personal communication, August, 2013).
- Families and students should work with the appropriate high school personnel (e.g., counselors, transition specialists) beginning in 9th grade to construct a plan to college that includes the skills and competencies required for self-advocacy. This should become part of each individual student's transition plan.
- K–12 educators should receive professional development to assist with developing skills to reach out to engage families as partners.

Engaging families and students as partners in the process can build capacity for educators and empowers each stakeholder. This step is necessary for students with disabilities to obtain the skills needed to function as a self-advocate and assume the adult roles that were once filled by multiple stakeholders in K–12 settings. Finally, taking action can help families to reframe how they view the abilities of their student. Instead of focusing on what their student cannot do, these strategies will help families understand how their child can survive and thrive in higher education.

Implications for Policy

Current educational policy seems to be developed in a vacuum: established without taking into consideration the multiple stakeholders who are obligated to implement the policy, and those for whom the policy was developed. As the federal Reach Higher Initiative (for more information at https://

www.whitehouse.gov/reach-higher) contends, all students are to graduate high school college/career ready, we ask, *How are students with disabilities included, as well as the administrators who must support them?* Educators need help understanding, within in their respective context and role, what it means to be *ready*, and in the absence of a secondary-postsecondary partnership, also restricted by federal mandates, how to facilitate this. Such clarification would frame how to support students according to their abilities and needs, allowing both K-12 and higher education administrators to better guide students' transition to college, and encourage key partnerships to ensure students' academic success.

The Reach Higher Initiative also expresses a societal need for an increase in postsecondary certificates, which dismisses the limitations of current policy that only obligates secondary systems to "identify students within their jurisdiction who have a disability and who may be entitled to services" (The US Department of Education Office for Civil Rights [OCR], 2011, p. 5). Federal initiatives seem to hold institutions of higher education responsible for increasing degree attainment rates, while at the same time restricting outreach from the institution to the student. How then can disability services administrators, as well as the college/university community, fulfill and support the students who need them, and uphold the federal policies that are in place? While the ADAA of 2008 (American with Disabilities Act Action Network, 2015) clarified who is considered to have a disability, it did not address the gap caused by FERPA legislation restricting how an institution can identify those who require accommodations in order to persist to postsecondary degree attainment. Contrary to the K-12 environment, which is obliged to adhere to the letter of the law, the postsecondary environment is contextual to the institution and individuality of the students it serves. Thus, disability services administrators must play an active role in the development of policies and federal mandates that hold them responsible for meeting the need of the greater good. Moreover, it is imperative that all stakeholders charged by federal and state mandates to serve students with disabilities be part of these federal policy developments. By doing so, all educators are given the opportunity to specifically develop a pipeline for students with disabilities to and through college to career establishment.

Federal initiatives strive to open the postsecondary pipeline to a broader pool of students from underserved communities. However, focus on students with disabilities is mostly absent from the college access conversation. This chapter has a significant purpose, as it elucidates the ways higher education disability services administrators can support students with disabilities to succeed. As we desire postsecondary institutions to be more inclusive, and federal mandates call for a more educated society, we will need to reconceptualize the ways in which we think about the traditional forms of diversity. We must reframe the extent to which we create collaborative partnerships outside of our institutions to be inclusive of all of the students we serve in order to support their transition to and persistence through college. Implementing innovative strategies to close this diversity disconnect will help all stakeholders move the institutional iceberg.

References

Americans with Disabilities Act National Network (2015). What is the definition of a disability? Retrieved from https://adata.org/faq/what-definition-disability-under-ada

Brown, K., & Broido, E. M. (2015). Engaging students with disabilities. In S. J. Quaye & S. R. Harper (Eds.), Student Engagement in Higher Education: Theoretical Perspectives and Practical Approaches for Diverse Populations, *Journal of College Student Development, 56*(3), 187–203.

Cooper, L. M. (2012). *Disability as diversity: Assessing the perceptions of students with physical disabilities regarding access and equal opportunity in postsecondary education.* (Doctoral dissertation). Retrieved from http://media.proquest.com/media/pq/classic/doc/2629237701/fmt/ai/rep/NPDF?_s=tYELQ%2F%2BlXSMCYfRrn5NNZXJNEQ8%3D.

Eckes, S. E., & Ochoa, T. A. (2005). Students with disabilities: Transitioning from high school to higher education, *American Secondary Education, 33*(3), 6–20.

Epstein, J. L., Sanders, M. G., Simon, B. S., Salinas, K. C., Jansorn, N. R., & Van Voorhis, F. L. (2002). *School, family, and community partnerships: Your handbook for action* (2nd ed.). Thousand Oaks, CA: Corwin Press.

Field, S., Martin, J., Miller, R., Ward, M., & Wehmeyer, M. (1998). Self-Determination for Persons With Disabilities: A Position Statement of my Division on Career Development and Transition. *Career Development for Exceptional Individuals, 21*(2), 113–128.

Fiedler, C. R., & Danneker, J. E. (2007). Self-advocacy instruction: Bridging the research-to-practice gap. *Focus on Exceptional Children, 39*(8), 1.

Fitchen, C. S., Goodrick, G., Tagalakis, V., Amsel, R., & Libman, E. (1990). Getting along on college: Recommendations for college participants with disabilities and their profession. *Rehabilitation Counseling Bulletin, 34*, 103–125.

Getzel, E. E., & Thoma, C. A. (2008). Experiences of college students with disabilities and the importance of self-determination in higher education settings. *Career Development for Exceptional Individuals, 31*(3), 77–84.

Gliedman, J., & Roth, W. (1980). *The unexpected minority: Handicapped children in America.* New York, NY: Harcourt Brace Jovanovich.

Harry, B., Kalyanpur, M., & Day, M. (1999). *Building cultural reciprocity with families: Case studies in special education.* Baltimore, MD: Paul H. Brooks.

Heiman, T. (2002). Parents of children with disabilities: Resilience, coping, and future expectations. *Journal of developmental and physical disabilities, 14*(2), 159–171.

Higbee, J., Katz, R. E., & Schultz, J. L. (2010). Disability in higher education: Redefining mainstreaming. *Journal of Diversity Management, 5*(2), 7–16.

National Center for Learning Disabilities. (2013). *Diplomas at risk: A critical look at the graduation rate of students with learning disabilities.* Retrieved from http://www.ncld.org/images/content/files/diplomas-at-risk/DiplomasatRisk.pdf?goback=.gmp_1916332.gde_1916332_member_242202183.

Paul, S. (2000). Students with disabilities in higher education: A review of the literature. *College Student Journal, 34*(2), 200–212.

Quaye, S. J., & Harper, S. R. (2015). *Student engagement in higher education: Theoretical perspectives and practical approaches for diverse populations.* New York, NY: Routledge.

Steinmetz, E. (2006). *Americans with disabilities: 2002.* Retrieved from http://www.census.gov/prod/2006pubs/p70-107.pdf.

Test, D. W., Fowler, C. H., Wood, W. M., Brewer, D. M., & Eddy, S. (2005). A conceptual framework of self-advocacy for students with disabilities. *Remedial and Special Education, 26*(1), 43–54.

The US Department of Education Office for Civil Rights. (2011). *Transition of students with disabilities to postsecondary education: A guide for school educators.* Retrieved from http://www2.ed.gov/about/offices/list/ocr/transitionguide.html.

The US Department of Education. (2005). *National longitudinal transitional study 2: Family involvement in the educational development of youth with disabilities.* Retrieved from http://www.nlts2.org/reports/2005_03/nlts2_report_2005_03_complete.pdf.

The US Department of Education Office of Special Needs and Rehabilitative Services. (2006). *Tool kit on teaching and assessing students with disabilities.* Retrieved from http://www2.ed.gov/admins/lead/speced/toolkit/index.html.

Tevis, T., & Griffen, J. (2014). Absent voices: Intersectionality and college students with physical disabilities. *Journal of Progressive Policy and Practice, 2*(3), 239–254.

Texas Guaranteed Student Loan Corporation. (1999). Retrieved from http://www.lib.utexas.edu/taro/tslac/30136/tsl-30136.html.

Tinto, V. (1975). Dropouts from higher education: A theoretical synthesis of recent literature. *A Review of Educational Research, 45,* 89–125.

Tinto, V. (1993). *Leaving college: Rethinking the causes and cures of student attrition.* (2nd ed.). Chicago, IL: University of Chicago Press.

United States Equal Employment Opportunity Commission. (2015). Americans with Disabilities Act Amendments Act of 2008. Retrieved from http://www.eeoc.gov/laws/statutes/adaaa_info.cfm.

Vargas, J. H. (2004). *College knowledge: Addressing information barriers to college.* Boston, MA: College Access Services: The Education Resources Institute (TERI).

Yin, R. K. (2016). *Qualitative research from start to finish* (2nd ed.). New York, NY: Guilford Press.

PART IV

Institutional Programs and Initiatives

12

DISABILITY, DIVERSITY, AND HIGHER EDUCATION

A Critical Study of California State University's Websites

Susan L. Gabel, Denise P. Reid, and Holly Pearson

This chapter is based on a study we conducted in 2012–2014 in which we asked how disability is constituted on the 23 California State University websites and whether disability is associated with diversity (Gabel, Reid, Pearson, Ruiz, & Hume-Dawson, 2015). The study's five team members were diverse based on disability identities and racial/ethnic backgrounds and had varying experiences with their identities in institutions of higher education (IHE). Throughout the study, and now as we write this chapter, we acknowledge our personal stakes in the constitution of disability on IHE websites. For example, the first author is a mother of two adults with intellectual disabilities. She is also a scholar with a hearing impairment who does research on disability in higher education. The second author was diagnosed with a visual impairment as an adolescent and has vivid memories of struggling to obtain information from college brochures in the early 1980s. When she applied to graduate school in the early 2000s, admission information was located on university web pages. She vividly remembers her experience navigating university websites. The third author identifies as a hard-of-hearing Korean adoptee female who spent most of her life navigating and negotiating the spectrum of racial and disability diversity in education institutions, in particular in higher education.

In this chapter we highlight the significance of utilizing mixed methods, including a critical discourse framework and what we call a snapshot click analysis, and provide evidence of the constitution of disability on institutional websites. We discuss the (dis)connection of disability with diversity within the context of the California State University (CSU) web pages; provide a summary of our theoretical framework and findings; discuss the relevance of our approach; and conclude with recommendations for research, practice, and policy in higher education.

As disability studies scholars, we recognize the multiple conceptualizations of disability (e.g., medical model, social model, disability rights model). In this chapter, we intentionally use "disabled students" identified as students who have been disabled by institutional barriers (e.g., inaccessible buildings, programs, housing, employment, education) rather than indicating that the disability is innate (Barnes & Mercer, 2008, Oliver, 1990; Titchkosky, 2001).

Context of Our Study

Our research team started with informal conversations about whether and how universities in the State of California associate disability with diversity. Considering diversity from a statistical lens, the U.S. Department of Education (U.S. DOE) indicates that African-American students make up 12% to 14% of the student population who are enrolled in 4-year institutions of higher education (IHE), and Hispanics students make up 9% to 13% of the student population in 4-year IHEs (U.S. DOE, 2013b). Similarly the U.S. DOE (2013b) notes that students who self-identify as disabled make up about 11% of the student body within postsecondary education (U.S. DOE, 2013b). Given that disability is present within all racial, ethnic, and cultural categories, it would follow that IHEs would recruit disabled students to the same extent that they do students from underrepresented racial/ethnic backgrounds (Government Accountability Office, 2009; Ralph & Boxall, 2005; Raue & Lewis, 2011). Yet, as Boyer et al. (2006) have observed, there is a glaring absence of visibly disabled people on IHE websites, raising the question of why disability is invisible and when it is visibly represented, what messages about disability are conveyed to prospective and current students.

We recognize that the dominant view of disability holds that it is an individual deficit rather than a difference that is associated with diversity. This is reflected in the educational practice of requiring disabled students to disclose and provide evidence of their diagnosis to Offices of Disability Services (ODS) in order to receive accommodations provided under the American with Disabilities Act (ADA) (Hunter, Reid, & Nishimura, 2014). In contrast, our approach uses a social model lens that allows us to examine how institutional structures constitute disability (Barnes & Mercer, 2005, Gabel, 2005; Low, 1996; Prowse, 2009).

Our unit of analysis is a state IHE located on multiple campuses and represented by the websites for each campus. We chose the California State University (CSU) system because it is one of the largest university systems in the country (Gerth, 2010). Comprised of 23 campuses located throughout California, CSU has over 325,000 students enrolled within its systems (Piland, 2004). The CSU system has been described as "The People's University" that "provokes the spark of human potential in all of the citizenry" (Gerth, 2010, p. xvii). Gerth (2010) describes students attending CSU as "coming to a campus of the CSU and being able to become whoever they want, engage however they want, and learn whatever they want—regardless [of] their race, creed, or economic background" (p. 309).

In the effort to achieve a diverse student body, the CSU actively recruits specific demographics. For example, the annual Super Sunday is a "day [Chancellor Reed], campus presidents, trustees and others ... speak in predominately Black churches in the major metropolitan areas of the state" (Gerth, 2010, p. 322).

Initially, we were interested in the association of disability with diversity in the CSU as an institution, but we realized that first we had to determine how disability is constituted within the CSU, and to answer that we chose to start with the campus websites. So, our research question became "How is disability constituted on CSU websites and how is it associated with diversity?" Universities use their websites to actively recruit prospective students by providing information about the institution, academic programs, student activities, student affairs, and residential life (Pippert, Essenburg, & Matchett, 2013). The university website, particularly the home page, is considered the "virtual face" of the university (Meyer, 2008; Wilson & Meyer, 2009; Tripp, 2008). Therefore, university websites are not merely a tool of recruitment, but they also serve as a way to communicate institutional mission to the general public. This purpose of websites raises questions about the categories or identities that comprise diversity on the website, whether or not the institution is marketing to potential disabled students, and in what way disability is constituted on the website.

Theoretical Framework

Our theoretical framework draws on discourse theory and institutional theory. Website content is a form of institutional discourse that has material effects (Foucault, 1973, 1980a, 1982). A major contributor to discourse theory was Foucault's (1973, 1980a, 1982) work on how discourses construct economic, political, social, and historical implications that influence lived experiences. In other words, discourse produces conditions that affect people's choices and experiences. While discourses occurs within multiple forms such as textual, visual, and enactment, it is important to recognize that the absence or presence both shapes meaning of one's lived experiences. One feature of discourse is containment, or the silencing of voices lacking value (Senzani, 2010). Containment is protective. It insulates the speaker, or in our case the institution, from problematic events or outcomes. For example, with disabled people, the use of language such as "special needs," being "challenged," or requiring "learning support" upholds the legitimacy of who can speak and under what circumstances, while concealing the discourse of deficits, abnormality, and exclusion (Gabel & Miskovic, 2014). By interpreting discourse as political, discourse theory is a useful tool which provides an opportunity to consider the role of institutional websites in the construction of disability in higher education.

We use institutional theory from Clemens and Cook (1999) and Phillips, Lawrence, and Hardy (2004), who argue that the institution is constituted through discourse or "the collection of texts that exist in a ... field and that produce social categories that shape the understandings and behaviors of actors" (Phillips et al., 2004, p. 638). For example, prospective students use the IHE web pages to make informed decisions on where to apply for admission (Pippert et al., 2013; Wilson & Meyer, 2009). Therefore, the web page's presence and absence of textual and visual content associated with disabled students could be instrumental in the student's decision to apply. This reflects the need to consider how the university markets its "virtual face" to its potential users. Institutional theory enables a means to consider how certain discourses are perpetuated and taken for granted in the representation of disability in IHE's web pages.

Analytic Strategies

We used analytic strategies from previous studies of website content. Following advice from Ha and James (1998) and Boyer et al. (2006), our initial unit of analysis was the home page of each CSU website but the home pages revealed minimal disability content. Therefore, we incorporated a second analysis stage that involved counting the number of clicks to obtain disability content. This "snapshot click" approach (Pauwels, 2012) refers to the collection of information at one point in time, the snapshot, and the counting of the number of clicks from the home page to disability content. According to Meyer and Wilson (2010), any content that can be attained within one to three clicks is considered to be satisfactory, therefore we used this parameter. Drawing from Astroff (2001) and Meyer and Wilson (2010), we categorized disability content as "found," which was content found in less than four clicks, and "not found," which was content not found in four or more clicks. In addition to the snapshot click approach, we also discussed which terms would be accepted as disability content and eventually decided that the words "disability" and "access" would be acceptable. The term "disability" enabled a more reliable search term compared to "access." However, the term "access" was used due to the strong association disability has with the American with Disabilities Act (ADA) and Sections 504 and 508 of the Rehabilitation Act of 1973. We tried to search for disability content with the search term "diversity," but we had minimal success.

When the snapshot click analysis phase of the project was completed we turned to the critical discourse analysis phase. During each research team meeting in this phase we started discussing our individual impressions or observations of assigned CSU web pages, with all 23 being observed at the completion of our data collection. Next we scrutinized the websites for topics or features related to disability content. The findings were grouped into the following four categories: (1) type of presence, (2) category associations, (3) descriptors, and (4) access. Categories 1–3 were identified by Pauwels (2012) as important; category 4 was identified by us as important due to its association with the ADA. Type of presence referred to the spatial location of the content on the actual web page. Category associations reflected the constructs or institutional units with which disability was affiliated (e.g., academic affairs, student services, diversity).

Descriptors (both visual and textual) presented insight into the words and phrases used to communicate meanings about disability (e.g., accommodation, accessibility, technology, compliance, policy, etc.).

Category 4, "access," referred to whether the website indicated it was accessible and if so, how. As a team, we navigated each site considering how accessible the websites were for Denise, the second author, as well as how they appeared to sighted team members (e.g., font size, color combinations, amount of text). We counted the number of clicks it took to reach related disability content and delineated the navigation structures that allowed us to arrive at disability content. During this process, we considered what it would be like for a prospective or current student to navigate the website. This raised the questions about the intended audience for the page and the focus of the content on each page. Furthermore, we noted the dominant disability discourse used on the page (e.g., medical, social, disability rights). For example, we considered whether the discourse "focused on the individual and individual problem solving or did the discourse view disability socially, as constituted by social structures, and perhaps as related to other categories of difference? Or did the discourse emphasize rights, policies, legislations?" (Gabel et al., 2015, p. 8). In order to locate patterns across all institutions, the first author converted the collective data into a table and double-checked the data to ensure accuracy of the screen captures of each website that was analyzed. In the remaining section of this chapter, we address what we found before moving into discussions, conclusions, and implications.

What We Found: Snapshot Click Analysis

The snapshot click analysis allowed us to determine whether or not disability content could be found on the website and to what degree finding it would be effective or efficient for the user. Our snapshot click analysis revealed that disability content was found in less than four clicks from the home page on two-thirds of the CSU websites, while one-third of the CSU websites included disability content on the home page. One institution, San Diego State University (SDSU), had no clickable disability content in two separate snapshot studies. On the SDSU home page we had to use the search term "disability" to locate disability content. This was the only CSU website that required such a search.

In addition to the number of clicks to disability content, we found an inconsistency in navigation structures, or the ways in which a user could search the website to find disability content. While one-third of the CSU websites had disability content readily accessible, six sites allowed multiple navigation strategies for accessing the same disability content, a feature that could allow the user greater likelihood of finding content. Furthermore, the websites used various navigational terms to link to disability content. Four CSU websites provided a link to disability content, labeled "A-Z index." On one site, a "student services" link navigated to disability content, while on another site "quick links" was used. Two sites used the term "campus life."

The numerous ways of accessing the information were frustrating for us as users and, to complicate matters, during the year of data collection the websites and their contents changed. For example, in the first snapshot CSU Long Beach initially had disability content on the home page, but in the second snapshot, four clicks were required to locate the content. Similarly, while Sonoma State's home page had information about the Disability Awareness in the first snapshot, one month later, one click was required to retrieve the information that had been moved. The numerous ways of accessing disability content and the changes within the content on the home pages caused us to wonder about the experiences of prospective or current students who interact with these web pages.

What We Found: Discourse Analysis

While the snapshot analysis approach presented intriguing insights, the approach had its limits. It allowed us to determine whether and how disability content could be found. It suggested whether or not the institution contained disability by making it difficult to find or invisible. However, it did not yield insight into the CSU websites' constitution of disability and its association with diversity. Thus, we used critical discourse analysis.

Category Association

Ninety-one percent of the CSU websites associated disability with student services. The association between disabilities and student services conveys a sense of a unit that provides support or service to students. In contrast, San Luis Obispo and Maritime housed disability within academic affairs. With San Luis Obispo website, the disability content easily accessed once the user clicked on "academic support," which presented a link to the "Disability Resource Center." Furthermore, the disability content was located by clicking on "current students" and "enhance my studies." Similarly, Maritime listed the "Office of Disability Services" within "Academic Resources." The association between disability content and academic affairs may suggest a perception of disability that stand in contrast with its association with student affairs. For example, "Enhance my studies" conveys a sense that disability support is part of the academic success rather than an accommodation or extracurricular service. Additionally, "Enhance my studies," suggest a sense of ownership in one's academic success. On the other hand, association with student services could broaden the sense of disability support, since student services also encompass extracurricular student life.

Descriptors

We identified 57 descriptors associated with disability and through discussion categorized the descriptors into three types of discourse: disability rights (language of ADA and legal rights), medical model (language of disability as a deficit within an individual), and miscellaneous (terms that could not be categorized). Terms that could be categorized as social model discourse were not found. For example, all websites used people-first language. The most common descriptors were "access/accessibility," "accommodations," "assistive technology," "resources," and "equality/equity." These terms were used by those who provide disability services or supports, or were found within mission statements, policies, and procedures referring to disability support. After grouping the 57 descriptors into types of discourse, it was clear that majority of the language used about disability was based on the disability rights model. This surprised us because we assumed the dominant discourse would be the medical model.

Diversity

CSU Fresno stood out as a model for providing easily found disability content that explicitly articulates the importance of disability access. CSU Fresno's home page was the only site that used the descriptor "diversity" in association with disability. The accessibility link at the bottom of the Fresno home page led to a page presenting Fresno's mission statement on accessibility. The statement includes: " . . . We also provide the leadership and structure for the campus to engage in assessment on issues of equity, inclusion, and diversity . . . " (CSU Fresno State, 2014, para. 1). The "Accessibility" web page also presented links to campus accommodations; "reports an access barrier" option; and information about the CSU President's committee on Disabilities and the Accessible Technology Initiative. Another feature that stood out was the spatial locality of the information on accessibility. All the links were posited on the accessibility page at eye level in medium readable sized font rather than being positioned on other pages, at the bottom of the page, or in small font. Between the easy access to the information, the language of the mission statement, and the spatial location of the information on the web page, the website conveyed a perception of the institution's approach to accessibility as a campus wide issue.

Visual Content

While textual information about disability was available on all but one CSU website, each website used different visual images. Visual images of diversity on campus are a tool for recruiting diverse prospective students. Ralph and Boxall (2005) observe that an absence of a particular population (e.g., disabled students, racial/ethnic minority students, or female students) may result in a missed opportunity to recruit prospective diverse students along with "missing out on the diversity and valuable contributions of an important group" (p. 371).

We examined the visual images on the websites (e.g., symbols, photos, illustrations, streaming videos) and noted a variety of visual images that reflected gender by race, age, and in one case, an image of a Muslim woman wearing a hijab suggesting religious diversity. Similar to Boyer et al.'s (2006) study, we found no images that represented visible disability (e.g., a white cane, a wheelchair user, a person wearing hearing aids, a person using crutches, etc.). While many disabled people may not appear disabled to others, the virtual lack of any signs of disabled people on campus is problematic.

Two campuses, CSU Channel Islands and CSU San Jose, portrayed images that reflected an association between diversity and disability. The Channel Island's disability support unit website had an image of seven multiethnic students who were located in front of a banner that depict "Dimensionally Able." Among the students, there was no clear indicator of disability, thus the viewer could assume the students may be invisibly disabled. Similarly, at San Jose's Accessible Education Center page, there was an image of a male and female student that did not physically indicate whether or not they were disabled. In the image, there was a text that stated, "I am empowered by my dis/ability." From the text, it could be assumed that this is a reference to disability.

Discussion

Methodologically, we made some useful and effective decisions. First, using the combination of critical discourse analysis and a snapshot click approach enabled us to present a multilayered understanding of how university home pages and websites could impact prospective and current student users. The snapshot click analysis provided insight into the user's experience. The number of clicks is a means of measuring satisfactory navigation. For example, Astroff (2001) and Meyer and Wilson (2010) noted that easily accessible information could be located within a timely manner. With CSU websites, the lack of a consistent way of finding disability content could be frustrating to users who are navigating multiple sites in an effort to learn about disability services prior to submitting an application or trying to locate information about disability support services. As a team, we experienced various degrees of frustration in locating disability content. After several trials of locating disability content, we became more aware of the different ways of finding the information. However, how often do users, especially prospective disabled students, search through a number of websites in a short time, or within a single website? In the course of data collection website content and home page layout changed. These changes could impact the user's ability to reliably relocate disability content in a satisfactory amount of time.

Second, using the snapshot approach of capturing still images of the website content enabled us to critically reexamine and reframe the disability content, which illuminated the significant functions of home pages. This approach allowed the researchers to analyze the websites at both an individual pace and collectively as a group. Each team member contributed his or her insights shaped by personal experiences with disability and race or ethnicity while also collectively learning from others as we worked toward a general consensus of the findings.

For example, the second author, Denise talked about how, as an African-American female, she had no options to pass as anything. During her early and middle childhood, Denise grew up in a predominantly African-American neighborhood. Her mother used the local public library as a refuge from the the slow and steady rise in crime. Denise became keenly aware that her identity as an African American who loved to learn would have to skillfully negotiate her identity as the African-American girl who knew the latest dance moves and hairstyles and the African-American who loved to read and learn because it was not a valued trait for those with whom she associated with in her community. Similarly, being diagnosed in her teenage years with a rare form of macular degeneration, she made a conscious decision not to use any social markers associated with visual impairments and/or blindness (i.e., white cane or guide dog), so she had the option to decide when and to whom to disclose or not to disclose. However, during her doctoral studies, Denise realized her experiences as an African-American female with a visual impairment was the topic of significant research. Through her research, she learned how to conceptualize the intersections of her race and disability and how both impacted her life and educational journey.

The third author, Holly, also had comparable experiences where she had the option to disclose or not to disclose due to the invisible nature of her disability. Growing up, she had exposure to a wide array of individuals who were deaf, hard of hearing, hearing, and those who could sign or communicate by oral means. As a result, Holly grew up using oral communication and American Sign Language, which meant she also learned early on how to adjust depending on who she was interacting with. At the same time, growing up as a Korean adoptee in a predominately White community meant she had little exposure to the implications of her Asian female physical appearance, which resulted in her having to catch up with "how to talk race" during her college years. Together, her racial physical appearance and her disability exposure enabled her to be able to navigate and, in a way, manipulate, the racial and disability landscape whether it's to pass being Asian-American female, Korean adoptee, deaf, hard of hearing, or hearing for the moment.

Disability discourse has material effects. For example, as a result of the categorization of descriptors, it became evident that the CSU website discourse of disability was the rights-based model of disability. Eighty-eight percent of the CSU websites associated disability with student services and terms associated with the ADA and Section 508 of the Rehabilitation Act, such as "access," "accommodations," and "assistive technology." To receive accommodations or assistive technology, a disabled student must self-disclose, provide medical verification of a private diagnosis, and be comfortable sharing an accommodation letter with instructors. Nationwide, 10.9% of postsecondary education students are disabled (U.S. DOE, 2013b), yet less than 1% of students in California's 4-year IHEs self-disclosed (California Postsecondary Education Commission, 2009). Gabel and Miskovic (2014) and Miskovic and Gabel (2012) also observed a similar stark discrepancy between the U.S. DOE data and the IHE data at a Midwestern institution, where less than 1% of students self-disclosed. Furthermore, Reid (2014) revealed that 79% of her participants did not disclose their disability, thereby opting out disability support services. The discrepancy in the number of disabled students enrolled nationwide and those who self-disclose in California CSUs reflects the need to reconsider the CSU home pages and websites. After all, they symbolize the "virtual face" of the university" (Meyer, 2008; Wilson & Meyer, 2009; Tripp, 2008). Spatially locating disability content "behind" a number of other requiring the user to click several times and navigate different pathways served to contain disability. In fact, 12% of the CSU websites had no disability content in less than four clicks. We interpreted the location of disability behind walls as a means of "insulat[ing] the [institution] from something disvalued or dangerous" (Irvine, 2011, p. 26). Difficult to find disability content could perpetuate the notion that disability should be invisible and marginal.

Several studies show that if web pages contain inactive or absent links, absence of content, or poor instinctual navigation skills, then the user may cease interacting with the website and look elsewhere (Abanumy, Al-Badi, & Mayhew, 2005; Baker, 2009; Wilson & Meyer, 2009). Throughout our study, user-friendliness emerged as a key issue and as a visually impaired scholar, Denise provided valuable insights. She described the most accessible font size, color contrast, and content organization. For example, she identified the home page of CSU Monterey Bay as inaccessible due to a dark background and font color. Waving the cursor over the page resulted in a fading of font color and background, which hindered her ability to navigate home page content. However, Denise noted that all the CSU system home pages were compatible with the adaptive software that she used. This reflects the need to acknowledge that it is not merely about the location of the disability content on the home page and website, but also it is user-accessible across all disabilities.

We took the standpoint that visual images are non-textual discursive constructions that can suggest the importance or relevance of disability within the IHE. Disability content can be found easily on 66% of CSU websites yet there are no visual representations of disability on any of the CSU websites. This should be surprising since statistically, African-American students, Hispanic students, and disabled students enroll at the CSU in roughly the same percentages (US DOE 2013a, 2013b). The absent visual and textual presence of disabled students on home pages and websites could have material consequences, as prospective disabled students may opt to not enroll at an institution (Boyer, Bruner, Charles, & Coleman, 2006). Increasing the visibility of the representation of disability could be not necessarily seen as a form of greater equality within diversity (Archer, 2007). However, it could be interpreted as disability being welcomed on campus the same way as the representations of racial, gender, or age diversity are used within the recruitment process.

Framing website content (e.g., text, navigation structures, visuals, categories) as a form of institutional discourse illuminates the significance of IHE websites. Symbolically, the home page is a door into the institution (i.e., home page) that reveals a map (i.e., links, navigation routes) leading the user to the institution's philosophy and approach (Meyer, 2008). Navigating a home page and website requires the ability to read between the lines textually, visually, spatially, and linguistically, and to interpret meaning through the act of physically navigating the site.

Conclusion and Recommendations

Our approach reveals the multiple ways in which websites are not neutral spaces. As digital spaces, home pages and websites can be locations wherein disability is constituted and contained (Olssen et al., 2006) through navigation strategies, management of information, and use of words and images (or absence of words and images). Containing disability within the landscape of accessibility, disability services, student services, and accommodations perpetuates the notion that disability is an innate characteristic that needs to be fixed on an individual basis. Furthermore, because it is something that needs to be fixed, this conveys a sense that disability is problematic or challenging, creating a need to minimize its impact or contain it. The individualization of disability suggests that there is no need for the broader university community to problematize and reexamine structural barriers that disabled students encounter. Segregating disability from diversity and other social differences reinforces and maintains the (dis)connect between disability and diversity.

Neither are home pages and websites static, which suggests possibilities in shifting toward constituting disability as diversity. Thus, we have recommendations stemming from working collectively in this research process. There is a need to increase the visibility of disability, along with being more transparent about the navigation and links to disability content. Web designers need to be conscious of the accessibility features of websites: font color and size, page color(s), dark/light contrasts, and location of content. The ease of use for sighted users is also something to consider. We found the lack of consistency and intuitiveness for locating disability content frustrating. Designing home pages and websites for users with a diverse array of abilities can increase the likelihood that prospective students feel welcome and can help them make informed decisions about which institutions would be best suited for them.

The representation of disability on IHE websites should be visible and multifaceted. It is important to include an array of visible representations of disability. It is true that disabled people often do not appear to be disabled, because their disability is hidden. Furthermore, some disabled students self-identify while others do not. This range should be reflected in institutional discourse. Location matters, too. Rather than situating disability within particular units, such as student affairs, or as associated with specific constructs, such as accessibility, it should be noted that disability is part of diversity. This could be as simple as reporting about disability related activities on the diversity web pages or holding disability awareness events hosted by the diversity office. We view the above strategies as recruitment strategies aimed at potential applicants.

There is a need to connect disability with diversity that enables the institution to acknowledge disability within the sociopolitical context of social differences. For example, the Association for Higher Education and Disability (AHEAD) defines diversity as "encompassing the variety of qualities, traits and characteristics that are inherent to humans, with a focus on the worldviews, communication styles, and unique ways of 'thinking, being, and doing' of individuals within our institutions and the communities we serve" (AHEAD, 2014, Sec. 2). This definition positions disability as a socio-political category aligned with other forms of diversity (e.g., race, gender, sexual orientation, religious affiliation) rather than an individual deficit requiring accommodations. However, in addition to the recommendations suggested, it is important to recognize that websites are only a piece of the bigger picture. To implement deeper community based social changes would involve changes across the many levels of the institution.

References

Abanumy, A., Al-Badi, A., & Mayhew, P. (2005). e-Government website accessibility: In-depth evaluation of Saudi Arabia and Oman. *Electronic: Journal of E-Government, 3*, 99–106.

AHEAD. (2014). *AHEAD's definition of diversity: Diversity initiative.* Retrieved from https://www.ahead.org/about/diversity#def.

Archer, L. (2007). Diversity, equality and higher education: A critical reflection on the ab/uses of equity discourse within widening participation. *Teaching in Higher Education, 12*, 635–653.

Astroff, R. (2001). Searching for the library: University home page design and missing links. *Information Technology and Libraries, 20*, 93–99.

Baker, D. L. (2009). Advancing e-government performance in the United States through enhanced usability benchmarks. *Government Information Quarterly, 26*, 82–88.

Barnes, C., & Mercer, G. (2005). *The social model of disability: Europe and the majority world.* Leeds, UK: Disability Press.

Barnes, C., & Mercer, G. (2008). *Disability: Key concepts.* Cambridge, UK: Polity Press.

Boyer, L., Brunner, B. R., Charles, T., & Coleman, P. (2006). Managing impressions in a virtual environment: Is ethnic diversity a self-preservation strategy for colleges and universities? *Journal of Computer-Mediated Communication, 12*, 136–154.

California Postsecondary Education Commission (CPEC). (2009). *California county comparison: Fiscal, economics, and population.* Retrieved from http://www.cpec.ca.gov/Fiscal Data/CACountyEconGraph.ASP.

California State University, Fresno State. (2014). Accessibility @ Fresno State. Retrieved from http://www.fresnostate.edu/accessibility/.

Clemens, E. S., & Cook, J. M. (1999). Politics and institutionalism: Explaining durability and change. *Annual Review of Sociology, 25*, 441–466.

Foucault, M. (1973/1994). *The birth of the clinic: An archaeology of medical perception* (A. Sheridan, Trans.). New York, NY: Vintage Books.

Foucault, M. (1980a). *Power/knowledge: Selected interviews and other writings 1972–1977* (C. Gordon, Ed.). New York, NY: Pantheon Books.

Foucault, M. (1982). The subject and power. *Critical Inquiry, 8*, 777–795.

Gabel, S. L. (2005/2009). *Disability studies in education: Readings in theory and method.* New York, NY: Peter Lang.

Gabel, S. L., & Miskovic, M. (2014). Discourse and the containment of disability in higher education: An institutional analysis. *Disability & Society, 29,* 1145–1158.

Gabel, S. L., Reid, D., Pearson, H., Luiz, L., & Hume-Dawson, R. (2015). Disability and diversity on CSU websites: A critical discourse study. *Journal of Diversity in Higher Education.* http://dx.doi.org/10.1037/a0039256.

Gerth, D. R. (2010). *The people's university: A history of California State University.* Berkeley, CA: Berkeley Public Policy Press.

Government Accountability Office. (2009). *Higher education and disability: Education needs a coordinated approach to improve its assistance to schools in supporting students.* Washington, DC: GAO.

Ha, L., & James, E. L. (1998). Interactivity reexamined: A baseline analysis of early business websites. *Journal of Broadcasting & Electronic Media, 42,* 457–474. http://dx.doi .org/10.1080/08838159809364462.

Hunter, D., Reid, D. P., & Nishimura, T. (2014). Postsecondary education for students with disabilities. In K. Storey & D. Hunter (Eds.), *The road ahead: Transition to adult life for persons with disabilities* (pp. 177–198). Amsterdam, The Netherlands: IOS Press.

Irvine, J. T. (2011). The unmentionable: Verbal taboo and the moral life of language. Leaky registers and eight hundred pound gorillas. *Anthropological Quarterly, 84,* 15–39. http:// dx.doi.org/10.1353/anq.2011.0011.

Low, J. (1996). Negotiating identities, negotiating environments: An interpretation of experiences of students with disabilities. *Disability & Society, 11,* 235–248. http:// dx.doi.org/10.1080/09687599650023254.

Meyer, K. A. (2008). The "virtual face" of institutions: What do home pages reveal about higher education? *Innovative Higher Education, 33,* 141–157. http://dx.doi.org/10.1007/ s10755-008-9071-2.

Meyer, K. A., & Wilson, J. L. (2010). The "virtual face" of planning: How to use higher education websites to access competitive advantage. *Planning for Higher Education, 38,* 11–18.

Miskovic, M., & Gabel, S. L. (2012). When numbers don't add up and words can't explain: Challenges in defining disability in higher education. *International Journal of Multiple Research Approaches, 6,* 233–244. http://dx.doi.org/10.5172/mra.2012.6.3.233.

Oliver, M. (1990). *The politics of disablement.* New York, NY: St. Martin's Press.

Olssen, M., Codd, J. A., & O'Neill, A. M. (2006). *Educational policy: Globalisation, citizenship and democracy.* London, UK: Sage.

Pauwels, L. (2012). A multimodal framework for analyzing websites as cultural expressions. *Journal of Computer-Mediated Communication, 17,* 247–265. http://dx.doi .org/10.1111/j.1083-6101.2012.01572.x.

Phillips, N., Lawrence, T. B., & Hardy, C. (2004). Discourse and institutions. *Academy of Management Review, 29,* 635–652.

Piland, W. E. (2004). Sabotaging the California dream. *Change, 34,* 21–25.

Pippert, T. D., Essenburg, L. J., & Matchett, E. J. (2013). We've got minorities, yes we do: Visual representation of racial and ethnic diversity in college recruitment material. *Journal of Marketing for Higher Education, 23,* 258–282. http://dx.doi.org/10.1080/0884 1241.2013.867920.

Prowse, S. (2009). Institutional construction of disabled students. *Journal of Higher Education Policy and Management, 31,* 89–96. http://dx.doi.org/10.1080/13600800802559302.

Ralph, S., & Boxall, K. (2005). Visible images of disabled students: An analysis of UK university publicity materials. *Teaching in Higher Education, 10*, 371–385. http://dx.doi.org/10.1080/13562510500122297.

Raue, K., & Lewis, L. (2011). *Students with disabilities in degree-granting postsecondary institutions.* NCES 2011–018. US Department of Education.

Reid, D. P. (2014). *Stuck between a rock and a hard place: Exploring the lived experiences of college students who do not request accommodations.* Dissertation, Chapman University. ProQuest, UMI Dissertation Publishing, #3665093.

Senzani, A. (2010). Class and gender as a laughing matter? The case of Roseanne. *Humor: International Journal of Humor Research, 23*, 229–253. http://dx.doi.org/10.1515/humr.2010.011.

Titchkosky, T. (2001). Disability: A rose by any other name? "People first" language in Canadian society. *Canadian Review of Sociology and Anthropology, 38*, 125–140. http://dx.doi.org/10.1111/j.1755-618X.2001.tb00967.x.

Tripp, P. J. (2008). Proactive recruitment strategies at CSU's increase FCS majors. *Journal of Family and Consumer Sciences, 100*, 18 –23.

U.S. Department of Education, National Center for Educational Statistics. (2013a). [Chap. three]. *Digest of Educational Statistics, 2014 –2015.*

U.S. Department of Education, National Center for Educational Statistics. (2013b). *Characteristics of postsecondary students.* Retrieved from http://nces.ed.gov/programs/coe/indicator_csb.asp.

Wilson, J. L., & Meyer, K. A. (2009). Higher education websites: The "virtual face" of diversity. *Journal of Diversity in Higher Education, 2*, 91–102. http://dx.doi.org/10.1037/a0015443.

13

ENCOUNTERING INSTITUTIONAL BARRIERS AND RESISTANCE

Disability Discomfort on One Campus

Heather Albanesi and Emily A. Nusbaum

In this chapter we investigate the process and extent to which disability has been incorporated into the diversity space on one college campus. In order to do this, we present two related mini-studies. First, we draw on a data set that helps depict the campus climate in terms of the relative marginalization of disability within existing strategies around diversity and inclusion. This data is drawn from a set of three consecutive inclusiveness student surveys (administered between 2009 and 2011) in which we utilize the qualitative responses. Secondly, we turn to a narrative account of a series of efforts pushing for the integration of disability into existing diversity work on campus. Here we describe a constellation of episodes that are places and points in time that the campus *could* have worked to address issues around disability differently—that is, to incorporate responses to disability-related issues within other diversity efforts on campus—but that, because of administrative decisions, framed the disability discourse in terms of compliance, and in some cases, established institutional barriers to moving discussions about disability into broader inclusiveness efforts on campus.

Our examination of these experiences demonstrates structural and institutional resistance to creating a place for disability with other types of diversity work on campus. We conclude the chapter by considering what both survey data and these "magnified moments" (Hochschild, 1994) reflect about resistance and silence at the institutional level. We consider parallels to anti-racism work at postsecondary institutions and the issue of burnout from those doing this kind of social justice work (Gorski & Chen, 2015; Vaccaro & Mena, 2011). Additionally, we explore how differing diversity constituencies are ultimately pitted against one another fighting for the allocation of limited diversity energy/resources and for airtime within the perceived narrow bandwidth for diversity messaging. Further, we contend that disability occupies a uniquely disadvantaged position within diversity work on college campuses for a number of reasons. First, disability is typically understood as a phenomenon that is highly regulated by law/compliance, which allows for and supports the discomfort around engagement with disability, and maintains the notion that it is expensive and requires specialization. As Shallish (2015) argues, within institutions of higher education over the last 35 years,

> attention to marginalized groups evolved to include larger networks of academic and co-curricular support such as formations of identity centers, cultural events, fields of study and scholarships yet disability is largely absent from this work as much of higher education maintains a singular focus on legal compliance.
>
> *(para. 1)*

Eschewing recognition of disability communities, cultures, and histories, and within curriculum, the dominant frame instead maintains individualistic narratives of disability as something that exist within a student's body/mind.

In the process of working on disability inclusion on our campus, we had expected to encounter some pushback from administration (with excuses like "It's too expensive" or "We can't afford to do this"). What was more disheartening, however, was pushback from those associated with diversity work and offices specifically created to champion other forms of student diversity on our campus. Institutionally, outside of academic departments, diversity advocacy has several campus locations: the Student Center for Diversity and Inclusion, the Diversity and Inclusiveness Office (which is part of the administrative structure housed under the Provost) and Faculty Assembly committees (e.g., Faculty Women's Committee). Our experience has been that at each of these "diversity tables," no room has been made for disability. Instead, disability has been stuffed in the "Disability Services" closet, with some obvious negative ramifications, such as a lack of disability programing or events, lack of social inclusion, "access" being framed as an individual issue, requiring documentation and individual accommodation, and lack of information, training, or support for faculty in practices such as Universal Design for Learning (UDL).

On our campus, the history of the Center for Diversity and Inclusion is an interesting (but perhaps not atypical) one. Originally focused on including underrepresented students of color on campus, it was expanded several years ago to include an institutionalized LGBT component. This expansion was a result of a LGBT task force convened to address inclusion of LGBT students and which included the hiring of a dedicated LGBT program director. Although this center has the word "access" in its mission, and includes "ability" as the last of a list of ten social identity markers the center says it works to include, there is no other reference on the website to any resources, initiatives, programs, or events about disability or that are targeted to disabled students, lacking even a link to the campus Disability Services office. The Center for Diversity and Inclusion organizes approximately ten events every semester, but all these events focus on race, ethnicity, gender, and sexual orientation (e.g., a series of events for Hispanic Heritage month or "Guess Who's Gay" panel). No event, to our knowledge, that addresses disability (or even intersectionality, including disability) from similar critical frameworks has come out of this center.

In addition to the Center for Diversity and Inclusion, the second institutional location for diversity advocacy is the Office for Diversity and Inclusiveness. This was the administrative office that disseminated the Inclusiveness Surveys in 2009–2011 (discussed below) that documented serious lack of access and inclusion issues for disabled students. Subsequent years have produced no movement from this office on the issue of disability. For example, the website for this office includes the mention of "abilities" in the list of twelve identity markers that are referenced in the campus mission. However, the website itself includes no other references or links to campus programs, events, or resources for people with disabilities (students, faculty or staff). Parallel exclusion is seen in the Faculty Assembly for the campus. No standing or advisory committee representing disability issues to the campus faculty assembly exists, unlike the separate committees that represent the issues of other social identity groups: women faculty, faculty of color, and LGBT faculty.

Another indication of the campus climate, related to disability, is reflected in its faculty demographics. Unlike other social identities (e.g., race, gender) captured in the hiring process by Human Resources, accessing comparable data on faculty with disabilities is difficult. Compliance with the ADA limits the data on faculty who identify as disabled to those who voluntarily disclose disability (versus calculation by those who request various accommodations). Clearly, in the higher education setting, the professional risks to faculty to either voluntarily disclose disability (especially mental disability, such as mental health issues and neurodiversity, or chronic illness/ health issues linked to exhaustion) or request accommodation are so high, even if the data were available, we would predict it to be underreported[1] However, we do find some evidence of a shared perception of lack of disability-based diversity based on disability. In a system level climate survey of faculty, staff and students conducted in 2014, respondents were asked "Do you agree or disagree that Mountain University has diversity among its FACULTY in each of the following social identities?" Compared with 59% who agreed with that statement for race/ethnicity, only 35% agreed for physical impairment and 18% agreed for mental impairment. These were the lowest levels of agreement among the 13 social identity categories included in that survey question. This is further exacerbated by the lack of presence of disability in campus spaces designed to address diversity, in curricular areas, or addressed openly by campus administrative offices or functions.

Inclusiveness Survey Data

In order to share a sense of the climate around the relative marginalization of disability on campus, from the student perspective, we examined the qualitative results of a set of three consecutive inclusiveness student surveys (administered 2009–2011). For the purposes of this chapter, we present only those comments shared by students (N = 253) who identify as either having a physical disability or a learning disability. These two demographics were the only ones related to disability elicited by the survey (with respondents being evenly divided between these two and about 13% checking both boxes). The student comments were coded following a grounded theory approach (Charmaz, 2014); five themes of exclusion/access for disabled students emerged from the data: (1) general exclusion, (2) built environment, (3) social exclusion, (4) professor/staff treatment, and (5) curricular exclusion.

General Exclusion

The most frequent comments were general statements suggesting disabled students experience lower levels of inclusion and/or access to a range of academic contexts than other students. Sentiments such as "Prominently display signs that say something like "all learners welcomed! Let us know if we can help you out!" were echoed throughout the data. Some of these comments framed the exclusion in terms of "discrimination," either utilizing that term or making statement like "Students with disabilities are not treated fairly." This theme pointed to subgroups within the broader disability umbrella who they perceived as facing particular exclusion. For example, "I would like to see more mentally disabled on campus without having to fight so hard to be there" and "[Mountain U] should make more accommodations [sic] for the mentally impaired."

Built Environment

The second theme that emerged from the survey data involved the lack of access due to the built environment. Issues related to parking, accessing what is a hilly campus, bathrooms, and the student recreation center were identified: "Give people with disabilities a better chance at parking spots and discounts because we are the ones who truly need it. Not the rich white folks that have the money to pay for a parking spot close to the school" and "fix/make sure that all the bathrooms and doors on campus have electronic opening devices so that they are accessible to all." Some responses linked stigma associated with size and physical access, such as, "Although health is important, it is not the only thing that makes people obese. I have a genetic problem. But Mountain U still makes the smallest restroom stalls and continues on with the super small old fashioned desks." Additionally, the lack of access in the built environment was specifically articulated as a barrier to educational access and equity:

> I find it very hard to get around campus as a disabled person. I cannot imagine what I would do if I were confined to a wheelchair. While there are elevators and handicapped buttons for doors, some of the ramps and

handicapped entrances are out of the way and little known. It should not be harder for a disabled person to get their education than it is for a non-disabled person.

Individuals with disabilities really have a problem on campus just getting to and from classes—I can't think what it would be like to have a worse disability than I have today. This is why I dropped out last spring when I broke my leg.

One student drew a connection between issues of physical access and broader micro-aggressions/social exclusion, referencing a campus "sustainability" signage campaign chastising the use of elevators and automatic doors: "I have a problem with my hips, and therefore I take the elevators. All over campus there are signs indicating that I am a lazy, power-squandering, fat-ass for not taking the stairs. I really don't appreciate it at all." The prominent display of these signs both powerfully demonstrated to disabled students that their presence on campus was invisible/not-valued and created a dynamic of increased surveillance and negative attention to those who used the elevators or electric doors. We believe that this reflects the general ableist attitudes, practices, and actions that are the norm on this campus, as well as the pervasiveness of normativity, as it relates to different body/minds.

Social Exclusion

The third theme referenced dynamics between students and social exclusion. Respondents referenced the lack of student groups recruiting disabled students, negative treatment within class group projects (particularly for those with invisible or less obvious disabilities), and social isolation: "It seems that people with physical disabilities are outcasted [sic] at Mountain U the way they are outcasted [sic] in the rest of society." This experience was more deeply articulated by multiple respondents:

Among students, the problem lies primarily with isolation. Students often discount the ideas of students with both physical and learning disabilities, or acknowledge them briefly before turning away. Many students with disabilities experience a profound sense of alienation because their peers are unlikely to enter into conversation with them, and spurn being spoken to. . . . For students, diversity seminars would likely do more harm than good—evoking pity rather than a true sense of friendliness.

Finally, as a result of my two accidents, I am registered with student disability services and often come to class with wires for a tens unit dangling out the bottom of my shirt . . ., but because I don't have a really obvious disability, other students don't understand and get upset with me for being a pansy. I have to move around so I don't get stuck in one position and lay down for breaks during the day and take more breaks to grab pills and food.

I get accused of again not being a team player or even malingering. I'm doing everything I can to be in school even if it hurts me and sets back my healing, I WANT to be here and finish my degree, but I have on more than one occasion gone home and cried, not just because of the pain in my neck, shoulder, back and leg but because of how I get treated on campus.

Treatment from Faculty and Staff

The fourth theme, perhaps the most disheartening, involved faculty and staff treatment of disabled students. References to staff primarily involved individuals from the parking office and campus police. A number of respondents pointed to the need for more nuanced faculty/staff training around disability (respondents specifically mentioned issues of invisible visible disability, chronic pain and illness), perhaps incorrectly assuming that there is systematic and non-voluntary training for faculty/staff on issues such as ableism and accessible pedagogy (UDL).

> Also, those with physical disabilities that may be rare (like extreme photosensitivity) are treated like freaks or liars when asking staff for accomodation [sic]. There is often a presumption that if you look healthy and are young, then you are able-bodied & some sensitivity training (especially for Parking services staff/ Police) would be great—so accomodation [sic] could be offered rather than requested.

There were considerably more references to faculty around access, such as, "Better access for students with disabilities. Professors should be more active in making classrooms inclusive to people with disabilities." More specifically, the accommodation letter interaction/process was situated as the primary point of contention. Some students challenged the process itself, for example, the documentations requirements:

> A person should not be forced to get doctor appointment and get letter for disability department in order to get help/accommodation. Each person differs based on life experiences and when an instructor's ego is so far to the point of being unwilling to communicate. ACTUALLY TEACH, WHAT IN THE HELL AM I PAYING FOR? How hard it is for learning disabled students to get respect and help from instructors. There are too many hoops that students have to go through and they almost have to beg the professors to respect their learning disabilities.

Others noted that even when armed with an accommodation letter, treatment by faculty varied widely in terms of both willingness to offer accommodation and macro-aggression of broadcasting a student's disability status to the rest of the students in the class:

> Professors are often unwilling to accommodate based on disability status; others use condescending language or make demeaning remarks about or in front of students with disabilities. Again, diversity seminars and a greater voice among students may help to prevent this. Also, tolerance for those with disabilities that [are] not so apparent. Fibromyalgia, MS, Chronic Fatigue syndrome, these are not seen as a disability on campus and it is only for a couple of professor that sympathize with the student that the student can be successful. Disability does not mean one has to be restricted to a wheelchair. I am TIRED of having to FIGHT for the rights of those of us who CANNOT HEAR lectures and don't KNOW sign language.

The following respondent links professor treatment (where professors ever emphasized his/her disability) to making student interactions more difficult:

> Despite the efforts of the Disabilities Department, few professors are as accommodating as they could be. Some are unavailable to address students' needs, while others confine students within a disability-related box. I am totally blind and have been asked by two professors to write solely about my blindness—during this semester alone. This seems quite limiting, considering that far more salient items could have been considered in each case. Professors should be encouraged during diversity seminars to think broadly, not placing students in any sort of proverbial box. They should also be encouraged to be both available and flexible. If professors did more to allow students with disabilities to have a normal, unhindered voice, many students would recognize this and include such students in intelligent discourse.

Disability Missing from the Curriculum

Some respondents pointed to the lack of inclusion of disability within the curriculum:

> When considering diversity, most people consider only a specific number of "prominent areas"—race, class, and gender. . . . With regards to students with physical disabilities, very little consideration has ever been given to this subject. I was once enrolled in a course in which the professor came near to insisting that little girls would be forever destroyed if given even one doll. Despite her revolutionary ideas concerning the "important" issues, this professor refused to discuss the social discrimination that was taking place in the life of one of her students, who happened to have a disability. Mountain

U is well-versed in diversity as it pertains to prominent groups; however, we as a university should now focus on more marginalized groups—those who are not experiencing the benefits of religious toleration, and students with both physical and learning disabilities.

Diversity and inclusiveness are lovely concepts. At Mountain U, however, they do not appear to be a blip on the radar screen. And I know, as a student with physical disabilities. The efforts of administration to "improve" diversity and inclusiveness might be better directed at expanding Mountain U's course offerings. That alone will bring a world of diversity to our campus.

Ensure Diversity Is Integrated into Coursework

These responses suggest that students, on the one hand, see the university as making visible overtures toward embracing diversity of certain social identities (whether these efforts are perceived as lip service or not) and, on the other hand, that disability is not a valued part of those efforts.

Magnified Moments

As faculty, our perceptions of the disability climate in many ways mirrored the range of themes voiced by the students with disabilities captured in these inclusion surveys. This reality drove us to engage in a range of efforts aimed at addressing the relative marginalization of disability on campus. Drawing on Hochschild's concept of "magnified moments" (1994), we reflect on a number of specific encounters where work to move disability into the campus "diversity project" in meaningful ways was blocked, deflected, or silenced. Hochschild (1994) defines magnified moments as "episodes of heightened importance, either epiphanies, moments of intense glee or unusual insight, or moments in which things go intensely but meaningfully wrong. In either case, the moment stands out; it is metaphorically rich" (p. 4). Other researchers have used analyses of highly salient "magnified moments" as the basis to explore the social world. For example, Messner (2000) uses the analysis of a single youth soccer game as a "magnified moment" to explore how children construct gender. Specifically, we describe a constellation of experiences or "moments" that demonstrate institutional resistance to calls for access. They include (1) blocked efforts to promote accessibility standards at a campus-hosted Diversity and Inclusion Summit and the response to recommendations for a disability studies (DS) scholar as keynote speaker, which was "We've already done disability, so we don't need to do it again"; (2) thwarted attempts to establish a mentoring program for students who identify as disabled; (3) failed efforts to move a campus student group for disabled students and their allies away from administrative oversight from the Disability Services office; and (4) the creation by the campus administration of an ADA compliance committee in response to survey data and faculty recommendations, and an external consultant ADA compliance report that was met with almost complete institutional silence.

Magnified Moment #1—The Diversity and Inclusion Summit

I [Emily] had just moved a thousand miles for a new job as an assistant professor in a special education department at Mountain U. It was August, and before the academic year even began, I was invited to be a part of a campus-level committee that would be meeting and planning a multi-day conference focused on issues of diversity, which was open to community members and those from other campuses in the state-wide university system. The Diversity and Inclusion Summit, as it was called, would take place the following spring semester, and the committee I was asked to join would be responsible for the planning and implementation of all aspects of the event; I thought it was a perfect fit for me—a professor whose research and teaching were focused on shifting pervasive, dominant, deficit-based ways of understanding and responding to disability—and with the invitation I imagined that this campus wanted to think about disability in new ways and that my work on the committee would be pivotal in "making my mark," so to speak, on the path to tenure.

At the first committee meeting I met faculty from within the college that I taught in, as well as faculty from departments such as history, women's and ethnic studies, psychology, and sociology, along with administrators from the two key offices on campus that worked to address diversity in a myriad of ways. I was optimistic that this group would be the place where I could share ideas and ways of thinking grounded in disability studies—the no longer nascent, but emerged academic field that had transformed my own thinking and scholarly work.

I remember that the first tension arose when talking about names for a keynote speaker. In the time allotted to keynotes, our committee had to choose two people to invite. The chair of the committee (a man and the campus's chief diversity officer) "suggested" a speaker whose work focuses on racial identity in higher education and had been a keynote at this event previously. When I suggested that we consider a disability studies scholar—one who could speak about the field in very accessible ways to an audience who would be new to considering disability within critical, diversity frameworks—the chair pointed me to his "suggestion," told me that she "did disability," and had already been invited anyway. Another faculty member on the committee from the women's studies department (whose work around marginalization of various groups has won public attention at the university and in the local community) responded, "We don't need anyone on disability because we've already done disability studies." I acknowledge that it is possible that these responses were representative of committee members' egos and the desire to control content of the event. However, paired with other disability-related experiences throughout the process, it seemed to reflect a general dismissal of disability-related content and lack of interest in bringing disability into critical conversations and spaces that the event intended to foster. In the end, although I was able to bring a senior scholar from humanities-based DS (and, despite an international reputation, her talk was positioned as secondary), this experience became emblematic of the kinds of micro-aggressions that I experienced on this committee from many of the faculty and administrators "doing" diversity work on the campus.

The issue of event accessibility, across a number of dimensions, had similar results. I was once again optimistic that for an event focused on diversity and inclusion, access would be a central concern. Beyond the lack of accessibility of the university website for the event, I was continuously challenged in my addressing access at committee meetings, and many faculty on the committee pushed back, citing accessibility as an individual problem for the individual with a disability. With input from a colleague at another university and from many readily available resources, I developed a small handbook of accessibility guidelines and sent it to the chair of the committee, asking if it could be distributed to all presenters. I was told that it was "too much to ask" presenters to do (following accessibility guidelines in preparing presentations and making them at the event) and was also too costly (he indicated that the keynotes would have sign interpretation, however). I countered that having a "little bit of access" didn't make the event "accessible." The committee's discussion of accessibility at the event was ended by the chair, and no accessibility standards were set.

Finally, in my role reviewing event proposals I was troubled by a proposal that promoted the creation of a business in the local community that was a segregated employer for disabled adults. The session was housed in a panel about promoting ethical businesses (this specific business provides an environmental service in the local community). I e-mailed other committee members who were reviewing proposals, and although the issue of being a segregated employer for disabled adults hadn't struck them as counter to promoting diversity and inclusion, they each then agreed that perhaps it should not be included. When I brought my concerns to the committee chair he refused to hear my concerns, and instead told me that the professor who proposed it was a senior faculty member who brought lots of money to the university, and that the session would remain. He offered, as my recourse, that I should attend the session and ask hard questions (knowing I was an untenured, new, junior faculty member at the time).

In the committee planning meetings, I felt that I had become the person that almost everyone looked away from when I started talking. Ignoring me or refusing to take up disability-related discussions was another type of microaggression that I experienced in my work on this committee. All of these instances seemed so counter to the notion of inclusiveness and the efforts of so many to advance diversity efforts on my campus. How "inclusive" or "diverse" could an event like this be if certain groups of people are not assured the ability to access and/or see themselves represented in non-stereotypical ways that were authentic?

Magnified Moment #2—Underrepresented Student Mentorship Program

I [Heather] contacted one of the directors of the Center for Diversity and Inclusion to discuss their existing mentorship program. This program was designed to match undergraduate students from various underrepresented groups with faculty/staff mentors, but did not include any category for students to identify as having a disability. I met in person with the director to discuss the addition of "disability" as well as the addition of "military/veteran." The director's reaction (throughout our exchanges on this issue) struck me as one of discomfort, particularly around the language change I was asking for on the forms around disability (she seemed fine with the veteran part). The program used two forms—one for the "mentors" (faculty/graduate students) and one for the "mentees" (undergraduates).

My sense was that her discomfort was coming from two places. First, given her role as a professional diversity "expert," her relative lack of familiarity with disability studies as an academic field, or a broader "disability literacy" (Dickens, Reamy, & Nusbaum, 2015) led to a protracted debate (that went on via e-mail for a few weeks afterward) over why I thought the terminology should be "disability" instead of "ability." Second, I believe some of her discomfort was around disability itself (leading to reluctance to add the category at all). I also asked that on the mentor form, there be an option to identify as "ally" or "disability ally," explaining why this would be a particularly important category in order to increase the chances of successfully finding faculty mentors for disabled students—as academia is, for a range of reasons, not a safe space for faculty to openly identify as disabled (cf. Margaret Price, 2011). When I left the meeting, she said she would have to discuss both of these issues with her staff. I then received a series of e-mails that said that after talking with her staff, they collectively decided the term added to the form should be "ability," not "disability." They also rejected the inclusion of "ally" or "disability ally." I was particularly disappointed when I saw the final forms. On the forms, at the top of the form in larger font, it had separate lines for "gender," "ethnicity/s" and "sexual orientation," and it was only at the bottom of the form (in smaller font) that "ability" was added as second to last in a list of possible qualities to be used in pairing mentors with mentees. The qualities, in order, were as follows: major, native language, LGBTQIA, ethnicity, hobbies, veteran, ability, other. I felt the valuation of various social identities was clear: the important social identities are gender, ethnicity, and sexual orientation. "Ability" falls somewhere below "hobbies." Following the addition of "ability" to the mentor/mentee categories, the whole mentorship program was ended.

Magnified Moment #3—All Access: Failed Efforts to Move a Campus Student Club for Disabled Students and Their Allies away from Administrative Oversight from the Disability Services Office

During my first year on campus Heather invited me [Emily] to join her as faculty advisor to the newly revived Disabled Students Union, a club for disabled students that had been defunct for a couple of years, but that in the past been associated with the Disability Services office. The faculty advisor for this group had also been the director of the Disability Services office. In our first meetings with the student club, the three women who attended regularly (and became the club officers) shared with us some of the history of the club. The student leaders wanted the new club to be more independent from certain administrators who in the past seemed to want to control and depoliticize the group's activities. While they were not sure of the motivation of these administrators, they were concerned they were being "risk managed" and felt vulnerable/at risk within any type of power struggle with the university. One of the student leaders shared that with the revitalization of the club she had already been contacted by an administrator asking about the club's activities and if he could attend the meetings, and this made her anxious and frustrated. As the club progressed, the members spent the majority of the meetings sharing their histories on campus and experiences with various offices and individual administrators and faculty. Their stories also reflected a range of methods through which they had learned to combat faculty who were resistant to providing accommodations, difficulty navigating social spaces on campus, and lack of representation of disability in campus environments outside of the DS office. Each of the women who attended the meetings regularly also seemed to have a highly internalized sense of oppression— as they wavered between anger at their (largely negative) experiences with the institutional structures on campus, and then communicating bad feelings about their anger and identifying all of the positives that they associated with individual people working within the institution. This pattern was especially pronounced in one woman's involvement, as she was very specifically concerned that the DS office director would have hurt feelings at being replaced by us, in addition to her confusion at working in the office of the chief diversity officer on campus, being financially dependent on this position (and also on a letter of recommendation for graduate school) and beginning to recognize the silence around issues of disabled students on campus by those working on other issues of diversity. Brief moments of anger-turned-activism spurred the official change in the name of the group to "All Access."

We understood our role with All Access to both provide information to encourage an alternate understanding of disability on our campus and to support student-initiated efforts to do this. We offered readings and documentary films that worked to shift broadly accepted, deficit-based definitions of disability and attending a campus–wide student club fair. We also shared models of similar campus groups that had been established for a longer period of time and had a highly politicized presence on the campuses where they existed. We attended most of the club meetings and often just listened to the life experiences shared by the three women. All Access met monthly for almost two years. During that time only a few other students attended a handful of the All Access meetings, in addition to the three female officers. After two years the group of women stopped meeting. One of them was graduating and was no longer interested in addressing disability-related issues. The two remaining women were unable to sustain momentum for the group. Without support from any of the diversity-related offices on campus, disability issues remained absent from other diversity initiatives on campus, and All Access was not able to develop, coordinate, and implement a disability-related event on their own.

Steps Forward, but More Steps Back

However, not all disability-related efforts on campus were blocked. The area that we felt most empowered to make some change was in curricular inclusion. As faculty at Mountain U, we retain important control over the content of our courses and certificate level programing (as long as new certificates do not require any additional resources). Thus, we successfully developed undergraduate and graduate disability studies certificates in the academic years following the administration of the "inclusiveness" surveys. Although there has been positive movement toward the inclusion of disability within the curriculum, it is worth noting that there was little institutional interest or resource allocation for this change (the Office of Diversity and Inclusiveness did award us with a small grant of $250 to show the movie *The Sessions* and bring together faculty from a range of departments on campus to form a discussion panel following the film), and resistance/silence from some faculty we approached. These new courses and certificates were built with a core group of faculty who were open to expanding an intersectional approach in their work to include disability and who wanted to engage in the mutual exchange of ideas, resources, and more to enhance all our content.

Not as successful was our attempt to follow the strategy employed by campus LGBT advocates (which resulted in an institutionalized center with dedicated administrative staff) and advocating for the creation of a Disability task force. In an attempt to think strategically about institutionally expanding the Center for Diversity and Inclusion to include disabled students, we met with the Chief Diversity Officer. As had happened with the LGBT task force, we suggested this task force contact a range of stakeholders to gather data on issues of access and inclusion for students, faculty, and staff with disabilities on campus. This suggestion caused something of a legal panic within the administration. Because we were the ones who asked for the creation of a Disability task force we were then asked to meet with campus lawyers. We explained to the lawyers what we view as the best practices approach, that is, a "beyond compliance" model. It was clear that as far as disability was concerned, the campus did not want to allow for the process to follow one similar to creation of the LGBT task force, which successfully led to the hiring of a LGBT program director. Instead, the administration assembled an ADA "compliance" committee with only one faculty representative (neither of us was invited to serve, despite our visibility as the ones requesting a Disability task force), one student, and no campus-facing charge nor transparency. The ADA compliance reports that were produced by an external consultant have not been shared with the campus community and have been met with almost complete institutional silence.

The relatively minute successes around curricular development had little impact beyond students enrolled in the courses and our own solidarity. Rather, our experiences on this campus and an analysis of student survey data about inclusiveness and disability as a case-study demonstrate deeply entrenched dynamics of institutional resistance. In this analysis we suggest that two broad dynamics might be in play. First, we believe that institutions of higher education, as large bureaucracies, are structured to resist change, and those doing diversity work push up against that reality. For example, attention has been called to the underrepresentation of minorities within faculty ranks and how those numbers have stayed relatively flat in recent years. At Mountain U, only 15% of tenured or tenure-track faculty are ethnic minorities, and there has been no increase in the last three years. We suggest institutional practices of "diversity management" (Jones 2006; Russell 2014) include the pitting of various diversity constituencies against one another, forcing a competition for constrained diversity energy/ resources as well as for airtime within the perceived narrow bandwidth for diversity messaging on campus.

We believe that the story of Mountain U is not unique. Rather, we believe similar processes of institutional resistance occur on campuses across the country. We suggest a second, more potentially pernicious dynamic function simultaneously. Here we offer the possibility that the same institutional structures and mechanisms that are responsible for the promotion of diversity in institutions of higher education can at the same time work to silence or block parallel efforts related to disability, keeping it within the limited confines of compliance. Despite the moment/space to use the real experiences of disabled students as impetus to move disability into conversations about privilege and inclusion (and interest among some faculty to do this work), our campus chose to eschew those opportunities.

Note

1   Margaret Price, in her book *Mad at School* (2011), states:

> The grim history of ADA lawsuits brought by professors with disabilities . . . indicates that employers do not rise enthusiastically to the challenge of access, nor do the courts support plaintiffs' efforts to gain access through legal channels. There is little current research on how well mental disabilities are accommodated outside the context of ADA suits; however, what research does exist seems to indicate that employees fear asking for accommodations, and when they do ask, report being further stigmatized (Goldberg, Killeen, and O'Day). . . . This creates what Goldberg, Killeen, and O'Day call a "disclosure conundrum": to obtain accommodation, a person with a mental disability must disclose; but the act of disclosure itself may bring about stigmatization and retaliation.
>
> (p. 118)

References

Charmaz, K. (2014). *Constructing grounded theory* (2nd ed.). Los Angeles, CA: SAGE Publications.

Dickens, B., Reamy, M., & Nusbaum, E. A. (2015, April). *Disability studies in education as a tool for transformation of the self and teaching.* Paper presented at the Second City: Disability Studies in Education annual conference: Chicago, IL.

Gorski, P. C., & Chen, C. (2015). "Frayed all over": The causes and consequences of activist burnout among social justice education activists. *Educational Studies: A Journal of the American Educational Studies Association, 51*(5), 385–405.

Hochschild, A. R. (1994). The commercial spirit of intimate life and the abduction of feminism: Signs from women's advice books. *Theory, Culture & Society, 11*, 1–24.

Jones, C. (2006). Falling between the cracks: What diversity means for black women in higher education. *Policy Futures in Education, 4*(2), 145–159.

Messner, M. (2000). Barbie girls versus sea monsters: Children constructing gender. *Gender and Society, 14*(6), 765–784.

Price, M. (2011). *Mad at school: Rhetorics of mental disability and academic life.* Ann Arbor, MI: University of Michigan Press.

Russell, L. (2014). Whiteness in Scotland: shame, belonging and diversity management in a Glasgow workplace. *Ethnic and Racial Studies, 37*(8), 1371–1390.

Shallish, L. (2015). "Just how much diversity will the law permit?": The Americans with Disabilities Act, diversity, and disability in higher education. *Disability Studies Quarterly, 35*(3). Retrieved from http://dsq-sds.org/article/view/4942/4059.

Vaccaro, A., & Mena, J. A. (2011). "It's not burnout, it's more": Queer college activists of color and mental health. *Journal of Gay & Lesbian Mental Health, 15*(4), 339–367.

14

ACCESS RYERSON

Promoting Disability as Diversity

Denise O'Neil Green, Heather Willis, Matthew D. Green, and Sarah Beckman

In the United States, legal challenges to race-conscious higher education policies have required that practitioners and researchers continue to focus on race/ethnicity to the exclusion of other diverse populations, including students with disabilities. In Canada, postsecondary institutions are not besieged with such challenges. On the contrary, instead of race/ethnicity, indigenous peoples, first generation, and persons with disabilities primarily occupy the diversity space.

The aim of this chapter is to show how Ryerson University, located in Toronto, Ontario, Canada, has integrated accessibility into an equity, diversity, and inclusion framework with a systemic, organizational approach called "Access Ryerson." The chapter will describe several key components of the Access Ryerson Initiative, which aims to make Ryerson fully accessible: (1) foundational principles, (2) leadership structure and components, and (3) working groups. Ultimately, this chapter demonstrates how the Ryerson community is addressing barriers to inclusion experienced by people with disabilities through the lens of disability as diversity, not deficit.

Ryerson is a public institution, with approximately 38,000 students located in the heart of downtown Toronto (Ryerson University, 2015). The Office of Equity, Diversity and Inclusion (EDI) is comprised of five core areas: Aboriginal Initiatives; Education and Awareness; Strategic Planning, Assessment and Special Projects; Human Rights Services; and Access Ryerson. Each area supports, overlaps, and has a synergy with the other four areas. In particular, Human Rights Services derives its policy of discrimination and harassment prevention from the Ontario Human Rights Code (OHRC). The OHRC speaks to prohibited grounds upon which people cannot be discriminated against or harassed based on gender, religion, race, disability, and so on (Ontario Human Rights Commission, 2015). This service primarily addresses complaints at the interpersonal level and is largely reactive. Access Ryerson takes this a step further and examines systemic, institutional structures, moving beyond complaints to proactively champion a more accessible environment. At Ryerson, within the EDI portfolio, disability and diversity are strongly connected. Access Ryerson is a critical institutional initiative that advances the notion of disability as diversity, with an even stronger rejection of disability as deficit.

Accessibility for Ontarians with Disabilities Act (AODA)

Whereas the United States has had the Americans with Disabilities Act (ADA) in place since 1990, the Ontarians with Disabilities Act (ODA) represented the first accessibility legislation in Canada. Passed in 2001, the ODA simply required that all provincial municipalities and publically funded organizations form accessibility advisory committees and make publically available an annual report outlining a plan to remove barriers. In 2005, the Accessibility for Ontarians with Disabilities Act (AODA) was enacted to replace the ODA with a more comprehensive approach that applies to both public and private sectors. The purpose of this current legislation is to enforce mandatory accessibility standards in five key areas of daily living, including customer service, information and communications, employment, transportation, and the built environment. The goal of the AODA is create an accessible Ontario by 2025 through the graduated implementation of these standards.

AODA Principles

The AODA legislation has four core principles that speak to the intention of the AODA and how persons with disabilities ought to be treated (see Table 14.1).

TABLE 14.1 Accessibility for Ontarians with Disabilities Act Values and Principles

Principles and Values	Description
Dignity	Providing service with dignity means the customer maintains his or her self-respect and the respect of other people. Dignified service means not treating persons with disabilities as an afterthought or forcing them to accept lesser service, quality, or convenience.
Independence	Persons with disabilities are enabled to do things on their own, without unnecessary assistance or intervention from others.
Integration	Services are provided in a way that enables persons with disabilities to benefit from the same service, in the same place, and in a similar way as others.
Equality of Opportunity	Goods and services are provided to persons with disabilities in a way that the opportunity to access goods and services, resources, and materials is equal to that given to others. This requires accessible formats and flexible approaches. It means inclusiveness and full participation.

Whereas the Ontario Human Rights Code requires that we "accommodate to undue hardship," the AODA principles clearly articulate that individuals with disabilities should not be treated, serviced, or conceptualized as problems or burdens, or marginalized as segregated entities. On the contrary, dignity, respect, independence, full integration, and equal access drive AODA legislation and implementation. It is within this spirit that Access Ryerson advances its agenda, rejecting a medical model and instead focusing on removing and preventing barriers to full inclusion.

Access Ryerson—Our Approach

Ryerson's university-wide accessibility initiative, Access Ryerson, is both welcoming and invitational. It welcomes students to "access Ryerson," a university that aspires to be both physically accessible and socially inclusive. Further, it speaks to the initiative itself, inviting everyone to play a part in creating a more inclusive environment in which we all live, work, and study. While the bricks and mortar are imperative in improving access to physical space, equally important are the people willing to address the less tangible but critically important social, cultural, and attitudinal changes required to realize the transformational power of the Access Ryerson initiative. We recognize that barriers exist not only within the physical realm, but also are hidden within policies, procedures, and the attitudes of those with decision-making power.

Ryerson's approach to furthering the principles of the AODA is that all members of the university have a shared responsibility to support access and inclusion. Underpinning this approach is a commitment to the practice of universal, or inclusive design and the Social Model of Disability, which systematically addresses accessibility. In short, Ryerson is committed to accessibility in the classroom, accessibility in the workplace, and accessibility on campus.

Defining the Problem

Historically, communities who experience marginalization have been both intentionally and unintentionally excluded from postsecondary education. This exclusion has been largely based on perceived individual deficits. According to Liasidou (2014), "as a direct result of the predominance of this individual pathology perspective, disability, unlike other sources of social disadvantage, has not been taken into consideration when discussing issues of unequal and discriminatory treatment" (p. 121). In order to achieve equitable opportunities for education, the policies and programs of postsecondary institutions must reflect inclusive practices. In research conducted by López Gavira and Moriña (2014), findings suggest that barriers faced by students with disabilities can outweigh available support and resources. Furthermore, their research suggests that teaching and learning environments that are inclusive of students with disabilities benefit the entire student population, providing opportunities for all to succeed.

Efforts aimed at creating campus environments that are more inclusive of students with disabilities should therefore incorporate a social justice approach with an emphasis on intersectionality (Gibson, 2015; Liasidou, 2014; Madriaga & Goodley, 2010; Madriaga, Hanson, Kay, & Walker, 2011). Madriaga et al. (2011) maintain that it is essential to confront the dominant sense of normalcy that persists in higher education. In working toward fostering a campus environment that is inclusive of students with disabilities, they argue that the notion of normalcy perpetuated at the institutional level can be associated with practices that prioritize students without impairments as the ideal norm. Creating attitudinal shifts in relation to the notion of normalcy can therefore help minimize the culture that perpetuates the perception of students with disabilities as inferior and marginal.

Mortimore (2013) suggests that any model of disability support that focuses on individual difference can be characterized as medical-oriented, focusing exclusively on the perceived deficits. Shifting the focus from the learner to the wider context of the learning environment can increase awareness and have broader positive implications for all students. A social justice approach would therefore be beneficial for removing barriers for student learners who experience marginalization by highlighting the needs of students rather than focusing on impairments. The current practice of isolating students creates an environment where students with disabilities who access learning supports are put in a vulnerable position to disclose perceived deficits, and as a result conceive of themselves as having needs that go beyond what is typically offered in the university classroom environment.

> A socially just pedagogy allows us to imagine inclusivity where these same disabled students do not have to disclose and seek "special" allowances to engage in higher learning ... it compels us not to settle, but to move beyond the minimum provision in our teaching, engagement and support of our students because it is "just."
>
> *(Madriaga et al., 2011, p. 914)*

Employing a social justice approach to address the experiences of students with disabilities on campus would also require an intersectional lens. More specifically, Liasidou (2014) suggests that it is essential to consider the intersecting and compounding sources of marginalization that can be experienced by students with disabilities such as socioeconomic status, race, culture, and sexuality. Disability should therefore be conceived as a human rights issue and institutions should respond by addressing these incremental sources of marginalization.

Preston, "a professor and disability rights advocate," (par. 3) maintains the defining feature of successful academic experiences for students with disabilities consist of encouraging students to be as involved as possible in their own academic goals and plan (Academica Group, 2015). A significant source of barriers can stem from accommodation and learning plans that are developed and implemented without the input of students. Providing a broader approach to delivering education will minimize the need for accommodation while also benefitting the broadest possible range of students (Academica Group, 2015). In addressing these issues, Liasidou (2014) strongly suggests the implementation of disability aware-ness initiatives across the postsecondary institutional level. Furthermore, supports and resources must be put in place to facilitate inclusive practices. Awareness alone will not make this happen.

In a review of the literature on inclusive strategies, Orr and Hammig (2009) insist on the value of providing a diverse range of inclusive teaching strategies and learner supports for students with disabilities. This intersectional approach reflects the diversity within the disability community. Importantly, these approaches must take into account the lived experiences of students with disabilities by including them in bringing about institutional change. To achieve this more inclusive environment, students with disabilities have expressed a need for opportunities for faculty training, as challenges faced in the classroom environment were often due to lecturers who were not prepared to meet their specific needs (López Gavira & Moriña, 2014). Inclusive strategies for students with disabilities should therefore personify the needs and desires specific to students who experience barriers. "Henry, Dean of Students at King's University College suggests that, in the near future . . . services for students with disabilities will operate as part of a holistic network of inclusive campus opportunities that no longer marginalize and isolate these students" (Academica Group, 2015, par. 7). Furthermore, "Henry and Preston argue for a strategy that brings students with disabilities out of segregated adminis-trative silos . . . [aiming,] 'to actively promote and naturalize services on campus to support students with disabilities in an effort to destigmatize the process'" (par. 9).

Education that is inclusive of students with disabilities must move beyond simply fulfilling legally required accommodations. (Finnis, Howell, Gorrie, & Finnis, 2014). As we begin to move away from individual accommodations, we can move toward universal inclusivity for all students (Redpath et al., 2012). This approach can empower students with disabilities to be active participants in creating change at the cultural level on campus. Access Ryerson builds upon this social justice framework. While the medical model of disability continues to be prominent, viewing disability from an inclusion or access lens speaks to those social justice paradigms that incorporate intersectionality and agency. Access Ryerson defines the "problem" as such, recognizing that organizational or cultural change is the goal. In sum, how we define the problem has a direct impact on how we address it.

Access Ryerson: Principles and Values, Leadership Structure, and Working Groups

As noted earlier, Access Ryerson was initially a response to the AODA legislation in Ontario. This initiative is comprised of three key components: (1) a framework guided by principles and values, (2) a senior leadership structure with key com-ponents, and (3) working groups that focus on implementation.

Access Ryerson Foundational Principles and Values

In addition to the principles of the AODA, Access Ryerson created its own set of foundational principles and values that underpin it. The importance of establishing access and accessibility work in specific guiding principles and values is threefold: it builds community and allies; it publicly articulates the rejection of a deficit paradigm; and finally, it creates a means of alignment with other university priorities.

Below are the ten Access Ryerson principles and values (see Table 14.2). These key elements of the Access Ryerson approach are often shared and reinforced in presentations, workshops, and one-on-one meetings. While several should be obvious, the principle of "accessibility and accommodation as distinct approaches" is critical to the basis of Access Ryerson's work. Accessibility aims to change the environment in the classroom, campus, and workplace so that there is less need for individual accommodation.

TABLE 14.2 Access Ryerson Foundational Principles and Values

Principles and Values	Description
Accessibility at the Start	By providing the highest degree of accessibility possible at the outset, we ensure no new barriers will be created, avoiding problems later on. Every individual plays a role in ensuring accessibility from the start.
Disability as Diversity, not Deficit	The experience of disability is typically and historically perceived negatively as a deficit. Instead we consider the perspectives of persons with a disability beneficial to a wider and more inclusive perspective.
Accessibility, not Disability	By recognizing the relationship between social and physical barriers and disability, our focus is shifted to the environment and solutions to remove barriers, rather than to any perceived deficit of the person.
Accessibility and Accommodation as Distinct Approaches	Individual accommodation is an essential component of accessibility; however, these are distinct approaches. The more accessible an environment/organization/process is from the start, the less need there will be for accommodation. Although a legal obligation may require only "accommodation as required," ideally permanent accessibility solutions will be sought, reducing the need for individual accommodation.
Intention	We need to act with intention. When we are not being actively inclusive, we may be unintentionally exclusive. In order to avoid accidental exclusion of persons with disabilities, we need to be attentive to inclusive practice at all times.
Fairness and Equitable Treatment	We understand that equitable treatment does not necessarily mean treating everyone the same. Treating people fairly may require different approaches that do not imply a lesser standard of performance.

(continued)

TABLE 14.2 (*continued*)

Principles and Values	Description
Leadership Commitment	Senior leaders are in a unique position to ensure accessibility is at the core of decision-making. As champions of accessibility, senior leaders promote the accountability and advancement of accessibility in their areas of responsibility.
Shared Responsibility	Successful learning and employment outcomes are the result of a shared responsibility and commitment on the part of students, staff and faculty. There is the expectation that all members of the community will advance and contribute to the ongoing development of an environment that is accessible and inclusive, while actively working to identify, remove, and prevent barriers to persons with disabilities.
Collaboration	We recognize that barriers are rarely the sole responsibility of a single department, faculty, or individual and can be addressed only with a collaborative approach.
Social Innovation	With creativity, energy, and optimism, we set our sights on altering perceptions, behaviors, and structures by inventing strategies for social change and using new and existing tools in innovative ways.

Access Ryerson Leadership Structure and Components

Prior to 2010, Ryerson had an Accessibility Advisory Committee which was initiated as a requirement of the 2001 Ontarians with Disabilities Act, the precursor to the 2005 Accessibility for Ontarians with Disabilities Act (AODA, 2011). It included representation from faculty, administration, and students with a primary mandate to provide advice to the university on accessibility and address issues as they arose. Its responsibilities under the ODA required only that there be an advisory committee that included people with disabilities, and its main role was community consultation, planning, and annual reporting.

This committee as it existed was not able to oversee the activities necessary to implement the standards under the AODA, so a separate Advisory Committee was set up to ensure Ryerson's compliance and engage in strategic planning for the future. As a result of this committee's recommendations, necessary training was put in place, an accessibility website was created, a statement of commitment was articulated, and an administrative policy was established.

In addition to implementing the steps required to fulfill the initial customer service standard, a formal recommendation was made by this committee to hire an Accessibility Coordinator as it was recognized this work could not realistically be accomplished by a committee comprised of members of the Ryerson community with full-time responsibilities. This role was filled in 2010 and within the Human Resources Division.

Access Ryerson was established in 2011 with the intention of embracing a more comprehensive approach to the AODA legislation. Access Ryerson then set out to renew the university's accessibility commitment with a mandate that expanded beyond consultation and reporting, to implementing and enhancing accessibility in keeping with the additional requirements of the AODA legislation. In addition, a leadership commitment was established with the appointment of a steering committee led by senior management.

At this time, most universities in Ontario had some type of AODA initiative. However, Ryerson University was unique with its inclusive, campus-wide structure. In the summer of 2013, the Access Ryerson initiative moved from Human Resources to the Division of Equity, Diversity and Inclusion. While being housed in Human Resources provided an excellent start to the coordinator's position and initiative, the EDI Division provided greater visibility, more opportunities for collaboration, and more importantly, Access Ryerson was also able to advance its social justice identity and address intersectionality.

Access Ryerson Structure—Version 2.0

Steering Committee

The former accessibility advisory committee reported directly to the Provost and Vice President Academic along with the Vice President, Administration and Finance. It was essential to maintain this bilateral reporting mechanism, however, to increase the leadership commitment across the institution, a more comprehensive steering committee of senior administrators representing key areas of the university was put in place. This included deans, directors, and assistant vice presidents responsible for human resources, libraries, financial services, student affairs, capital projects, academic affairs, and facilities.

The primary function of the Steering Committee is to take responsibility for implementation of the AODA standards and to address any related, major business issues. Another key function is to promote accessibility at Ryerson. The Steering Committee provides oversight of the Ryerson Accessibility Advisory Group, including approval of terms of reference, recommendations, plans, and projects. The Steering Committee also monitors the risks, quality, and timeliness of Advisory Group activities and establishes benchmarks.

Advisory Committee

The Advisory Committee itself was expanded to ensure representation from all departments and faculties. The key responsibility of its members is to serve as a liaison between the area they represent and Access Ryerson. Therefore the former committee was disbanded, and the Deans and department directors were requested to appoint a representative from their divisions and/or faculties. An intentional effort was made to include additional representation from staff, faculty and students with lived experience of disability. Given the advent of an accessibility coordinator responsible for coordinating initiatives across the university, this position took on the co-chair role for the administrative side while a representative from Ryerson's School of Disability Studies, with a strong background in disability rights and a foundation in the social model of disability, fulfilled the new academic cochair role.

Working Groups

In order to expand the mandate of the original committee, working groups were created to address barriers in particular areas. More specifically, they proactively plan ways to identify, remove and prevent barriers to inclusion for those with disabilities. These groups vary widely in size and are led by the department under which the responsibility would naturally fall. For example, the Built Environment Working Group is led by Campus Facilities, the Information and Technology Working Group led by Campus Computing Services, while the Employment Working Group is led by Human Resources, and so on. Working groups meet and carry out specific activities focused on initiatives as identified by the Advisory Group and partners within the university. In Table 14.3, the vision and commitment of each working group are described. Each vision statement implicitly or explicitly aims for total inclusion (i.e., built environment—public spaces accessible to all) and/or eliminating the creation of new barriers (i.e., procurement—no new barriers to access are created). Ensuring such lofty commitments can be challenging in a highly decentralized, unionized environment whereby resources are scarce. While collectively, these working groups have been successfully advancing Ryerson's accessibility agenda, dedicated coordination is constantly needed to keep all groups on track. Open, transparent communications and establishing and maintaining relationships are the glue that makes the cogs in the accessibility wheel operate.

TABLE 14.3 Access Ryerson Working Groups

Working Group	Vision	Commitment
UNIVERSAL DESIGN FOR LEARNING (UDL)	A Ryerson teaching community that adopts a universal approach to designing, developing, and implementing courses that reach out to every student on campus.	The UDL Working Group is committed to introducing universal design for learning principles through the Learning and Teaching Office's programs and services, expanding the current UDL web resources and developing faculty training.

Working Group	Vision	Commitment
BUILT ENVIRONMENT	A campus where the physical environment and public spaces are accessible to all.	Accessibility at Ryerson is a priority and as such accessibility criteria and features will be considered in all aspects of renovation, development and redevelopment of campus facilities and spaces.
COMMUNICATION AND AWARENESS	A university culture that appreciates the experience of disability as a matter of diversity rather than deficit; that embraces the principles and practices of embedding access from the start; and that recognizes the role we each play in creating a barrier-free Ryerson community.	We are committed to promoting accessibility at Ryerson University.
INFORMATION & TECHNOLOGY	A fully accessible information and technology (IT) environment for all Ryerson University stakeholders, including students, faculty, staff and the general public.	We are committed to creating an IT environment that aligns with the POUR (perceivable, operable, understandable, robust) principles of the Web Content Accessibility Guidelines, including content (documents, images, audio, video, multimedia), systems (e.g., Blackboard, email, etc.), and processes, policies, and procedures.
PROCUREMENT	Integrated accessibility criteria and features when procuring goods, services and facilities for Ryerson University, ensuring that no new barriers to access are created.	We are committed to embedding accessibility criteria into all procurement practices and policies, ensuring that processes, from the procurement of a chair to the procurement of a building, are accessible to the Ryerson University community.
EMPLOYMENT	A university employment environment that is fully accessible and inclusive to all stakeholders, including students, faculty, staff and prospective employees.	We are committed to eliminating existing barriers in HR policies, programs, processes, systems, documents and communications and ensuring that new employment initiatives and services are designed to be inclusive, with no new barriers.

Chairs Coordinating Group

It was recognized early that a key challenge to address was a culture of working in silos that commonly exists in large organizations, particularly universities. To address this, a coordinating group was formed in which the chairs of the individual working groups along with the Access Ryerson cochairs share current projects and challenges. This allows the working groups to identify common areas and crossover issues. As such, groups can work together and avoid working at cross-purposes. This group has proven to be a very useful form of communication and mutual support, facilitating synergies and collaborations to support accessibility.

Student Testimonials

In 2015 greater efforts have been made to incorporate more student voices and increase engagement and as a result, the student engagement working group was created. While student engagement forums had been held on an annual basis, incorporating the students as a distinct working group within the Access Ryerson structure embedded them in the initiative as partners. As with the other working groups, they participate in the coordinators group providing an opportunity to provide input into the work of the other groups while also allowing the other working groups to hear their needs directly from them. Recently, members of the student engagement working group convened and shared their thoughts about Ryerson with respect to Access Ryerson, the campus, classroom, and workplace. Their area of study, student status, and disability have been shared to provide further context for their remarks.

Equity and Diversity Studies—Visual Impairment

This student underscores that "there has never been a better time to be a university student with a disability." As such, the classroom has become more inclusive; nevertheless, students' attitudes continue to make the campus environment and even the classroom a challenge for visually impaired students.

> I remember being told that university was not for "people like me" and as a result when I was accepted into Ryerson University wasn't really sure what to expect. What I came to learn quite quickly is that thanks to many on campus organizations like Access Ryerson, there has never been a better time to be a university student with a disability. That being said my experience has not been all rosy. I certainly face barriers on a daily basis but fortunately for the most part I find them outside of the classroom. Most of the barriers I come to face are attitudinal and if you weren't paying attention you might even miss them. I use a guide dog and there have been many occasions where either I get pointed and stared at by other students. When

I walk into classrooms the limited accessibility seating is taken up by able bodied students who refuse to move, or when I need to take the elevator to move between floors I get shoved out of the way by my able bodied peers. This last academic year a new student group launched called the Student Engagement Working Group and I have never been more positive about a group making change for students like me. Even in its infancy, this group had a powerful impact on students specifically through the launching and running of the first set of accessible campus tours. Every time I attend one of these meetings I feel like the voices of students just like me are being heard and the challenges that we face on a daily basis are being understood and addressed by those in charge. I have high hopes that with this new group in place that eventually students like myself will be able to walk across campus and be accepted and welcomed by other students, that building and development plans will consider accessibility in the planning stages as opposed to after the fact, and that in the classroom professors will learn how they can tailor their lectures to enhance our learning experience to the fullest.

According to this student, there are opportunities through Access Ryerson to directly impact students (e.g., accessibility campus tour), building projects and pedagogy so that students with disabilities can be fully included in the classroom, campus spaces, and student interactions.

Creative Industries—Wheelchair User

Similarly, a student who is a wheelchair user noted the significance of the accessibility campus tours and how it led her to direct involvement in the working group:

I got involved in this student group because as a first year student I really wanted to get involved at Ryerson, and I thought this was a great way. It was a way for me to meet new friends, but also to make a real difference in the Ryerson community. I was first approached to join this group during Frosh Week. I was taking an Access Tour that highlighted the accessible routes around campus and also the barriers. I thought that . . . was really important and a really useful tour to have, especially during my first week. After I went on that tour I thought it would be great to join this group, that way with future students I could get involved with not just . . . the tours, but with everything else related to accessibility around campus.

Further to this student's discussion of the tours and making a difference for students, she aims to make a difference in her chosen career in the arts. While she does not speak directly to Ryerson's workplace, the student's point is clear. Workplaces should be accessible no matter what the venue.

I'll definitely take my knowledge about accessibility into my career. . . . I'm a Creative Industries student. I'm in my first year right now, and that's basically the business side of the arts; so right now I'm doing a lot of classes on the music industry. One of the barriers I've already faced in the music industry is that so many venues are inaccessible, . . . especially the more underground, bar-type venues. There are steps and they're not accessible at all. In my career I definitely hope to make a difference in that community and make that accessible to everyone.

Again, physical spaces are barriers to pursuing specific careers. Students with disabilities recognize these challenges will continue beyond their university experience.

Accessibility Practices: AODA and Beyond

While students who participate in the working group are very motivated and wish to change the system, there are many more students who are just trying to have a relatively good classroom experience with their professors and peers. Nonetheless, there are attitudes that students with disabilities confront both outside and inside the classroom. This student expresses the core premise of Access Ryerson, access and integration, not barriers and marginalization:

When I moved to Toronto and enrolled in Ryerson University, attending class was a bit of a challenge. Aside from actually getting there, the thing I hated most was sitting in class. Typically there are two spots for persons in wheelchairs: the front or the back. Neither are bad places to sit or stay in class, but other students usually do not sit next to these designated spots. The number one purpose of class is to learn to get better at your craft or major, but in spite of that, there is also a significant social aspect of university life many students with disabilities lose out on.

As I mentioned, seating for me was, and still is, primarily in the front, back, or off to the side of a row of desks. I'm essentially on the fringe no matter what. It wasn't that people treated me poorly, but there was practically no interaction from my other classmates unless I very purposefully flagged people down during breaks and repeatedly did so each class. In the big scheme of things, saying hi to someone you haven't met in class isn't a big deal, but nonetheless it can feel socially weird. Again, the main goal of university should be to excel in one's studies, but the community aspect is a big part of that experience too. It would be fairly hard to change things because tiered-seating classes (theatre style) for example usually have steps, but for other classes, having openings in different spots aside from the usual front or back would be a solution for sure; something to make disabled students feel more integrated.

One of the mature students of the group articulated systemic barriers of discrimination, attitudes, or lack of access to counseling or adequate testing services:

> I got involved with this student group because I have been part of the Accessibility Advisory Committee right from the beginning, and I saw the progression of all the other groups—the Communications group, the Employment group, physical barriers—and they all make a difference, really. What I did not see was the actual engagement from the students. I understand that, as a person with a disability, the biggest barrier we face is attitude. So, it is the students who are going to bring their personal experience of discrimination, or barriers, and when everyone realizes that, "oh, it's not just me who's facing this barrier in my classroom," in this group I can hear that other people are actually facing the same barrier. The courses, the exams, are only in writing rather than alternative modes of evaluation. Or my professor doesn't want to accommodate my needs. Then you realize that there're systemic barriers. But we'll never know if it's only one person speaking. So this student engagement group is really a vital key for the university to move forward. Because the university without students is really not a university, so the students need to be accommodated. The students of the university experience the problems; the inaccessibility to class courses . . . to counseling, if that's what they need for mental illness. So, this is basically what I wanted to do by participating.

Allowing students with disabilities to come together and discover they are not alone in this struggle is important to this student. Bringing the voices together also provides "a vital key for the university to move forward." Truly this was the missing piece to Access Ryerson, student voices.

Conclusion

The combination of foundational values and principles, leadership structure and working groups speak to the multi-faceted approach that is needed to change any decentralized organization with respect to accessibility. First, values and principles attempt to shape how the problem is framed—shifting from disability as deficit to disability as diversity. They also provide the foundation for accessibility education and training, policies, communications and the like as it relates to students, faculty, and staff with disabilities. Lastly, it disrupts the perception of persons with disabilities as medical problems that need fixing, and shifts to a focus on the removal of physical and social barriers in classrooms and workplaces on campus. Making these spaces accessible ultimately benefits everyone, not just persons with disabilities.

Higher education research consistently shows that leadership is critical for diversity efforts to success. The leadership structure developed over the last five years at Ryerson University reaffirms the need to have executive and senior level administrators at the table. Furthermore, leadership cannot be limited to the administrative or academic side of the institution. Because both administrative and academic streams of the university impact students' experiences, both must have ownership and be invested in the initiative's success. Additionally, bringing key leaders together on a regular basis maintains visibility such that accessibility issues and concerns remain action items, beyond lip service.

To address systemic problems institutional structures must be put in place. A comprehensive, proactive approach is required. Hiring an accessibility coordinator and forming working groups from specific areas needed to accessibility barriers was critical to Ryerson's accessibility agenda and preliminary success. With the addition of the student engagement working group, Access Ryerson will gain more ground and credibility because it will ultimately respond to students' concerns, challenges, and systemic barriers to access and inclusion.

References

Academica Group. (October 28, 2015). Working with, not on behalf of students with disabilities. Retrieved from http://forum.academica.ca/forum/working-with-not-on-behalf-of-students-with-disabilities.

Accessibility for Ontarians with Disabilities Act (AODA). (November 17, 2011). Nonprofits and The Act. Retrieved from http://www.aoda.ca/nonprofits-and-the-act/.

Finnis, E., Howell, J., Gorrie, R., & Finnis, E. (2014). Some reflections on improving accessibility and the classroom experience. *Transformative Dialogues: Teaching and Learning Journal, 7*(3), 1–13.

Gibson, S. (2015). When rights are not enough: What is? Moving towards new pedagogy for inclusive education within UK universities. *International Journal of Inclusive Education, 19*(8), 875–886. http://doi.org/10.1080/13603116.2015.1015177.

Liasidou, A. (2014). Critical disability studies and socially just change in higher education. *British Journal of Special Education, 41*(2), 120–135. http://doi.org/10.1111/1467-8578.12063.

López Gavira, R., & Moriña, A. (2014). Hidden voices in higher education: Inclusive policies and practices in social science and law classrooms. *International Journal of Inclusive Education, 19*(4), 365–378. http://doi.org/10.1080/13603116.2014.935812.

Madriaga, M., & Goodley, D. (2010). Moving beyond the minimum: Socially just pedagogies and Asperger's syndrome in UK higher education. *International Journal of Inclusive Education, 14*(2), 115–131. http://doi.org/10.1080/13603110802504168.

Madriaga, M., Hanson, K., Kay, H., & Walker, A. (2011). Marking-out normalcy and disability in higher education, *32*(April, 2015), 37–41. http://doi.org/10.1080/0142 5692.2011.596380.

Mortimore, T. (2013). Dyslexia in higher education: Creating a fully inclusive institution. *Journal of Research in Special Educational Needs, 13*(1), 38–47. http://doi.org/10.1111/j.1471-3802.2012.01231.x.

Ontario Human Rights Commission. (2015). The Ontario Human Rights Code. Retrieved from http://www.ohrc.on.ca/en/ontario-human-rights-code.

Orr, A. C., & Hammig, S. B. (2009). Inclusive strategies learning literature for teaching students with learning disabilities: A review of the literature. *Learning Disability Quarterly*, *32*(3), 181–196.

Redpath, J., Kearney, P., Nicholl, P., Mulvenna, M., Wallace, J., & Martin, S. (2012). A qualitative study of the lived experiences of disabled post-transition students in higher education institutions in Northern Ireland. *Studies in Higher Education*, *38*(December), 1–17. http://doi.org/10.1080/03075079.2011.622746.

Ryerson University. (2015). Accessibility—Ryerson University. Retrieved 20 November 2015 from http://www.ryerson.ca/accessibility.

Ryerson University. (2015). Quick Facts—News & Events—Ryerson University. Retrieved from http://www.ryerson.ca/news/media/quickfacts/.

15

THINKING AND PRACTICING DIFFERENTLY

Changing the Narrative around Disability on College Campuses

Sue Kroeger and Amanda Kraus

In the United States, approximately 56.7 million citizens report having at least one physical, sensory, cognitive, or emotional impairment. Disabled individuals[1] have the lowest levels of educational attainment and are most likely to be under- or unemployed, leading to lower socioeconomic status and higher poverty rates (Brault, 2012). The National Center of Education Statistics reports that eleven percent of American undergraduates have a disability (2014), yet beyond reasonable accommodations, campuses do not readily support the disability community or disability identity development through cultural programming or organizations, bringing into question how inclusive or welcoming our campuses are to disabled students. Another important population to look at when attempting to understand the landscape for disabled students in higher education is student veterans. With over five million service members expected to transition out of the military by 2020, we can expect to see a continued increase in the enrollment of student veterans. It is estimated that veterans or military-connected students represent 4% of undergraduates, and 10% of all student veterans report at least one disability (Molina & Morse, 2010). Many veterans acquire a disability later in life, sometimes through military service, and struggle to navigate a college campus, or specifically disability services (Kraus & Rattray, 2011). While these numbers are compelling, we must acknowledge that all disability data is collected via self-report at the postsecondary level. Given that we do not necessarily have an accurate sense of disabled students in higher education, relying on numbers to determine practices around campus accessibility is shortsighted. In a piece in the *Chronicle of Higher Education*, disability studies leader Leonard Davis (2011) asks why disability is missing from the discourse on diversity:

> While our current interest in diversity is laudable, colleges rarely think of disability when they tout diversity. College brochures and Web sites depict

people of various races and ethnicities, but how often do they include, say, blind people or those with Parkinson's disease? Or a deaf couple talking to each other in a library, or a group of wheelchair users gathered in the quad? When disability does appear, it is generally cloistered on the pages devoted to accommodations and services. It's not that disability is simply excluded from visual and narrative representations of diversity in college materials; it is rarely even integrated into courses devoted to diversity.

(Davis, 2011)

Higher education must challenge what we have been socialized to understand about disability. This chapter will examine how disability is framed in higher education, explore disability as a sociopolitical category, share strategies to reframe disability on college campuses, and consider disability-related access an institutional responsibility rather than a special need.

What Do We Think We Know?

Medical and Tragedy Models

Disabled people share a history of oppression that included abuse, neglect, sterilization, euthanasia, segregation, and institutionalization. Elements of this history continue to inform our understanding and perception of the disability experience today. Historically, scholars, professionals, politicians, and much of the public have responded to disability as a measurable limitation in function linked to an underlying physiological deficit that prevents a person from performing "normal" tasks. They did not distinguish between impairment and disability and above all seek to cure, correct, or eradicate it. The medical model, as coined by disability studies, holds that disability is the result of a physiological difference, that the individual is the problem, in need of intervention or a cure (Swain, French, & Cameron, 2003).

Though this model certainly presents a disempowering and limited perspective on disability, it is sadly the most prevalent way in which disability is framed in society. Related to the medical model, is the tragedy or charity model, which holds that because of their physiological difference, disabled people are in need of help, pity, or prayer. Though not through medical intervention, disability is a problem that must be fixed. Because our societal standards for disability are so low, we also frame disabled people as inspirational for doing ordinary things. We objectify disabled people for the benefit of non-disabled people, an emerging concept called "inspiration porn." One example of this phenomenon is an image of a disabled athlete with a caption that reads: "What's your excuse?" Positioning disability as an object of inspiration may be well intended but reinforces lower standards for disabled people by celebrating how they have risen above our very low societal expectations. Most of us are not conscious of it, but we intersect regularly with medical or tragedy model thinking about disability. Language and media consistently represent disability this way and in turn inform our design of environments, policy, curriculum, and so on. In higher education, there are few models that challenge dominant thinking on disability.

Language

Consider language used to describe disability or disabled people. How often do we describe disabled people as having a deficit; being courageous and overcoming; wheelchair-bound; having suffered an injury; or special. Also, in our use of metaphor, we use disability to describe exceptionally good or exceptionally bad conditions: he is a stand-up guy, I ran circles around you, or she does not have a leg to stand on, the economy was crippled by.... Such language perpetuates thinking that disability is a condition that must be cured, and that disabled people are victims, helpless, and needy.

Media

As an important source of knowledge and insight, media and popular culture interpret human events (Haller, 2010; Longmore, 2003). The media reflect values, beliefs, and norms. In movies, television, books, and news, disabled people are often rendered invisible, leading to the mistaken belief that such people do not exist, or are insignificant in society. Or, disabled people are superheroes, the high-achieving "super-crip" (Haller, 2010), so awesome that we no longer see disability. The media present disabled people as one-dimensional, objects of ridicule, pity, and humor, or sources of inspiration, rarely as ordinary individuals living ordinary lives.

Curriculum

From kindergarten through postsecondary education, disability is regularly ignored in curriculum, and when included disability is represented as a personal tragedy or as an inspiration to non-disabled people. On syllabi, disability content is usually isolated to a specialized applied field, like medicine, special education, and rehabilitation, where it is pathologized and individualized and where treatment is emphasized.

Design

The designs of our spaces, buildings, information systems, policies, and procedures reinforce norms that exclude rather than include. Examples are uncaptioned videos, exams with strict time limits, print-only textbooks, separate and limited entrances, parking or seating for wheelchair users, and data systems that are incompatible with adaptive technology.

Impact

These images and ideas on disabled and non-disabled people are significant and certainly impact our practice and policy in higher education. Society's beliefs about disability are pervasive, consistent, and clearly locate the problem of disability within the individual or as the individual. In higher education, we respond to disability-related access as "special needs," we develop programs to raise awareness about disability by service work or simulation, and we design policies that exclude disabled people from full participation. While we should be problematizing such messages, there are few campuses that model something different or better.

Disability Rights and the Social Model

Disabled people have been politically active and engaged for more than a century, but it was not until the 1970s that disability truly emerged as a civil rights issue. American disability rights advocates have made significant victories to ensure accessible and equitable experiences for disabled individuals, most notable is the passage of the Americans with Disabilities Act (ADA) of 1990, and more recently the ADA Amendments Act of 2008, that seek to end discrimination based on disability status in employment, public services, and public accommodations, such as educational institutions. Alongside this political movement, Disability Studies has emerged as a critical, academic discipline to examine how disability is presented and represented across various disciplines (disstudies.org).

While impairment has been recognized since antiquity, disability is a relatively new sociopolitical category. Shakespeare (1997, 2012) describes new thinking on disability through a social model that distinguishes impairment from disability and responds to access systemically through design rather than individual interventions. Disability Studies challenges the dominant narrative on disability by discerning impairment from disability, focusing on the conditions that disable or create disability: the physical, technological, educational, social, political, economic, medical, and legal structures that create barriers for disabled people. Scholars challenge conceptualizations of disabled people as deficient and less than human and instead celebrate impairment as a natural facet of human diversity (Society for Disability Studies, n.d.). Disability Studies promotes disability as a sociopolitical experience, shaped by power and oppression. This emerging perspective elucidates how individuals designated "disabled" are treated collectively in a manner that diminishes their economic, interpersonal, psychological, cultural, political, and physical well-being, relegating them to membership in a socially marginalized, disadvantaged group. By moving away from the idea that impairment is the problem, we can understand disability as the interaction between the individual and larger social values, practices, and systems.

Universal Design

Universal Design (UD) presents promising strategies to operationalize social model thinking about disability. UD is the design of products and environments to be usable to all people without the need for specialized design or modification (Center for Universal Design, 1997). We must look at the design of our environment and understand who is excluded and who is included. UD rejects the need for individual accommodations because access is achieved broadly and systemically. UD has seven principles that can be applied to a variety of environments: (1) Equitable Use; (2) Flexibility in Use; (3) Simple and Intuitive Use; (4) Perceptible Information; (5) Tolerance for Error; (6) Low Physical Effort; and (7) Size and Space for Approach and Use. An offset of UD, and a construct particularly relevant to educators, is UD for Learning with three main tenets: multiple means of participation, engagement, and representation (Steinfeld & Maisel, 2012). These principles encourage flexible curricular design by providing various ways for students to interact and intersect with the instructor, the content and with one another, as well as offering a variety of methods by which to demonstrate and assess learning. Though in higher education, administrators, faculty, and staff may not readily consider themselves designers, they do in fact design policy, curriculum, events, programming, and communication, all of which reflect values about diversity, inclusion, and access.

Disability in Higher Education

Diversity in higher education is an ever-important issue. While we may agree on a working definition of diversity that includes race, class, gender and sexual orientation, disability has a precarious seat at higher education's table of social justice. Our practices are very much informed by the dominant societal narrative on disability—disability is stigmatized, something to be hidden or avoided, hence the lack of disability cultural centers, dedicated space, or programming on campuses as compared to resources put toward other social identity groups. Though institutions of higher education take seriously their obligation to provide access to disabled students and employees, they often do so by interpreting the ADA very narrowly and reactively by responding to requests for reasonable accommodations once an individual has encountered a barrier. Our practices suggest that disabled students and employees are responsible for their own access on campus, whereas for other groups, the institution has a more pronounced and proactive role in ensuring an inclusive experience.

Disability Services

Campus disability services (DS) offices or resource centers are designated by an institution to monitor ADA compliance and determine reasonable accommodations. Through their service delivery and campus partnerships, DS offices have the power to influence the larger campus culture around disability and access. When situated to work proactively to facilitate the institution's federal obligation to accessibility, the impact of a DS office should be quite far reaching. Consumed with responding to requests for reasonable accommodations, DS offices are typically positioned to work individually and reactively, reinforcing a narrative on campus that positions disabled students as needy and burdensome. Given their focus on compliance, DS professionals engage in practices that do not reflect progressive thinking on disability or access, and yet are considered to be the leaders for the disability experience on campus. Without consistent exposure to Disability Studies and Universal Design, DS professionals will continue to perpetuate disempowering ideas about disability and disability-related access, and because this is consistent with the way society has been socialized to understand disability, most faculty, students, and administrators will continue to engage in this narrative without question.

Reimagining and Redesigning Disability Services: A Case Study

The University of Arizona has an enrollment of over 40,000 graduate and undergraduate students. Approximately 2,500 students identify as disabled, and about 1,800 utilize disability-related accommodations. The Disability Resource Center (DRC) has been an integral part of the campus community for over 40 years. For the last 15 years, UA DRC has been working to shift professional thinking and concomitant practices to reinforce a more progressive concept of disability and accessibility.

In 1999, with the arrival of a new director, the DRC staff began the arduous process of examining its values about disability. In its efforts to reframe disability on campus, DRC first worked to ensure that all of its staff understood and could articulate the core concepts of disability studies, that is, social model and UD. Not unlike the broader public or campus community, DRC staff were steeped in medical model thinking, perhaps highlighted by the reality that many DS professionals come from applied educational fields such as rehabilitation counseling, special education, and social work. While they understood social justice, they conceptualized it mainly in terms of race, class, gender, and sexual orientation. The challenge became not simply how to articulate new thinking on disability, but how to operationalize it through practice. We began the ongoing work to infuse social model thinking into every aspect of the department, so that we could easily and fluently model these ideas to the campus.

Informed by the social model, the office promotes a view of disability that is social, cultural, and political. DRC uses the social model of disability and principles of UD to inform its departmental practices so as to model a progressive concept of disability across campus. Toward that end, the DRC has shifted its focus away from the individual and more to the environment, operationalizing an institutional commitment to access for all students. DRC strives for simpler, less burdensome practices, and to ensure access through proactive and sustainable approaches. Specific departmental goals include the following:

- Provide leadership to the campus community by modeling a social model of disability.
- Align departmental practices with social model values.
- Ensure a campus experience for disabled students that is comparable, if not identical, to that of their non-disabled peers.
- Promote social justice, sustainability, access, and inclusion; and alleviate the necessity for individual accommodations.

Language

The first area that DRC addressed in the implementation of the social model was language. Staff analyzed its use of disability-related and helping language. We recognized that throughout our materials we used words like "need," "support," "allow," "service," "assistance," "special," "compliance," "needs," "able," and "able-bodied." As staff analyzed the use of these words, we recognized that we were inadvertently reinforcing deficit and charity thinking by implying that the individual is the problem and that professionals had the power to remedy the situation individually. As a result, we made changes in language across our websites and materials in the descriptions of our office mission, job titles, job descriptions, eligibility, service delivery practices, and also in conversations with disabled students, faculty, and colleagues.

The previous departmental mission statement follows:

> *The mission of the Disability Service Office is to provide and coordinate support services and programs that allow students with disabilities to receive equal access to an education within legal mandates (ADA) and to be judged on their abilities not their special needs.*

Our revised mission statement now reads:

> *Disability Resources works to create inclusive and sustainable learning and working environments and facilitate access, discourse, and involvement through innovative services and programs, leadership, and collaboration.*

The DRC mission statement now represents disability as an aspect of diversity and access as an issue of social justice, and equity.

Job titles and job descriptions were also updated to support new thinking. For example:

- Disability Specialists are now Access Consultants.
- Student Testing Coordinator is now Exam Administration Coordinator.
- Student Assistive Technology Coordinator is now IT Accessibility Consultant.

To expand, the previous job description for "Disability Specialist" was as follows:

> *The Disability Specialist establishes student disability status and eligibility for accommodations. Reviews disability documentation, determines accommodation plan, coordinates services, and provides advice, advocacy, and referrals to students. Ensures best practice with legal mandates and University policies while minimizing the University's exposure to risk.*

The current job description for "Access Consultant" is as follows:

> *Informed by Disability Studies and Universal Design, the Access Consultant works directly with students to identify barriers in the environment and respond to requests for reasonable accommodations. The Access Consultant works with students, staff, and faculty to improve accessibility on campus with the ultimate goal of ensuring that disabled students have full access to their University experience.*

The job description now emphasizes identifying and responding to problems or barriers in the environment and ensuring access through increased collaboration.

Service Delivery Practices

Our goal is to ensure a similar, if not identical, campus experience for disabled students to that of their non-disabled peers. We do not believe disabled students should have the additional burden of advocating for access that non-disabled simply get by virtue of enrollment. The Association on Higher Education and Disability (AHEAD), the international professional organization that offers guidance and practical standards for disability services, recently revised its guidance on how to utilize documentation in determining reasonable accommodation (AHEAD, 2012). Where previously students were required to provide medical documentation so a professional could determine eligibility and reasonableness, now AHEAD advises a more holistic, individualized process that relies on good conversation with the student about where and how she/he experiences disability-related barriers. That conversation alone might be sufficient to implement an effective accommodation. Should questions remain, the DS professional could ask for documentation or consult with a colleague to make a determination. Not only is this revised procedure less medical or clinical, but also it dismantles the power dynamic between professional as gatekeeper and student as disempowered.

While DRC staff could verbally articulate this new guidance, our practices were not designed to reflect our values:

> *Services are available to students with diagnosed disabilities. Examples of such disabilities include: Learning Disabilities and Attention Deficit Disorders, Mobility and Sensory Impairments, Neurological, Psychological and Medical Disabilities. Federal laws governing access for students with disabilities stipulate that educational institutions may require documentation of disability prior to delivering services.*

Previously, the focus was on the individual by requiring appropriate medical documentation, to prove disability and identify a specific diagnostic category to determine eligibility. The revised eligibility statement now reads:

> *Everyone is unique. A conversation about your experiences and expectations will help identify the information necessary to support your accommodation requests. Helpful information may include: medical records, psychoeducational test reports, or school records. Don't delay completing the Accommodation Request Form if you don't have any formal disability-related paperwork.*

Today, DRC acknowledges that individuals are unique and that they are the experts regarding their disability experience. Their story is validated. Students are not burdened with proving they are disabled and DRC staff have the opportunity to develop relationships with them as individuals before being biased by professional documentation.

Through this process, DRC staff came to appreciate that its practices placed a great deal of the burden for access on students, reinforcing the notion that disabled students were the problem and were responsible for ensuring access that non-disabled student were given. The risk here, we quickly realized, was that not only were we reinforcing these ideas to students and our staff, but to faculty and administrators on campus.

The typical process to arrange testing accommodations is as follows:

1. Student must schedule exam, often in person.
2. Student must make testing arrangements weeks in advance.
3. Student must negotiate and confirm with faculty.
4. Student must get exam and deliver to testing center.
5. Student must return exam to instructor.

The process informed by the social model of disability is as follows:

1. Student schedules exams online.
2. Student shows up to take exam.
3. DS staff make all arrangements with faculty before, during, and after testing.

This process, though very consistent with practice across the country at most colleges and universities, was cumbersome and inequitable. Students using testing accommodations were required to take many steps that their non-disabled class-mates were not. A non-disabled peer needs only to get out of bed and show up to the classroom to access their exam, while disabled students were required to plan weeks in advance.

True to the social model, DRC staff reflected on how the design of an exam often presented disability-related barriers. With this new understanding, we increased our outreach with faculty to address course design and accessible learning assessments. More and more faculty now design more accessible exams or provide accommodations on site, to provide a more similar experience for all enrolled students. Should faculty continue to design exams or assessments that present barriers, students are welcome to test at DRC. They would use our online portal to provide exam dates, while DRC staff work with faculty to procure their exams and any specific information about test-taking. Staff communicate with faculty and make a plan to return their exams. Historically, DRC administers over 12,000 exams each year. We are beginning to see a decline in these numbers and believe this decrease is due to more consistent and effective outreach with faculty.

Campus Outreach

Campus outreach is critical to changing the narrative on campus with regard to disability and difference. In order to operationalize our commitment to good design and equitable access, we must identify systemic barriers and remove them. The DRC has become more proactive in its outreach efforts through more pro-active strategies and developing a more effective web or online presence.

Faculty and the Curricular Environment

Our previous communication with faculty previously entailed providing disabil-ity-specific information about a particular student, detailed disability etiquette, reiterated legal requirements, and related roles and responsibilities. Now the focus of our outreach with faculty is Universal Design for Learning and how to reduce or eliminate barriers in the design of their courses. Staff consult with instructors on how to redesign their learning assessments and activities or on how to pro-vide accommodations as seamlessly as possible. We target large-enrollment classes with high numbers of disabled students well before the start of each semester to connect with faculty and discuss how to maximize access. Large-venue faculty alone represent over 70 unique consultations. Many instructors with whom we have consulted on course design remark that these changes have increased opportunities for engagement and participation broadly, have maximized teaching time, and have helped them provide a more equitable and meaningful experience to all students (Burgstahler, 2007).

To address curriculum and study, UA hosts a disability studies collaborative. Housed in the College of Social and Behavioral Sciences in Gender and Women's Studies, this interdisciplinary group of faculty and practitioners come together to identify disability-related research and implement events with disability studies authors. A goal is to impact curriculum broadly, by identifying opportunities to infuse disability and disability studies into general education courses and electives and to increase disability-specific courses, especially outside of applied fields. According to a 2009 study, there are 21 disability studies programs across American colleges and universities (Cushing & Smith, 2009). Until we are able to procure faculty lines and offer proper disability studies major, the collaborative is way to keep wwdisability on our curricular radar.

Physical and Technology Environments

UA DRC is fortunate to have dedicated staff positions to coordinate and consult on campus-wide physical and technology access. Both positions consult on major projects and purchases to ensure the highest levels of accessibility and usability. Staff consulted on the planning and design of ten new construction and major renovation projects in academic year 2013–2014, as well as consulted on the design of major campus events that saw participation of thousands of diverse students, employees, and community members (University of Arizona Disability Resource Center, 2014). Relative to technology, in collaboration with Procurement and Contracting Services, DRC worked to implement procedures to assess and ensure the accessibility of university-wide purchases of electronic and information technology and other goods and services. While the individual campus DS office may not have dedicated staff to spearhead this kind of outreach, building relationships with key partners can bring the campus together around the goal of ensuring good, seamless access systemically.

Campus Events and the Social Environment

Events and engagement opportunities reflect not only ideas about disability, but an idea of who is invited and welcomed to participate. We must look at what messages each event sends about disability as well as the accessibility in its design. A popular way to program or raise awareness about disability is to create a simulation or immersion activity. However, within the disability community, simulations are highly controversial (French, 1992; Swain, French, & Cameron, 2005;

Herbert, 2000; Straumshein, 2013). Simulations cannot truly or completely replicate the disability experience. Focusing on only certain pieces of the disability experience, simulations tend to leave participants with increased negative perceptions of disability—feelings of pity for disabled folks or relief that they are not disabled—rather than engender a feeling of pride or respect for the community.

We work with event planners and student leaders to identify programmatic outcomes such as what they hope for participants to gain, learn, or appreciate as a result of having attended an educational program. We ask how they might program around another cultural group. Rather than try to simulate a complex cultural experience, we encourage the exploration of one specific aspect of the experience, for example, accessibility, sports, or activism. Disability awareness events seek to increase sensitivity toward people with disabilities, yet they mostly focus on etiquette, simulation, understanding disabilities, myths, and compliance, which do not tend to encourage participants to consider disability from a sociopolitical perspectives.

Programming that is informed by social justice and the social model include reading and discussing first-person narratives; studying the impact of design; hosting disabled authors, artists, or performers; attending a wheelchair sports event; or engaging in disability activism. One example of an effective program that invited students, staff and faculty participation is "Disability in the Academy," an annual event that hosts disability studies authors and poets to do readings and writing workshops. Another example, our Disability Justice Project, invited disabled and non-disabled students to come together under the umbrella of justice and looked specifically at disability on campus and in the community.

Conclusion

UA DRC continues to spend a great deal of time reviewing our website, communications, and practices to ensure that our language, service delivery, and outreach efforts are aligned with disability studies and the social model of disability. DS providers in higher education are influential in shaping how campus communities define and conceptualize disability; they can and should be hub for progressive thinking about disability and access on campus.

When we reflect on the student experience on campus, from recruitment to enrollment through graduation, disability must be represented progressively and consistently. It is not enough to cite the ADA and advertise that we facilitate individual accommodations so as not to discriminate on the basis of disability. In order to cultivate a campus culture that is truly welcoming and inclusive to disabled students, individual accommodations should be the institution's minimal response, a foundation upon which to build. Accommodations do not ensure an equitable experience, or necessarily a positive or respectful one. Access and equity are institutional responsibilities and values that should guide the design of our campus environments. Good access is seamless, and available without individual requests. In an ideal world, we would not need the term "universal design," because it is what good design would be (Preiser & Ostroff, 2001).

We must also be critical of how disability is represented in institutional marketing and communications, through curriculum and events. What is the narrative we produce on campus through images and language? Is it one of compliance and pity or one of community and pride? How does an institution communicate that disability is a valued and welcome perspective? What would a prospective disabled student understand about her/his disability identity from campus materials?

Changing the narrative on disability on campus and in higher education requires a paradigm shift in the way we conceive of the disability experience. The DS office can be a good resource, but it is incumbent on all community members to challenge what they think they know about disability and develop attitudes and behaviors that are informed by social justice.

Notes

1   Consistent with social model thinking on disability, the authors have chosen to use "disabled" and "non-disabled" versus person-first language ("person with a disability") throughout this chapter to reinforce that it is the environment that disables individuals with impairment.

References

AHED (Association on Higher Education and Disability) (2012). *Supporting accommodation requests: Guidance on documentation practices—April 2012*. Retrieved from https://www.ahead.org/learn/resources/documentation-guidance.

Brault, M. (2012). Americans with disabilities: 2010 household economic studies. U. S. Census Bureau.

Burgstahler, S. (2007). Who needs an accessible classroom? *Academe, 93*(3), 37–39. http://eds.b.ebscohost.com.ezproxy2.library.arizona.edu/ehost/detail?sid=2b25d422-aa02-440a-85dc-808667783867%40sessionmgr112&vid=2&hid=116&bdata=JnNpdGU9ZWhvc3QtbGl2ZQ%3d%3d#db=eric&AN=EJ765979.

Center for Universal Design, North Carolina State University (2008). Retrieved from https://www.ncsu.edu/ncsu/design/cud/about_ud/udprinciples.htm.

Cushing, P., & Smith, T. (2009). A multinational review of English-language disability studies degrees and courses. *Disability Studies Quarterly, 29*(3).

Davis, L. J. (2011) Why is disability missing from the discourse on diversity. Retrieved from http://chronicle.com/article/Why-Is-Disability-Missing-From/129088/.

French, S. (1992). Simulation exercises in disability awareness training: A critique. *Disability and Society 7*(3), 257–267.

Haller, B. A. (2010). *Representing disability in an ableist world: Essays on mass media* (pp. 25–48, 49–66, 137–154). Louisville, KY: Advocado Press.

Herbert, J. (2000). Simulation as a learning method to facilitate disability awareness. *Journal of Experiential Education, 23*(1), 5–11.

Kraus, A., & Rattray, N. (2011). Understanding disability in the student veteran community. In C. Rumann & F. Hamrick (Eds.), *Called to serve: A handbook on student veterans in higher education* (pp. 116–138). San Francisco, CA: Jossey Bass.

Longmore, P. K. (2003). Screening stereotypes: Images of disabled people in television and motion pictures. In *Why I burned my book and other essays on disability* (pp. 131–148). Philadelphia, PA: Temple University Press.

Molina, D., & Morse, A. (2010). Military-conencted undegraduates: Exploring the differences between National Guard, reserve, active duty, and veterans in higher education. Retrieved from https://www.acenet.edu/news-room/Documents/Military-Connected-Undergraduates.pdf.

National Center on Universal Design (2014). About UDL. Retrieved from http://www.udlcenter.org/aboutudl/whatisudl.

Preiser, W., & Ostroff, E. (2001). *Universal Design handbook.* New York, NY: McGraw-Hill.

Shakespeare, T. (1997). The social model of disability. In L. J. Davis (Ed.), *The disability studies reader* (pp. 266–273). London and New York, NY: Routlege.

Shakespeare, T. (2012). Understanding the social model of disability. In N. Watson, A. Roulstone, & C. Thomas (Eds.), *Routledge handbook of disability studies.* London: Routledge.

Society for Disability Studies (n.d.). What is disability studies? Retrieved from http://www.disstudies.org/about/what_is_ds.

Steinfeld, E., & Maisel, J. L. (2012). *Universal Design.* Hoboken, NJ: John Wiley & Sons.

Straumshein, C. (March 7, 2013). Disability awareness draws scrutiny. Retrieved from http://www.insidehighered.com/news/2013/03/07/clemson-professors-criticize-trivializing-disability-awareness-event.

Swain, J., French, S., & Cameron, C. (2003). *Controversial issues in a disabling society.* Buckingham: Open University Press.

Swain, J., French, S., & Cameron, C. (2005). Practice: Are professionals parasites. In J. Swain, S. French, & C. Cameron (Eds.), *Controversial Issues in a Disabling Society* (pp. 131–140). New York, NY: Open University Press.

University of Arizona Disability Resource Center (2014). Annual Report. Retrieved from http://drc.arizona.edu/sites/drc.arizona.edu/files/DRC%20Annual%20Report%20AY%202013-2014.pdf.

ABOUT THE CONTRIBUTORS

Heather Albanesi is an Associate Professor at the University of Colorado Colorado Springs. She received her Ph.D. in sociology from the University of California at Berkeley, and she completed her undergraduate studies at Wesleyan University in Middletown, Connecticut. Her research interests include heterosexuality, gender, disability, privilege, parenting, and education. She is the author of *Gender and Sexual Agency: How Young People Make Choices about Sex* (2010, Lexington Books), and her current research look at the intersections of disability, veteran status, and transitions to higher education.

Taghreed A. Alhaddab is an independent researcher from Saudi Arabia with research interests in college access, degree-job match, and minorities' college retention. A recent graduate of Seton Hall University (USA) with a Ph.D. in Higher Education Research, Assessment, and Program Evaluation, Taghreed has several publications in related journals and conferences, including the *Journal of First-Year Experience and Students in Transition, Journal of International Students*, IEEE Conference, NERA Conference, and many others.

Cali Anicha (aka Colleen McDonald Morken) is a public school teacher and adjunct instructor. She received her Ph.D. from North Dakota State University (NDSU) and holds additional degrees from Minnesota State University Moorhead (B.S. and M.S.), and NDSU (M.S.). Cali's teaching and research interests include educational equity, social justice, and complex systems. As a graduate assistant with NDSU's National Science Foundation–funded ADVANCE FORWARD Institutional Transformation program, Cali served on a Faculty with Disabilities Task Force, and she continues to work as a Research Associate with that program.

Katherine C. Aquino holds a B.S. in psychology from Fordham University, an M.A. in school psychology from Georgian Court University, and a Ph.D. in Higher Education Leadership, Management, and Policy from Seton Hall University. Her research interests include the socio-academic transitioning into and throughout postsecondary education for students with disabilities and other underrepresented student populations. Her work appears in the *Journal of the First-Year Experience and Students in Transition*, the *Journal of Postsecondary Education and Disability*, and the *Review of Higher Education*.

D. Eric Archer, Ph.D., is an Assistant Professor of educational leadership higher education in the Department of Educational Leadership, Research, and Technology and a faculty affiliate of the global and international studies program at Western Michigan University. He received his Ph.D. in educational leadership and policy studies from Oklahoma State University. His research interests include issues of diversity and inclusion in postsecondary education and globalization in higher education.

Sarah Beckman is originally from Ottawa, Ontario, but has lived in a variety of regions throughout the world, including East Africa, Nepal, and England. Her background consists of working in community health, community outreach, and education in communities that experience marginalization. Currently, Sarah is a Midwifery student at Ryerson University in Toronto, Ontario. She plans to employ her social justice perspective in her future work as a Midwife by prioritizing pregnant individuals who frequently experience marginalization when accessing the health-care system.

Eric R. Bernstein is an Assistant Professor of Educational Leadership and Adult Learning at the University of Connecticut Neag School of Education. He holds a joint appointment in the School of Dental Medicine as Director of Curriculum Advancement. In collaboration with the University of Pennsylvania Graduate School of Education, Dr. Bernstein serves as Associate Director of the Penn Educational Leadership Simulation Program. Prior to UCONN, Dr. Bernstein was on the faculty at the University of Southern California Rossier School of Education. He holds an Education Doctorate from the University of Pennsylvania and a Juris Doctor degree from the University of Connecticut.

Canan Bilen-Green is Vice Provost at North Dakota State University. She is also Dale Hogoboom Professor of Industrial and Manufacturing Engineering. She received her Ph.D. from the University of Wyoming. She holds additional degrees from Middle East Technical University (B.S.), Bilkent University (M.S.), and University of Wyoming (M.S.). Dr. Bilen-Green's primary teaching and research interest is in quality engineering and management of people systems. As lead investigator and director of the National Science Foundation–funded

ADVANCE FORWARD Institutional Transformation program, Dr. Bilen-Green formed and served on NDSU's Faculty with Disabilities Task Force and Commission on the Status of Women Faculty.

Rachel E. Friedensen is a doctoral candidate at the University of Massachusetts Amherst in Educational Leadership & Policy Studies with a concentration in Higher Education. Rachel is interested in feminist and poststructuralist theory, faculty development and faculty life, and issues of access and equity in higher education. In addition to current research about the climate for students with disabilities in STEM fields, she is also working on her dissertation, a policy discourse analysis of the construction of the "Diverse Other" in policies and strategic plans at a public research university.

Susan L. Gabel is Professor of Teacher Education at Wayne State University in Detroit, Michigan, where she teaches courses on inclusive education. Her research focuses on structural exclusion, inclusion, and the institutional production of disability.

Matthew D. Green III is an undergraduate student at Ryerson University, majoring in Radio and Television Arts (RTA). He is also a freelance writer, editor, and photographer. Single-handedly landing hundreds of thousands of views for videos on YouTube, he undoubtedly enjoys what he does. While not yet an award-winning writer, the potential is most certainly there.

Denise O'Neil Green is the inaugural Assistant Vice-President/Vice-Provost Equity, Diversity, and Inclusion at Ryerson University in Toronto. Prior to Ryerson, she was the Associate Vice President for Institutional Diversity at Central Michigan University. Before taking on a senior leadership post, she was faculty at the University of Illinois Urbana-Champaign and the University of Nebraska–Lincoln in higher education administration and educational psychology, respectively. She is the 2016 Pioneer for Change award recipient for Women in Leadership, co-author of *100 Accomplished Black Canadian Women— 2016 Edition*, and is Executive Editor for InstitutionalDiversityBlog.com.

Jacalyn Griffen is a Visiting Assistant Professor and Coordinator of Teacher Credentialing in the Benerd School of Education. Through critical and social justice frameworks, she employs an action-inquiry focus to bring change to the status quo of institutionalized barriers that hinder the engagement of historically marginalized students and families in the educational system. Her research studies the complex issues faced by students, families, and the educational systems they must navigate in a localized context. She employs a social justice lens when teaching action research and pluralism to graduate level students. Collaboration and collegiality with peers, faculty, scholars, P-12 administrators, students, and families are the hallmark of her scholarship and practice.

Wanda Hadley, Ph.D., LPC, is an Assistant Professor of educational leadership higher education in the Department of Educational Leadership, Research, and Technology at Western Michigan University. She received her Ph.D. in educational leadership from the University of Dayton in Dayton, Ohio. Dr. Hadley is also a Licensed Professional Counselor in the State of Ohio. She has researched extensively the academic adjustment issues first-year students with learning disabilities experience in their transition to college.

Eunyoung Kim is an Associate Professor in the Department of Education Leadership, Management and Policy at Seton Hall University. Her recent scholarship focuses on the transition experiences of students within organizational and institutional environments and socio-cultural contexts. This focus is applied to three interrelated topics of research inquiry: (1) college access and success for underserved student populations, (2) equity issues within the Unite States and global context, and (3) intersectionality of the individual within diversity framework. She holds an M.A. and Ph.D. from the University of Illinois at Urbana-Champaign.

Ezekiel Kimball is an Assistant Professor of higher education at the University of Massachusetts–Amherst. In his work, he studies the roles that individual agency, institutional practices, and social structures play in the construction of student experience. His recent research has examined the way that student affairs professionals use scholarly knowledge in practice and the way that disability status shapes student success in higher education.

Amanda Kraus received her M.A. and Ph.D. from the University of Arizona (UA) in Higher Education. She currently serves as Deputy Director at UA's Disability Resource Center. Dr. Kraus is Assistant Professor of Practice in the Center for the Study of Higher Education at UA, where she coordinates the Master's program and instructs courses on student affairs, student development, and disability. Dr. Kraus serves on the board of directors for the Association on Higher Education and Disability and has delivered numerous keynotes and workshops at institutions nationally and internationally, including Duke University, Wake Forest University, and Singapore Management University.

Sue Kroeger is currently the Director of Disability Resources at the University of Arizona. She received her doctorate in human rehabilitative services from the University of Northern Colorado. In addition to her administrative duties, she has presented at numerous conferences, published articles, and co-edited a book entitled *Responding to Disability Issues in Student Affairs*. She has been President of the National Association of Higher Education and Disability. She holds adjunct faculty status in the Department of Disability and Psychoeducational Studies, where she teaches undergraduate courses in disability studies. She has been principal investigator for numerous federal grants and has consulted nationally and internationally.

Adam R. Lalor is a doctoral candidate in the Department of Educational Psychology at the University of Connecticut and holds an M.Ed. in Educational Policy, Planning, and Leadership–Higher Education Administration from the College of William and Mary. Adam's research focuses on the transition of students with disabilities to higher education and the preparation of college administrators to meet the needs of this student population. He has experience as a higher education administrator and is an active member of the American College Personnel Association, the National Association of Student Personnel Administrators, and the Council for Exceptional Children.

Allison R. Lombardi is an Assistant Professor at the University of Connecticut. She teaches undergraduate and graduate courses in the Special Education Program within the Department of Educational Psychology in the Neag School of Education. She's also the director of the graduate certificate program in Postsecondary Disability Services. In her research, Dr. Lombardi studies the transition from adolescence to adulthood, with a particular focus on college and career readiness (CCR) and higher education experiences of underrepresented groups, including students with disabilities. Dr. Lombardi currently serves on the editorial boards of the *Journal of Diversity in Higher Education, Career Development and Transition for Exceptional Individuals*, and the *Journal on Postsecondary Education and Disability*. She earned her Ph.D. from the University of Oregon in 2010 and her M.A. and B.A. degrees from the University of California, Berkeley, in 2003 and 2000, respectively.

Ryan A. Miller, Ph.D., is Assistant Professor of Educational Leadership (Higher Education) at the University of North Carolina at Charlotte. His research focuses on creating inclusive campus cultures in higher education. Ryan's dissertation on intersections of disability and LGBTQ identities received the 2016 Melvene D. Hardee Dissertation of the Year award from NASPA Student Affairs Administrators in Higher Education. He holds graduate degrees in education from the University of Texas at Austin and Harvard University.

Emily A. Nusbaum is an Assistant Professor at University of San Francisco and coordinator of a doctoral program focused on disability and equity. Her current research is focused on developing critical, qualitative methods related to disability, as well as understanding the experiences of disabled students on post-secondary campuses. She has used ethnographic methods to uncover the tenuous commitments of teachers to inclusive schooling within accountability pressures, concluding with the need for inclusive education to be taken up as an ideological stance and examined within critical frameworks, moving beyond literature that focuses on technical implementation of practice.

Holly Pearson recently earned her doctorate in Education with a Disability Studies emphasis from Chapman University. Dr. Pearson's research focuses on intersectionality and diversity in higher education. From a critical spatial and architectural standpoint, she is interested in the experiential dynamics of space(s) and identities as a means of critically re-approaching design with diversity and intersectionality.

Chris M. Ray is Associate Professor and Coordinator of the Education Doctoral Programs at North Dakota State University. He received his Ph.D. in Educational Psychology from Oklahoma State University and holds additional degrees from Missouri University of Science and Technology (B.S.) and Oklahoma State University (M.S.). His primary teaching and research interest is in defining, measuring, and improving quality in educational institutions. Dr. Ray serves as an NSF-funded ADVANCE FORWARD Gender-Equity Advocate. He also co-chaired the campus climate team and has chaired university committees to eliminate gender-related bias from the assessment of teaching policy and the Student Rating of Instruction instrument.

Denise P. Reid has the honor of serving as Assistant Professor in the School of Education at Biola University in La Mirada, California. Dr. Reid earned a Ph.D. in Education with an emphasis in Disability Studies from Chapman University. She has served students in the education systems for nearly three decades. Dr. Reid has been instrumental in providing educational services and accommodations to students with disabilities to ensure the successful transition from high school to postsecondary education and college retention of students with disabilities.

Michelle Samura is Assistant Professor and Associate Dean for Undergraduate Education in the College of Educational Studies at Chapman University. She also is the founding Co-Director of the Collaborate Initiative. Dr. Samura's research focuses on the intersections of space, race, and education. She is particularly interested in how a spatial approach offers a unique lens to more effectively examine varying levels of power and a more accessible language to talk about the related dilemmas with which people wrestle.

Lauren Shallish is an Assistant Professor of Special Education at the College of New Jersey. Her work appears in *Disability Studies Quarterly*, the *IGI Handbook of Global Education, Equity and Excellence in Education*, and the Disability Studies in Education section of the *Encyclopedia of Educational Philosophy and Theory*. She previously worked as Chief of Staff at Hobart and William Smith Colleges and as a qualitative research assistant for the Center for Institutional and Social Change at Columbia University.

Elton Silva is a Senior Consultant of Strategic Product Development at CVS Health and a graduate of Curry College. As an undergraduate, he researched a variety of topics, most notably students with learning disabilities. His research outlines numerous strategies that institutions can employ to facilitate the learning process for students with learning disabilities. In his current role, he supports operational work plan development, assists in the conducting of consumer research, and develops business cases to demonstrate overall program value.

Tenisha Tevis is an Assistant Professor in the College of Education, Adult and Higher Education Leadership at Oregon State University. Tenisha explores issues related to students' transition to college and the role administrators play in this process. Through a critical-advocacy lens, she develops research that improves practice, informs policy, converges theoretical frameworks, and gives voice to underserved and marginalized populations. Utilizing both quantitative and qualitative methodologies, her scholarship encourages educational leaders to assuage systemic challenges related to institutional climate, student engagement, and cultural disconnect. By analyzing the social, cultural, economic, and political forces that influence agency and change, she is better able to understand the mindset and preparedness of historically underrepresented groups and the context to which students transition.

Annemarie Vaccaro is an Associate Professor in the College Student Personnel Program within the Department of Human Development and Family Studies at the University of Rhode Island. Her teaching and scholarly interests focus on intersectionality, diversity, and social justice issues in higher education. Her most recent research focuses on how diverse college students with all types of disabilities define and develop a sense of purpose while in college.

Kristine W. Webb, Ph.D., is a Professor at the University of North Florida in the Department of Exceptional, Deaf, and Interpreter Education. Her interests are transition to postsecondary education for students with disabilities, inclusion on college campuses, and student empowerment. Kris was the UNF 2015 Distinguished Professor, and she was the co-editor of the *Handbook of Adolescent Transition Education for Youth with Disabilities* and co-author of *Transition to Postsecondary Education for Students with Disabilities*.

Heather Willis joined Ryerson University in 2010 as Ryerson's inaugural Accessibility Coordinator. Heather has been an advocate in the area of accessibility and improving the lives of persons with disabilities since she was a teenager growing up in an institution for disabled children. She leads Ryerson's accessibility initiative—*Access Ryerson*—with a goal to identify, remove and prevent accessibility barriers for all members of the Ryerson community. Heather is a proud graduate from Ryerson's Disability Studies Program and has a post-graduate diploma in Disability Studies from the University of Leeds.

Richmond D. Wynn, Ph.D., is Assistant Professor and Director of the Clinical Mental Health Counseling program at the University of North Florida. His research focuses on intersectionality of identity, traumatic stress, and health outcomes with an emphasis on historically marginalized social identity groups. He is specifically interested in the ways in which culturally diverse, lesbian, gay, bisexual, and transgender (LGBT) people negotiate their identities and manage their health.

Christina Yuknis is an Associate Professor at Gallaudet University in Washington, D.C. She was a middle school teacher in programs supporting students with learning disabilities and students who are deaf, and she worked as a policy evaluation specialist for her school system. She is the president of the Convention of American Instructors of the Deaf. Dr. Yuknis holds a Doctorate of Philosophy in Education Policy Studies from the University of Maryland, a Master of Science in Education Studies from Johns Hopkins University, and a Master of the Arts in Deaf Education: Multiple Disabilities from Gallaudet University.

INDEX

21st century skills 123–124

ableism 20, 26, 27, 82–83
academic integration 47–48
academic supports 76
ACCESS *see* Assessment of Campus Climate to Enhance Student Success (ACCESS)
accessibility 41, 90, 93–94, 123, 130–131, 157
Accessibility for Ontarians with Disabilities Act (AODA) 201–202, 212–213
Accessibility of Campus Computing for Students with Disabilities Scale (ACCSDS) 115
Access Ryerson 200–214; Advisory Committee 207–208; approach of 202; Chairs Coordinating Group 210; leadership structure and components 206–210; principles and values 204–206; problem addressed by 202–204; Steering Committee 207; student testimonials 210–213; Working Groups 208–209
Accommodation of University Students with Disabilities Inventory (AUSDI) 116
accommodations 5–6, 26–28, 75–76, 79–80, 85, 94, 108, 143–145, 159–160, 172
accountability 15, 124–125
ACCSDS *see* Accessibility of Campus Computing for Students with Disabilities Scale (ACCSDS)

ACPA *see* American College Personnel Association (ACPA)
ACT Framework 128–132
ADA *see* Americans with Disabilities Act (ADA)
ADD *see* attention deficit disorder (ADD)
ADHD *see* attention deficit hyperactivity disorder (ADHD)
administrators: decision-making tools for 114–117; disability service professionals 109–110, 112–113, 155–157, 165; knowledge and attitudes of, toward disability 107–118; professional development for 112–114; resistance by 185, 186; student affairs 70, 110–111, 113–114, 138–149; treatment of students with disabilities by 190–191
ADVANCE initiative 130
advocates 154–155, 156, 161
Affordable Care Act 32
African American students 53, 54, 56, 57, 58, 172
AHEAD *see* Association on Higher Education and Disability (AHEAD)
alienation 40
American College Personnel Association (ACPA) 113
Americans with Disabilities Act (ADA) 7, 20–22, 32, 76, 79, 85, 124, 154, 157, 172, 197, 219
Americans with Disabilities Act Amendment 154, 161, 219

antidiscrimination law 21–22, 32, 50,
    75–76, 78–79, 83, 85, 124, 154,
    201–202, 219
AODA *see* Accessibility for Ontarians
    with Disabilities Act (AODA)
ARCHSECRET 115
Asian students 54, 55–56
assessment 13–15, 114–117
Assessment of Campus Climate to
    Enhance Student Success
    (ACCESS) 117
Association on Higher Education and
    Disability (AHEAD) 79, 110, 223
attention deficit disorder (ADD) 80
attention deficit hyperactivity disorder
    (ADHD) 78, 85
attitudes, disability-related 7–8, 107–118
AUSDI *see* Accommodation of University
    Students with Disabilities Inventory
    (AUSDI)
authenticity 39–40
autism spectrum disorder (ASD) 77–78, 85

Beginning Postsecondary Students
    Longitudinal Study 48–49
belonginess 51–53, 58
biases 34–36, 41, 55–57
body, role of 5
built environment 95–98, 130–131,
    188–189, 218, 226

California State University
    websites 171–182
campus climate 51–58, 65, 107, 116,
    122–123, 129–131, 162, 185–198, 203
campus events 226–227
campus layout 97–98
campus outreach 225
Campus Survey of Faculty and
    Student Perceptions of Persons
    with Disabilities 117
carnal sociology 5
Center for Diversity and Inclusion
    186–187
charity model of disability 217–219
Chief Student Affairs Officers (CSAOs) 84
Civil Rights Act 21
civil rights movement 19, 125
classroom entrances 97
classroom environment 13–14, 99;
    engagement in 64–67; physical aspects
    of 95–98, 130–131, 188–189, 218, 226
climate *see* campus climate

collaboration 41
college experiences, students' satisfaction
    with 47–58
college persistence 159–160
college student departure theory 159
College Student Educators International
    (ACPA) 138, 139
college transition 78–82, 153–155
coming out 26, 39
competencies 110; cultural 10; disability
    148–149; multifocal development
    of 148–149; for student affairs
    professionals 138–140
Confirmatory Factor Analysis (CFA) 51
contexual variable, disability as 83
course content 65
critical disability studies 5, 125–126
critical theory 5, 125
cultural competence 10
cultural conceptions, of disability 83–84
culturally relevant disability pedagogy 4,
    15–16; definition of 9–12; important
    of, in higher education 15; in
    practice 12–15
culturally relevant pedagogy 4, 8–15
culturally responsive classrooms 8–9
cultural norms 147–148
culture plan 128
curriculum 191–192, 218, 226

deficit-based views 28, 36–37,
    82–83, 89, 172
depression 54
descriptors, of disability 176–177
design, of physical spaces 218
desk styles 97
developmental course work 76
developmental theory 80–82
difference 97–98
difference-as-deviance 125–126
differentiated curriculum
    enhancements 14
disability advocacy movement 83
disability identity 68–70
disability(ies): attitudes toward 7–8,
    107–118; changing narrative on
    216–228; competency 148–149; as
    contextual variable 85; convergence
    with queer identity 31–42; cultural
    dimensions of 3; in the curriculum
    191–192, 218, 226; diagnosis of 144;
    disclosure of 5–6, 26–27, 70, 94, 147,
    172; discrimination and 125–126, 131;

diversity and 142–149, 171–182, 185–186, 200–214, 216–217; in higher education 220–227; history of 124–125; identity 68–70, 95, 171; on institutional websites 171–182; intersectionality of 3–5, 31–32, 61, 89–99, 138–150, 154; knowledge of, by faculty and administrators 107–118; medical evidence of 21–22, 24–25; medical model of 82–84, 89, 217–219; non-disclosure of 3–16; social construction of 23, 26–27, 82–84, 89, 154, 219; socio-spatial dynamics of 89–99; spatial approach to 89–99; stigma and 7–8, 13, 50, 94, 147, 154, *see also* people with disabilities; students with disabilities
disability rights movement 219
disability service professionals 109–110, 112–113, 155–157, 165
Disability Services Office 195–197
disability studies 5, 19–28, 98–99, 125, 219, 226
disability support services 6, 49, 50, 84–85, 155–157, 220–227; access to 66–67
disablement process 23
disclosure: of disability 5–6, 26–27, 70, 94, 147, 172; self-determination and 40
discourse analysis 176–180
discourse theory 173
discrimination 7, 21, 50, 55–57, 124, 125–126, 129
Diverse Learning Environment (DLE) survey 48–58
diversity: of accommodation needs 143–145; benefits of 125–128; of diagnoses 144; disability and 61, 90, 142–149, 171–182, 185–186, 200–214, 216–217; in educational settings 21; faculty 127–128; in higher education 91; institutional commitment to 53–55, 60; learning disabilities as construct of 82–84; resources 185–186; of self-advocacy skills 145–146; of social identities 147–148; training 148–149
Diversity and Inclusion Summit 193–194
diversity discourse 216–217
diversity workers 23–24
dyslexia 52, 77, 78

earning potential 123
educational attainment 123
educational opportunities 19–20
educational policy 164–165

education disparities 123
employment opportunities 32, 75
employment skills 123–124
empowerment 40, 161–162
enabling environments 124
engagement: disability identity and 68–70; importance of 62–63; institutional support and 66–67; peer networks and 67–68; recommendations to support 72; role of disability in mediating classroom 64–65; of students with disabilities 61–72
equal access and opportunity 79
equality 32
essentialism 22
exclusion 188, 189–190
Expanding Cultural Awareness of Exceptional Learners (ExCEL) survey 117

faculty members: attitudes toward people with disabilities of 8, 107–118; benefits of diverse 127–128; decision-making tools for 114–117; demographics of 187; diversity training for 148–149; knowledge of disability of 5–6, 107–109; mentoring by 42; outreach to 225–226; professional development for 111–112, 122–132; teaching practices of 111–112; tenure policies 123, 131–132; treatment of students with disabilities by 190–191
Family Educational Rights and Privacy Act (FERPA) 154
flexible body 36

gender 32–33, 89, 90, 124, 125
graduation rates 61, 75, 107
grounded theory 140, 141
group identity 22

HERI *see* Higher Education Research Institute (HERI)
higher education: access to 90, 107, 158; accountability in 15; disability in 220–227; disability studies and 19–28; diversity in 21, 91; persistence in 159–160; queering disability in 31–42; students' satisfaction with 47–58; students with learning disabilities and 75–86; transition to 78–79, *see also* students with disabilities

Higher Education Research Institute (HERI) 48, 57–58
Hispanic students 54–55, 56, 57, 172
human rights 125

IDEA *see* Individuals with Disabilities Education Act (IDEA)
identity 22, 24, 27; descriptions of 40–41; development 39–40, 41; disability 68–70, 95, 171; intersections of 31–42; majority-minority 94–95; minority 49, 91–92; personal 4, 5; positive 51; privileged 84; social 147–148; social construction of 82
IEPs *see* Individualized Education Plans (IEPs)
iEvaluate 115
in/accessibility 93–94
inclusion 37–39, 111–112, 116, 139–140, 185, 186
inclusiveness survey data 187–192
Individualized Education Plans (IEPs) 22, 78, 158, 163
Individuals with Disabilities Education Act (IDEA) 75, 78, 83, 154
Individuals with Disabilities Education Improvement Act (IDEIA) 75, 78
industrialization 124
inequality 97–98
inspiration porn 10–11, 217
institutional barriers 185–198
institutional commitment to diversity 53–55, 58
institutional iceberg 153–165
institutional integration 47–53
institutional support: access to 66–67, *see also* disability support services
institutional theory 173–174
instructional methods 14–15, 28, 111–112, 116–117
integration 159
intellectual and developmental disabilities (IDD) 40
intellectual disabilities (ID) 77, 78, 85
interdisciplinary research 41–42
international students 147–148
intersectionality 31–32, 61, 89–99, 154; concept of 4–5, 139–140; of disability 138–150; of disability with other identities 3–5; social identities and 147–148

K-12 students 22, 154, 156, 161–162, 163, 164
knowledge, disability-related 107–118

language, used to describe disability 218, 222–223
learning disabilities 7, 52, 69–70, 75–88; as construct of diversity 82–86; defined 79; diagnosis of 81; documentation of 81; as social construct 84–85
legal discourse 21–22, 32
LGBT students 26, 31–42, 55–56, 186–187, 197
lifetime earning potential 123

magnified moments 192–197
majority-minority status 94–95
marginality 138–150
marginalization 157–158, 185, 187–188, 192, 202–203
marriage equality 32
masculinity 27
media 218
medical model of disability 23–25, 27–28, 82–84, 89, 217–219
mental health disorders 7, 27, 50, 54
mentorship programs 194–195
merit 26
minority identities 49, 91–92
minority/majority 94–95
minority students 77, *see also specific minority groups*

narratives 33–40, 41–42, 63, 216–228
National Association of Student Personnel Administrators (NASPA) 113–114
National Center for Education Statistics (NCES) 75, 216
National Center for the Study of Postsecondary Education Supports (NCSPES) Survey 116
negative stereotypes 13
non-disclosed disabilities, supporting students with 3–16
normalcy 126
normality 5
normativity 26

Office for Students with Disabilities (OSD) 76, 79
Office of Disability Services (ODS) 80, 172
Ontario Human Rights Services (OHRC) 200
oppression 126, 217

parents 156, 161, 163
pedagogy: culturally relevant 4, 8–15; culturally relevant disability 4, 9–15
peer-mediated instruction 14
peer mentoring 40, 76
peer networks 67–68
people with disabilities: attitudes toward 7–8, 107–118; deficit-based views of 28, 36–37, 82–83, 89, 172; defined 158; diversity of 92; exclusion of 19–28; hiring of 28; labeling of 22; marginalization of 157–158, 185, 187–188, 192, 202–203; oppression of 126, 217; statistics on 216, *see also* students with disabilities
personal biases 34–36
personal identity 4, 5
physical environment 95–98, 130–131, 188–189, 218, 226
positionalities 34–36
postsecondary education *see* higher education
power relations 91
privileged identities 82
professional development: administrators 112–114; faculty 111–112, 122–134; multifocal 148–149; in service to institutional transformation 128–130; student success and 122–132
psychiatric disabilities *see* mental health disorders
psychoeducational assessments 79
psychosocial disability 27

queering disability 31–42
quotas 28

race 27, 90, 91, 124, 125, 200
racial space 91
Reach Higher Initiative 165
Rehabilitation Act 20, 76, 78–79, 83
relationship development 154
remedial support 76
resistance 185, 186
right of inclusion 37–39
Ryerson University 200–214

scholarly personal narratives (SPNs) 33–40, 41–42
Scholarship of Teaching and Learning 14
seating location 96

segregation 20, 47
self-advocacy skills 145–146, 153, 156, 157, 160–162
self-authorship 81
self-determination 40, 76–77, 79
self-efficacy 77
self-segregation 47
sense of belonging 51–53, 58
SERVQUAL 116
sexuality 32–33, 90
sexual orientation 26, 89
snapshot click analysis 174–176, 178–179
social activism 32
social construction of disability 26–27, 82, 83–84, 89, 154
social environment 226–227
social exclusion 189–190
social groups 19, 24
social identities 147–148
social justice 11–12, 15, 125–126, 139–140, 185, 203, 227
social model of disability 23, 219
social networks 67–68
social spaces 89–90
socioeconomic status 48, 123, 158
socio-spatial dynamics 89–91
space 93–99, 218, 226
spatial lens 89–99
special education services 3, 37, 78, 158
SPNs *see* scholarly personal narratives (SPNs)
stereotype threat theory 7
stigma 7–8, 13, 50, 94, 147, 154
strengths-based view 37
structured disability support program (SDSP) 66–67
Student Affairs Administrators in Higher Education (NASPA) 138, 139
student affairs professionals 70, 110–111, 113–114, 138–150; competencies for 138–140; diversity training for 148–149
student development theory 80–82
student engagement theory 62–72
student mentorship program 194–195
students with disabilities: access to higher education by 90, 107, 158; accommodations for 5–6, 26–28, 75–76, 79–80, 85, 94, 108, 143–145, 159–160, 172; advocates for 154–155, 156, 162; attitudes toward 10, 107–118; barriers for 20, 90,

157–158, 185–198; diversity of 61, 89, 90, 155; engagement by 61–72; experiences of 26–27, 41–42; faculty and staff treatment of 190–191; graduation rates of 61, 75, 109; in higher education 19–28, 40, 153, 216–228; identity development for 39–40; integration of 47–53, 160; labeling of 9–10, 155; LGBT 31–42; marginalization of 157–158, 192, 202–203; non-disclosed disabilities 3–16; perspectives of 36–37; policies and practices for 153–165; satisfaction with college experiences of 47–58; self-advocacy skills of 145–146, 153, 156, 157, 160–162; self-determination for 76–77; self-perceptions of 26–27; social exclusion of 189–190; success of 122–132, 158; support for 66–67; transition to college by 78–82, 153–155, *see also* students with learning disabilities
students with learning disabilities 75–86; accommodations for 75–76, 79–80, 85; challenges of serving 85–86; developmental theory and 80–82; enrollment of, in higher education 75–77; higher education experiences of 77–80; misconceptions about 80; support for 77–78, 80, 84–85; transition

to college by 78–82, *see also* students with disabilities
student veterans 216
study skills 154

taboo mentality 39–40
teaching strategies *see* instructional methods
technology 226
tenure policies 123, 131–132
time management 154
tokenism 28
tragedy model of disability 217–219
transgender persons 32

United Nations Convention on the Rights of Persons with Disabilities 124
Universal Design (UD) 130–131, 220
Universal Design for Learning (UDL) 13, 28, 111–112, 130–131, 186
University of Arizona 221–227

veterans 216
visual impairments 94–95

website content 171–182
Wechsler Adult Intelligence Scale (WAIS-IV) 79
Woodcock-Johnson Cognitive Battery 79

 Taylor & Francis eBooks

Helping you to choose the right eBooks for your Library

Add Routledge titles to your library's digital collection today. Taylor and Francis ebooks contains over 50,000 titles in the Humanities, Social Sciences, Behavioural Sciences, Built Environment and Law.

Choose from a range of subject packages or create your own!

Benefits for you

» Free MARC records
» COUNTER-compliant usage statistics
» Flexible purchase and pricing options
» All titles DRM-free.

Benefits for your user

» Off-site, anytime access via Athens or referring URL
» Print or copy pages or chapters
» Full content search
» Bookmark, highlight and annotate text
» Access to thousands of pages of quality research at the click of a button.

REQUEST YOUR **FREE** INSTITUTIONAL TRIAL TODAY

Free Trials Available
We offer free trials to qualifying academic, corporate and government customers.

eCollections – Choose from over 30 subject eCollections, including:

Archaeology	Language Learning
Architecture	Law
Asian Studies	Literature
Business & Management	Media & Communication
Classical Studies	Middle East Studies
Construction	Music
Creative & Media Arts	Philosophy
Criminology & Criminal Justice	Planning
Economics	Politics
Education	Psychology & Mental Health
Energy	Religion
Engineering	Security
English Language & Linguistics	Social Work
Environment & Sustainability	Sociology
Geography	Sport
Health Studies	Theatre & Performance
History	Tourism, Hospitality & Events

For more information, pricing enquiries or to order a free trial, please contact your local sales team:
www.tandfebooks.com/page/sales

 Routledge
Taylor & Francis Group

The home of
Routledge books

www.tandfebooks.com